2005

Oral
Storytelling
&Teaching
Mathematics

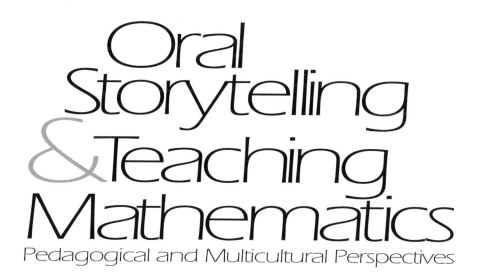

Oral Storytelling & Teaching Mathematics

Pedagogical and Multicultural Perspectives

MICHAEL STEPHEN SCHIRO

with Doris Lawson

SAGE Publications
International Educational and Professional Publisher
Thousand Oaks ▪ London ▪ New Delhi

For information:

Sage Publications, Inc.
2455 Teller Road
Thousand Oaks, California 91320
E-mail: order@sagepub.com

Sage Publications Ltd.
1 Oliver's Yard
55 City Road
London, EC1Y 1SP
United Kingdom

Sage Publications India Pvt. Ltd.
B-42, Panchsheel Enclave
Post Box 4109
New Delhi 110 017 India

Printed in the United States of America

Library of Congress Cataloging-in-Publication Data

Schiro, Michael Stephen.
Oral storytelling and teaching mathematics : pedagogical and multicultural perspectives / by Michael Stephen Schiro.
     p. cm.
Includes bibliographical references and index.
ISBN 0-7619-3009-4 (cloth : acid-free paper) — ISBN 0-7619-3010-8 (paper : acid-free paper)
     1. Mathematics—Study and teaching (Elementary)—Methodology. 2. Oral tradition. 3. Storytelling.
I. Title.
QA135.6.S42 2004
372.7'044—dc22   2003026081

This book is printed on acid-free paper.

04   05   06   07   08   10   9   8   7   6   5   4   3   2   1

Acquisitions Editor:	Diane McDaniel
Editorial Assistant:	Margo Crouppen
Production Editor:	Kristen Gibson
Copy Editor:	Robert Holm
Typesetter:	C&M Digitals (P) Ltd.
Indexer:	Naomi Linzer
Cover Designer:	Michelle Lee

CONTENTS

PREFACE

Oral storytelling dates back to ancient times. The first written description of it, found in the Egyptian Westcar Papyrus, was recorded sometime between 2000 and 1300 BCE (Baker & Green, 1987).

Early oral storytellers were historians, entertainers, bringers of news, religious and moral teachers, and educators. In the broadest sense the early storyteller was the medium through which a society passed on its culture. The teacher, the priest, the artisan, and the parent, as well as the professional "resident" and "traveling" storyteller, all used oral stories to pass on their traditions (Baker & Green, 1987). Professional oral storytellers were found throughout the world: in America, Europe, Africa, and Asia. Some of the more well-known oral stories familiar to Western cultures that have since been recorded include *Gilgamesh* (from the Middle East), the *Iliad* and the *Odyssey* (from Europe), and the *Ramayana* (from India). Bards of the British Isles often sang their stories or put them in poetry, as did those in Russia, Asia, North America, and Africa. Religious storytellers of India, China, and the Middle East often used physical manipulatives and pictures to aid them in their endeavors. Theatrical storytellers of China, Japan, Russia, and North America often performed their stories with the help of audience participation (Pellowski, 1990).

Once writing was invented, the educated had a new medium through which to pass on their culture. After printing became inexpensive in the fifteenth century, oral storytelling gradually began to wane in its influence as a medium for the transmission of culture.

When Friedrich Froebel founded the kindergarten movement in 1837, he introduced oral storytelling as a critical component for passing on culture to the young. By 1900 oral story-telling had found its place in American libraries in the form of the library hour, and in 1905 the first book was published in the United States on instructional uses of oral stories (Bryant, 1905). Gradually the power of oral stories was rediscovered by language arts teachers. It is now time for those of us concerned with the teaching of mathematics to begin to explore the instructional power of oral stories.

This book is largely about how mathematics and oral storytelling can be woven together to provide an exciting method of teaching mathematics. This instructional method grows out of the movement that advocates using children's literature to enrich mathematics instruction. Mathematical oral storytelling takes a giant leap as it abandons the written word and picture book for the oral word. In so doing, it alters many of the fundamental assumptions of our highly literate culture about the nature of school mathematics and the roles of teachers and students during mathematics instruction. Oral storytelling transforms the abstract, objective, deductive mathematics we all have experienced in school into a subject surrounded by imagination, myth, and subjective meanings and feelings. It allows teachers to personalize mathematics and connect it with their own creative powers and fantasy life. And it allows children to bring to bear their creative and imaginative powers in making mathematics meaningful to themselves.

Many different types of oral stories can be wrapped around mathematics, including science fiction, historical fiction, fairy tales, detective stories, adventure tales, and autobiographical accounts. Similarly, different types of mathematics can be embedded in oral stories, including arithmetic, geometry, measurement, statistics, and algebra. They can be used to teach algorithms, concepts, problem solving, connections, and communication. In addition, epic oral stories can be used to teach content areas other than mathematics.

This book is also about mathematics and culture. It explores the highly literate culture of school mathematics, the mathematical conceptual systems embedded in the more oral cultures of many urban and rural families and communities, and the reasons why children from more oral families often have difficulty learning the highly literate school mathematics. It also explores the instructional practices and theories of multicultural mathematics education and the contributions that oral storytelling can make to that field.

Another contribution of this book is to the area of mathematical problem solving. It examines mathematical problem solving from the perspective of multicultural mathematics. In so doing, it extends currently popular models of mathematical problem solving by adding dimensions that incorporate new stages, the cultural backgrounds of learners, and how interactions between learners can contribute to their problem-solving abilities.

ORGANIZATION OF THIS BOOK

This book is organized into two parts. To give concrete meaning to theoretical discussions, each part of the book begins with a case study of how a real teacher told an oral story, and then succeeding theoretical discussions constantly reference the stories.

The first part of this book begins with a description of how a fourth grade teacher told a story called "The Wizard's Tale" to her students. This story is designed to help second, third, and fourth graders learn multidigit addition. It is a search and rescue story in which children develop understanding and skills while pretending to be a mute bulldozer, talking parrot, and writing gorilla. It takes 5 sessions to complete. The teacher is Doris Lawson, who teaches in an urban area not far from Boston.

The first part of this book describes the essential elements of oral storytelling and shows how they can be used as the foundation for a new instructional methodology for teaching mathematics. It examines the nature of epic oral storytelling, how the relationships between teacher, students, and content function during oral storytelling, and pedagogical assumptions and techniques of oral storytelling. The first part of the book concludes with a chapter in which Doris discusses her experiences telling "The Wizard's Tale" to her classes between 1993 and 1997.

The second part of *Oral Storytelling and Teaching Mathematics* begins with a description of how a sixth grade teacher told "The Egypt Story." This story follows two children who travel back in time 3,500 years. It is designed to help fifth, sixth, and seventh graders learn problem solving and multicultural mathematics during an instructional unit that integrates the teaching of mathematics and social studies. It contains 11 sessions that explore topics in arithmetic, geometry, and the history of mathematics. Doris Lawson also tells this story (in 1997 she moved from teaching all subjects to fourth graders to teaching mathematics and social studies in Grades 6, 7, and 8).

The second part of the book examines a variety of topics: the culture of school mathematics; the relationships between children's home cultures and the culture of school mathematics; how oral storytelling can help children who frequently have difficulty learning mathematics because of the knowledge base they acquire from early family and community interactions; the assumptions underlying, and the practices utilized by, multicultural mathematics; the nature of mathematical problem solving during oral storytelling; and the ideological battles currently being fought over the purposes and methods of multicultural mathematics instruction. This part of the book also includes an interview with Doris about her experiences teaching "The Egypt Story."

The complete texts for both oral stories, with all student handouts, are included on a CD that accompanies the book.

It needs to be mentioned that mathematical epic oral storytelling is not being presented as the salvation of mathematics education. It is only one of many powerful media that educators can use as part of their teaching repertoire. Oral stories provide an exciting alternative to current instructional practices, an alternative that complements existing methods.

A PERSONAL NOTE

After creating a number of mathematical epic oral stories, teachers began to ask me where the stories came from. At first my answer was that I used to tell my children bedtime stories almost every night for about 6 years. Gradually over time, certain heroes and heroines became their favorites, and I told more stories about those characters. There was the wise old Gandalf who arrived in my memory from *The Lord of the Rings* (Tolkien, 1954/1981). There was Tinkerbell, whom I created by combining the *Peter Pan* fairy (Barrie, 1904/1982) and Ged from *A Wizard of Earthsea* (Le Guin, 1968/1975). Over time, stories that began as separate adventures started to evolve into epics. One epic I remember, which probably had twenty installments, was about how Tinkerbell learned to do magic.

Recently teachers pushed me further to explore where my stories came from. They asked me to think about my childhood and try to remember who told me stories and when I told my first story. I cannot remember anyone telling me stories; I do remember, however, that over a period of about 3 years, I used to tell my brother and a friend occasional bedtime stories about Donald Duck and Scrooge McDuck. I used to love to read and daydream about Donald's and Scrooge's adventures.

I also remember that as a child the stories I read and the movies I watched were very real to me. I could not watch monster movies because they frightened me so. Even now my children laugh at me because I cannot watch a movie thriller without jumping around. The same happens with the mathematics epic oral stories I tell. As I tell them—as they arise out of some mysterious place in my subconscious that integrates fantasy and mathematics—they become real to me, and I see myself accompanying my heroes and heroines on their adventures. It is in this context that I invite listeners of my stories and readers of this book to suspend their grip on reality and join me on my adventures.

ACKNOWLEDGMENTS

Special credit needs to be given to several educators who worked with me from the beginning on epic oral storytelling: to Doris Lawson for her courage in asking me to create stories that met her needs, trying out the experiments I gave her, and telling me about everything that occurred in her classroom; to Rainy Cotti and Laura McBride for trying "The Wizard's Tale," building an entire third grade mathematics curriculum around wonderful oral stories that they created, and telling me about all the exciting things that occurred in their classroom; to Joann Greenwood, Pamela Halpern, Theresa Hupertz, Mary Mahoney, Christine Moynihan, and Sheila Rinaldi for creating and trying out oral stories with their students and sharing their thoughts with me and the educators mentioned above. Credit also needs to be given to Beth Casey, Anne Goodrow, Karen Anderson, and Pat Paugh for accompanying me on quite a journey, the creation of six books of early childhood problem-solving stories published by Wright Group/McGraw-Hill. And special thanks need to be given to Rainy Cotti, Natalie DiFusco, Naomi Gottlieb, and Elizabeth Greenwood for reading the manuscript and offering suggestions that significantly improved it.

To Stephanie and Arthur Schiro, who listened with delight to hundreds of bedtime stories that I created at their request. In so doing they ignited my interest in oral stories, which eventually resulted in the creation of this book.

Part I

"The Wizard's Tale":
Foundations of Mathematical
Epic Oral Storytelling

Chapter 1

"THE WIZARD'S TALE"

Doris Lawson Tells Fourth Graders an Oral Story

This chapter provides an example of how a fourth grade teacher, Doris Lawson, uses oral storytelling to present an epic mathematics tale.

Doris Lawson describes herself as a regular teacher—that is, before she changed the way she teaches mathematics. Doris used to follow her mathematics textbook. She would present her fourth graders the lesson in their textbook, give them practice problems, and then assign homework. Homework was checked at the beginning of every math lesson, and a test was given at the end of each week.

About 1990, after teaching this way for 10 years, Doris decided to reinvent the way she taught in order to make teaching more enriching for both her students and herself. First, Doris started using manipulatives. She used base ten blocks, geoboards, pattern blocks, and fraction bars to help give meaning to her lessons. Later she discovered math games: social games with names like addition war, division bingo, and multiplication dominoes. Doris created twenty to thirty math games that reinforced and extended the ideas presented in each chapter of her textbook using materials such as egg cartons, poster board, tongue depressors, and wood cubes.

By 1992 Doris discovered children's literature and began using mathematical stories with her class. She felt, however, that few children's storybooks developed the mathematical skills that she wanted her students to learn and that when she read a book to her students they were outsiders looking in on the world of others. She wanted to get her class more involved in mathematical stories—involved in ways that deeply stimulated their fantasies and more fully developed the mathematical skills that she wanted them to learn.

As a result, I began writing mathematical oral stories for Doris, and Doris began to develop her ability to tell those stories. We began to learn how to weave fantasy tales around mathematical topics in such a way that Doris's students could listen in to the mathematical thoughts of the characters in the stories and participate in the stories by helping those characters overcome mathematical obstacles and challenges. The stories gradually became

3

epics—stories that lasted for many days—that guided students through several stages of learning in order to help them develop mathematical skills.

One of the stories that I wrote for Doris is "The Wizard's Tale." It is designed to help children understand the multidigit addition algorithm and acquire the skills needed for adding multidigit numbers. Doris told the story four times to four classes between 1993 and 1997 before moving from teaching fourth graders all subjects to teaching sixth, seventh , and eighth grade mathematics. Other teachers have used "The Wizard's Tale" with second, third, and fourth graders.

Let us now listen to Doris as she tells "The Wizard's Tale." It takes her 5 days to tell the story. In what follows, indented text indicates what Doris actually says while telling the story. Italicized type identifies a comment about what Doris is saying or doing. Type that is not indented describes what is occurring in Doris's classroom. The accompanying CD provides a full description of what occurred in Doris's classroom.

DAY 1

This first session of "The Wizard's Tale" takes Doris about an hour and a half to tell. She tells it during two of her scheduled periods: mathematics and language arts. Doris announces the story by stating rather matter-of-factly, "OK, you guys, settle down. I want to tell you a story." She waits until the class is quiet and then begins. As she speaks she moves about the class gesturing with her arms and changing the tone of her voice to accentuate what she is saying.

Once upon a time there lived two wizards named Gandalf and Tinkerbell, who had one exciting adventure after another. In fact, they are still alive, are still friends, and still have awesome adventures.

Gandalf is an old man who has been a wizard for many years. Some say he is several thousand years old. Some say his story was first told by Tolkien in *The Lord of the Rings*. Tinkerbell is a fairy who is 11 years old and who has only been a wizard for 5 years. Some say her mother's story was told in *Peter Pan*. Both Gandalf and Tinkerbell are the type of wizards who can do magic. Gandalf is about 6 feet tall, has a long white beard, gray eyes, and wears old, baggy, gray clothes and a conical wizard's cap. [*Doris says this while speaking in a deep male voice.*] Tinkerbell is four inches tall, has long, straight hair, has a ring of stars that float above her head like a halo, and wears dazzling clothes with stars, lace, sparkles, and rainbows on them. [*Doris says this while speaking in a high female voice.*] Both Gandalf and Tinkerbell have the ability to change their sizes and forms. Tinkerbell can make herself as big as a giant. Gandalf can make himself into an ant and crawl through small spaces. [*Doris gestures to portray large and tiny.*]

One day Tinkerbell is daydreaming in a hammock next to her home, an enormous, old oak tree. All of a sudden, there is a big boom over Tinkerbell's head. It is so loud that Tinkerbell jumps out of her hammock and hides under a leaf. Then fireworks start to go off over Tinkerbell's head, big red and blue and yellow flowers and fountains. Tinkerbell knows what is happening now, for this is the way Gandalf communicates with her when he is in trouble. Suddenly words appear among the fireworks, in bright red letters. They say "Help, I am trapped in Thoughtful Mountain. Come . . ." Then the fireworks and the message end abruptly.

Tinkerbell has heard of Thoughtful Mountain. It is a place where wizards and witches sometimes go to test their magic powers. It is alive and magical and poses problems, riddles, and puzzles to visitors. Many a wizard and witch have disappeared forever upon entering Thoughtful Mountain. Tinkerbell has never been there and does not want to go, but Gandalf is in trouble in Thoughtful Mountain.

So Tinkerbell runs into her tree house and then into the room that holds all of her magic powders and devices. Hurriedly she takes out her crystal ball so she can see what is happening to Gandalf, puts it on a table, claps her hands three times, utters magic words to the crystal ball, and claps her hands three more times.

Tinkerbell always claps her hands three times before and after saying magic words to make her magic work. You, from right here in our classroom, can help Tinkerbell make her magic more powerful by clapping your hands in unison three times before and after she says magic words. I will signal you when you should clap by moving my hands in front of me, like this, to indicate a silent clap.

Doris now has her class practice clapping in unison three times after she gestures a silent clap. After two tries her class can clap loudly in unison three times. She then has them help Tinkerbell activate her crystal ball by clapping in unison before and after she says the magic words, "Gamble, grumble, groumble Gandalf."

Saying those magic words and clapping make the crystal ball show what is happening to Gandalf. It shows him being slowly turned into stone inside a dark cavern. Suddenly the ball's image disappears. This means that someone or something magical—probably Thoughtful Mountain—has turned off the crystal ball's seeing power.

Tinkerbell is worried. She quickly fills a small pouch with magic devices and runs outside her house. She gets ready to do magic. [*Doris signals for magic clapping, and her class responds.*] "Tiba, diba, riba." [*Doris signals and her class produces more magic clapping.*] This turns Tinkerbell into a giant red hawk, one of the fastest flying birds in the world. And into the air Tinkerbell jumps, and off she flies toward Thoughtful Mountain [*Doris flaps her arms as though they were wings as she continues.*]

Tinkerbell flies for 5 hours to get to Thoughtful Mountain. As she flies she thinks of everything she knows about the mountain. It isn't much. But Tinkerbell knows where the entrance is and the magic words that will allow her to enter the mountain. She also knows that the mountain has many caverns within it, including a history cavern, a mathematics cavern, and a science cavern.

When Tinkerbell arrives at the mountain she flies to its entrance and prepares to turn herself from a red hawk back into Tinkerbell. [*Doris signals and magic clapping occurs.*] "Tiba, diba, riba." [*more magic clapping*] Suddenly Tinkerbell looks like herself again.

Tinkerbell now gets ready to do the magic that will allow her to enter Thoughtful Mountain. [*Doris signals and magic clapping occurs.*] "Double fuffle, guffle, truffle." [*Doris signals and more magic clapping.*]

There is a great creaking sound from the mountain and a small door, just Tinkerbell's size, appears and opens. Above it are written the words in very small print: "DO NOT ENTER, unless you can answer my questions. Incorrect answers will turn you into stone."

Cautiously Tinkerbell climbs up the mountain and walks through the small door. The door slams shut behind her and she is in complete darkness.

Tinkerbell takes a deep breath and gets ready to do magic. [*Doris signals and magic clapping occurs.*] "Twinkle, twankle, twinkle." [*more magic clapping*] A halo of stars begins to glow above Tinkerbell's head so brightly that she can see all around her. In front of her is a great cavern with many tunnels leading out of it. This is no ordinary cavern. One wall of the cavern, which seems to be made out of polished marble, is covered with a beautiful picture of a flower garden. The garden is constructed out of small bits of gold, diamond, rubies, sapphires, and emeralds that all seem to grow out of the wall. Tinkerbell can hardly believe her eyes, particularly when several silver butterflies fly across the wall.

But Tinkerbell did not come to Thoughtful Mountain to look at beautiful stones. She came to find her friend Gandalf. She looks at the many tunnels leading out of the main cavern and wonders aloud, "Which tunnel did Gandalf go down?" She takes her magic compass out of her pouch and tells it to find where Gandalf had walked. The magic compass is like a bloodhound tracking dog. Its needle turns around and around until it finds the scent of Gandalf's footprints. Then it points in the direction that Gandalf walked. Tinkerbell follows the magic compass and goes into one of the tunnels. She walks down the tunnel for an hour. Then the tunnel ends.

There is nothing but a wall in front of her. But her magic compass says that Gandalf walked through the wall. Tinkerbell studies the wall and sees some markings engraved on it. This is what they look like. [*Doris draws this on the chalkboard.*]

Exhibit 1.1

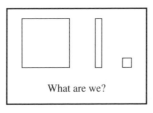

What are we?

"What do the marks mean?" Tinkerbell wonders. She thinks and thinks, but can think of nothing.

Doris tells her students that Tinkerbell needs their help to figure out what the marks mean. She puts her students into groups of two and asks them to discuss in their small groups what they think the marks mean. Doris has previously introduced her class to base ten blocks, and they have many ideas. After a few minutes of class discussion Doris continues the story.

> After thinking for the longest time, and not coming up with any ideas, Tinkerbell takes out her magic slate. The slate usually answers any questions that she has. It is sort of like a magical encyclopedia. Tinkerbell draws a picture of the wall markings on the magic slate and prepares to do magic. [*Doris signals and magic clapping occurs.*] "Sedle, sedelie, see. What are thee?" [*more magic clapping*] Tinkerbell watches the slate as it searches for an answer.

To involve her students in helping the story progress, Doris asks them to telepathically send their answers to Tinkerbell. She signals for her class to clap three times. Students then concentrate while they telepathically send the answer to Tinkerbell. Doris then signals for her class to clap three more times to complete the magic transmission.

> As soon as Tinkerbell's magic slate receives our telepathic thoughts, it[*] responds in a metallic, squeaky voice [*that Doris imitates*], "We are base ten number blocks. We are used in math. Our names are hundred, ten, and one. Ten ones equal a ten. Ten tens equal one hundred."
>
> Now Tinkerbell remembers. Tinkerbell announces to the wall, "You are hundred, ten, and one. If ten ones are put together, they make a ten. If ten tens are put together, they make a hundred."
>
> A great groaning echoes through the cavern as the wall at the end of the tunnel gradually melts away into nothing. On the other side of where the wall used to be is another cavern.
>
> Tinkerbell slowly walks into the new cavern. Inside Tinkerbell sees something. It is Gandalf, three other wizards, and a witch, all of them turned to stone and frozen into the cavern's wall. Tinkerbell stands still and quietly looks around her.
>
> On the floor not far away is a magic place value chart that looks like this. [*Doris holds up a 2- by 3-foot (0.6- by 0.9-meter) piece of cardboard with a place value chart drawn on it.*]

Exhibit 1.2

hundreds	tens	ones

All of a sudden, a deep, booming voice says [*and Doris delivers this in a deep, booming voice*], "Hello! So you have come to test your thoughtfulness against me, the Thoughtful Mountain. Well, prepare yourself! Solve my problems, or you will become stone! Here is your only hint: 'Talking Bulldozer adds.'"

Suddenly the room starts to glow pink, the shape on the floor begins to glow red, and from two different parts of the ceiling, orange pieces of stone fall to the floor. This is what the two sets of orange stone pieces look like. [*Doris places these configurations of base ten blocks on a table, so that all of her students can see them.*]

Exhibit 1.3

After that, there is no sound . . . just quiet. . . . In the silence Tinkerbell begins to think.

These are some of the things that Tinkerbell thinks [*and that Doris describes while pretending to be in a dream with her eyes closed*]: The stone pieces must be used with the magic place value chart on the floor. The hint "Talking Bulldozer adds" must mean that a bulldozer is to move the stone pieces and not me. I also think that the bulldozer will have to talk and explain everything that is occurring because this is Thoughtful Mountain. The bulldozer should add the orange stone pieces together. There are three columns on the magic place value chart and three types of stone. Each type of stone piece must go in its own column—nothing should ever be in the wrong column. Hundreds must go in the hundreds column, tens must go in the tens column, and ones must go in the ones column. Ten little stone cubes are the same size as a stone long, and ten stone longs are the same size as a stone flat. I wonder if there is a special way that a talking bulldozer adds stones.

[*Opening her eyes and coming out of her dream, Doris continues.*] Suddenly a jingle pops into Tinkerbell's mind that she once heard children sing. It goes something like this. [*Doris now sings "Tinkerbell's Addition Song," after hanging its words up on her wall on a large piece of chart paper.*]

Tinkerbell thinks for a long time before deciding what to do. She does not want to make a mistake and be turned into stone, like Gandalf. And this is what Tinkerbell does.

Doris now provides her class with a demonstration, which they will later imitate. She puts the place value chart, which she previously showed her students on the table, next to the base ten blocks. She positions it so that everyone can easily see it. She then performs the following activities on the place value chart while she speaks in such a way that her students can see the correspondence between her verbalizations and the actions she performs with base ten blocks on the place value chart.

Tinkerbell gets ready to do magic: [*Doris signals and magic clapping.*] "Brump, flump, clump." [*more magic clapping*] All of a sudden, Tinkerbell turns herself into a bulldozer.

Tinkerbell's Addition Song

Ones in ones
Tens in tens
Hundreds in hundreds
From right to left
    And down each column we go
    Down each column we go
    Column by column
    Column by column.
Slide them down
Then add them up
Make our trades
Each column we add
    And down each column we go
    Down each column we go
    Column by column
    Column by column.
Leave some behind
Some go up and over
All in their place
Always legal
    And down each column we go
    Down each column we go
    Column by column
    Column by column.

Doris now pulls a plastic bulldozer from her book bag and holds it up for her class to see. She purchased it from a local toy store. Its scoop is almost the same width as the columns on the place value chart. (A third grade teacher, Laura McBride, who told "The Wizard's Tale" to her class, made bulldozers inexpensively. She cut shoe boxes in half to make two bulldozer scoops that she spray painted. Each bulldozer was about 4 by 4 by 4 inches, or 10 by 10 by 10 cm.)

Exhibit 1.4

Laura McBride's
bulldozer scoop

With a great roar of her engines Tinkerbell the Bulldozer drives over to one pile of stones, picks them up, and deposits them in a row on the cavern's magic place value chart. She is careful never to let a stone fall into the wrong column. [*Doris acts this out with the bulldozer and the base ten blocks on the table, making loud "vrrroom" sounds whenever she moves the bulldozer forward.*] Tinkerbell the Bulldozer then does the same for the other pile of orange stone pieces. [*Doris also acts this out with the bulldozer and the base ten blocks with accompanying sounds.*] The orange stones are then arranged on the magic place value chart like this.

Exhibit 1.5

hundreds	tens	ones
☐ ☐ ☐ ☐	❙❙❙❙ ❙❙❙	□ □ □ □ □ □ □ □ □ □ □

Tinkerbell roars her motors, backs off so that she is above the ones column with her shovel pointing toward the column, and says some magic words so that her shovel adjusts itself in size so that it is the same width as the ones column. [*The diagram below shows how Doris positions her bulldozer (that represents Tinkerbell) with respect to the ones column.*]

Exhibit 1.6

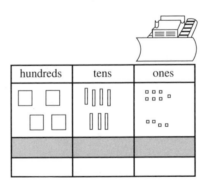

hundreds	tens	ones
☐ ☐ ☐ ☐	❙❙❙❙ ❙❙❙	□ □ □ □ □ □ □ □ □ □ □

Tinkerbell, the talking bulldozer, then yells out "Ones!" and moves slowly forward pushing all of the orange stone cubes before her until they are in the shaded box near the bottom of the ones column. [*Doris acts this out with the bulldozer and the base ten blocks on the till, making loud "vrrroom"* sounds whenever she moves the bulldozer forward.] Tinkerbell now has eleven stone cubes in her scoop. [*This is how the stones are now located above the place value chart. The arrow indicates where Tinkerbell traveled.*]

Exhibit 1.7

hundreds	tens	ones
□ □ □ □	❘❘❘❘ ❘❘❘	↓
		▫▫ ▫▫▫▫

Tinkerbell calls out, "Seven cubes plus four cubes equals eleven cubes." She then yells, "Trade ten ones for one ten." To her delight, ten of the orange stone ones disappear in a puff of smoke and an orange stone long falls out of the ceiling and into the scoop of her bulldozer. [*Doris demonstrates this trade.*]

Exhibit 1.8

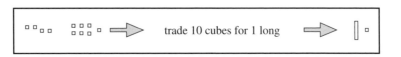

"Ah," Tinkerbell exclaims aloud, "Eleven cubes are the same as one long and one cube." [*This is how the stones (base ten blocks) are now located on the place value chart.*]

Exhibit 1.9

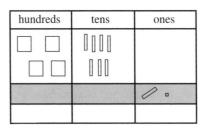

Carefully Tinkerbell drives forward a little and drops the stone cube in her scoop into the small rectangular area at the bottom of the magic place value chart, making sure not to let the long fall into the ones column. [*Doris demonstrates this.*] She says, "One cube." [*This is how the stones are now positioned. The arrow indicates where Tinkerbell traveled.*]

Exhibit 1.10

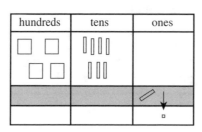

Tinkerbell then backs up the ones column, and when she reaches the top where the writing is, she rotates 90 degrees clockwise and drops the stone long into the tens column on top of the word "tens"—making sure that it is entirely in the small rectangular area surrounding the word "tens." [*Doris acts this out with the bulldozer and the base ten blocks on the till. This is how the till and stones now look. The arrow indicates Tinkerbell's travel route.*]

Exhibit 1.11

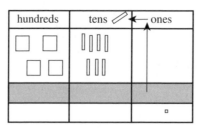

As the one stone long that is carried over to the tens column hits the magic place value chart, Tinkerbell says, "One long carried over into the tens column." [*This is how the till and stones now look.*]

Exhibit 1.12

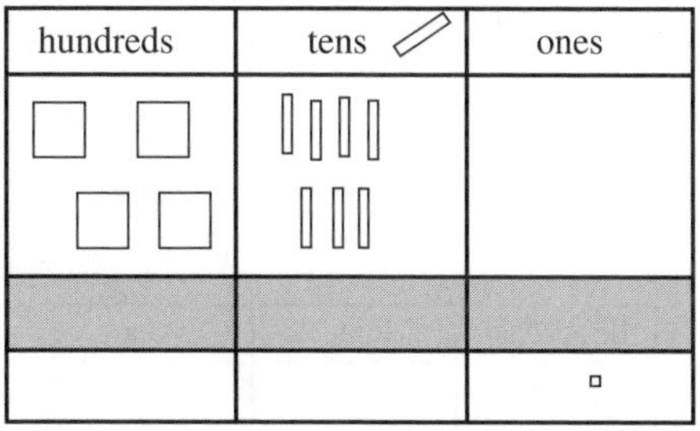

hundreds	tens ✎	ones
☐ ☐ ☐ ☐	▯▯▯▯ ▯▯▯	
		▫

Tinkerbell then backs herself around so that she faces down the tens column. [*The diagram below shows how Doris positions her bulldozer.*]

Exhibit 1.13

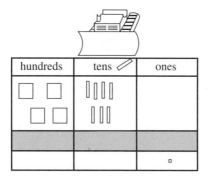

hundreds	tens ✎	ones
☐ ☐ ☐ ☐	▯▯▯▯ ▯▯▯	
		▫

Tinkerbell now roars her engine with a great "roarrrr," yells out "Tens!" and pushes the stone longs down the tens column to the shaded rectangular area near the bottom of the column.

Exhibit 1.14

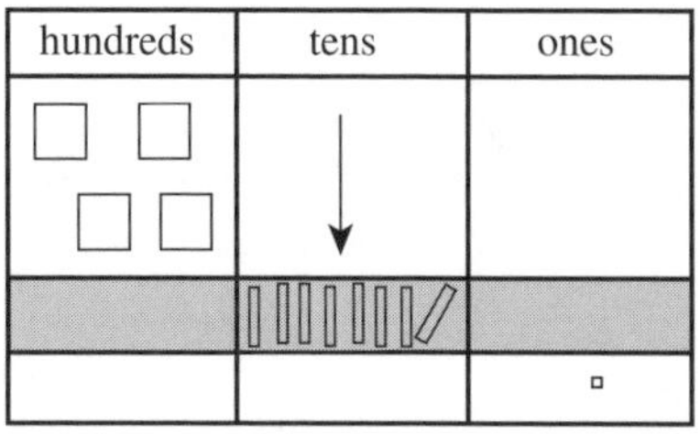

hundreds	tens	ones
☐ ☐ ☐ ☐	↓	
	▯▯▯▯▯▯✎	
		▫

Then Tinkerbell yells, "Eight longs and thus no trades!" She then moves slightly forward and dumps the eight stone longs in her scoop into the small rectangular area at the bottom of the magic place value chart and exclaims, "Eight longs!"

Exhibit 1.15

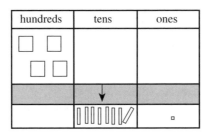

Tinkerbell then backs up the tens column and moves herself around so that she is facing down the hundreds column. She roars her engine with a great "roarrrr," yells out "Hundreds!" and pushes the stone flats down the hundreds column to the shaded rectangular area near the bottom of the column. Tinkerbell then yells, "Four flats and no trades!"

Exhibit 1.16

hundreds	tens	ones
↓		
□ □ □		
	‖‖‖‖‖╱	▫

Next she moves slightly forward and dumps the four stone flats in her scoop into the small rectangular area at the bottom of the place value chart and calls out, "Four flats!" [*Doris demonstrates this, making loud "vrrroom" sounds.*]

Exhibit 1.17

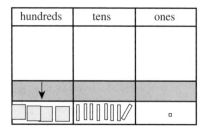

Tinkerbell then spins herself around, drives off of the magic place value chart and turns herself back into her normal fairy Tinkerbell form and yells, "Four flats, eight longs, one cube!"

As soon as she says that, the color of the room flashes pink and purple for one full minute as the stones on the floor's place value chart float up into the air and disappear by quietly exploding into glorious sprays of red, green, and blue fireworks. [*While saying this Doris clears the place value chart of base ten blocks.*]

Tinkerbell feels very proud of herself. But when the lights stop flashing . . . two more sets of stones fall out of the ceiling, representing the numbers 467 and 355.

Doris writes 467 and 355 on the chalkboard, asks her students which base ten blocks should be set out to represent these numbers, and, under the guidance of her students, puts out the appropriate blocks in two piles next to the place value chart.

Tinkerbell now prepares to do magic. [*Doris signals and magic clapping occurs.*] "Brump, flump, clump." [*more magic clapping*] Tinkerbell again turns herself into a bulldozer, roars her engines, and moves off to solve the problem while singing the "Addition Song."

Doris now gives her students copies of "Tinkerbell's Addition Song" and has her class sing the song with her, as loud as they can, while she points to its words on the larger copy hanging on the wall.

After singing, Doris asks her students what they think the song's words mean, for the words guide Tinkerbell's actions. Doris reinforces correct interpretations of the song's words and correctly rephrases incorrect interpretations.

Next, Doris demonstrates with base ten blocks how to solve the problem 467 + 355 by telling the story of how Tinkerbell places base ten blocks on the place value chart, solves the problem column by column, calls out in words the result of each action, and announces the final answer. During this demonstration, Doris asks students the following key questions, which they answer and which she in turn clarifies:

- Can cubes go in any other columns than the ones? Can longs go in any other column than the tens? Can flats go in any other column than the hundreds?
- Do the base ten blocks that represent each of the two numbers in the problem have to be placed in rows on the upper part of the place value chart in such a way that they can be seen as two separate numbers?
- Can the bulldozer push base ten blocks down more than one column at a time? (This is critical to clarify, for many children want to push all of the blocks to the bottom of the chart at once and then trade, but this does not parallel the addition algorithm she teaches.)
- Must the bulldozer stop in the shaded rectangle, called the thinking and trading area, to make trades before proceeding to dump blocks at the bottom of each column? (Doris emphasizes that this thinking step is important.)
- When cubes or longs are traded for longs or flats, can the traded blocks be placed any-where other than on the words at the top of their respective columns? (This is impor-tant if actions performed are to parallel written work.)

When this problem is complete, one more set of blocks falls from the ceiling representing 383 + 278. Doris tells her students that they have to solve this problem themselves, with her guidance, in order to help Tinkerbell.

Doris gives each group of two students base ten blocks, a place value chart, and a plastic bulldozer. She then carefully leads her class through the process of solving the problem, by providing verbal guidance while her students act out the problem using the bulldozers, base ten blocks, and place value charts. Doris's method of proceeding parallels the demonstration of the addition process that she has previously provided her students. As they work on the problem, Doris

- first asks students to sing "Tinkerbell's Addition Song," and then later during the addi-tion process she asks them to sing relevant parts of the song,
- asks students to describe what to do at each step of the problem,
- clarifies responses to her questions received from students,
- encourages students to make sounds, such as "vrrroom, vrrroom" while moving their bulldozers forward down columns, and
- monitors students' actions to correct any incorrect behavior.

Doris encourages students to work together cooperatively because doing so will help Tinkerbell. She tells them that they must work cooperatively with their partner and help their partner whenever possible, for the success of their group in helping Tinkerbell depends on both partners being able to solve the mathematics problem and not just one of them. She tells them that part of helping each other involves quietly saying out loud all of their mathematical thoughts. This means verbalizing or describing in words their actions and the reasons for their actions. Doris tells her students that they must also carefully listen to what each other says and check each other's manipulations with the blocks. Doris emphasizes that if they think their partner makes a mistake or if they do not understand why their partner does or says something, it is their job to politely and respectfully ask their partner questions and make sure that they both understand, either by teaching each other or getting help from her.

As her students work in their small groups under her direction—answering questions, singing "Tinkerbell's Addition Song," moving bulldozers and base ten blocks, making loud "vrrroom" sounds, and discussing each other's behavior—Doris circulates among them reinforcing how to work in groups, answering questions, and helping them with the mathematics. At one point, while a student is backing a bulldozer up a column, the student utters, "beep, beep, beep, beep." Before long several other students are uttering the "beep, beep, beep, beep" noise whenever their bulldozer backs up. (Within two days the whole class is making the "beep, beep, beep, beep" noise whenever their bulldozer backs up, and reminding each other that if they do not make the "beep, beep, beep, beep" sound, they will be turned to stone by Thoughtful Mountain.)

When the problem is complete, Doris continues the story:

> When the third problem is complete, the room flashes from pink to purple to red over and over again for one full minute as the stones on the cavern's magic place value chart disappear. Then the room becomes completely dark and the mountain speaks to Tinkerbell, "Very good, little fairy. You can now either be released from me to go in peace, or have any wish that is in my power to grant."
>
> Tinkerbell yells, "My wish is that you release my friend Gandalf!"
>
> There is a great sound of breaking stone and Gandalf falls out of the stone wall, fully human again. Tinkerbell examines Gandalf closely to see if his true essence was changed in any way. Is he still wise, and will he still rather share his wisdom with some boys on a baseball field than be in a television program? Is he still gentle, and will he still refuse to step on ants? Is he still honest, and will he do magic to find the owner of a lost dollar rather than keep it himself? Is he still the champion of all creatures in need, who would rather save a mouse in need of help than be cheered at a king's banquet?
>
> When Tinkerbell sees that the person who fell out of the wall is the same Gandalf she has loved and respected for years, she flies to him, pulls on his beard, and yells, "Gandalf, Gandalf, how did you ever get yourself into this predicament?"
>
> Gandalf tells her how smart she is to have figured out how to do the mountain's problems and that he came to save one of his good friends, Habble. Habble is one of the stone wizards who is frozen in the cavern's wall.
>
> Before they can say more, the mountain rumbles and booms, and Tinkerbell and Gandalf prepare themselves for something earth-shattering.

Doris now stops telling the story and tells her students that she will continue it tomorrow. She then asks them to discuss in their small groups two of the following questions and to record their answers on a sheet of paper:

- How did the story make you feel (and why)?
- What did the story remind you of in your own life?
- Did you like the story (and why)?
- If you were to tell a friend about the story, what are two things that would be most important for your friend to know (and why)?
- Do you think you know what will happen at the end of the story (and if so, what is it)?

Before discussion begins, Doris emphasizes the importance of cooperatively discussing the questions and listening to each other, learning from each other, and teaching each other. Doris stresses that the success of their group depends on both members of the group contributing to the discussion rather than just one person dominating the discussion.

During the discussions Doris circulates among students reinforcing cooperative behavior and stimulating discussion. Afterward, she draws students together for a whole-class discussion during which selected small groups report their results by reading and explaining what they recorded.

DAY 2

This is the third year that Doris is presenting "The Wizard's Tale," and she tells the story from memory, only occasionally referring to notes. She says that this telling of the story is different from the last two. She feels freer to alter, elaborate upon, and embellish the story—to stimulate specific interactions with her class or elaborate on events that occur in her classroom. (One of the ancient traditions of oral storytelling is the altering of stories to stimulate audience interaction and involvement.)

Multidigit addition is part of the second and third grade curriculum in Doris's school. Doris has found, however, that her fourth graders arrive knowing the procedures required for multidigit addition but that they do not have a good understanding of why they juggle digits as they do during addition—that is, they have procedural skills but inadequate conceptual understanding. She wants her students to acquire conceptual understanding, efficient performance of procedural skills, and the ability to relate the two to each other. Therefore, she reteaches addition.

When Doris announces that she is about to continue "The Wizard's Tale," her students give a yelp of delight. Doris tells them to get a partner and a tub of base ten blocks, a bulldozer, and a place value chart from her storage area. When students complete this and are sitting quietly, she begins.

> "The Wizard's Tale" ended yesterday in Thoughtful Mountain with Tinkerbell sitting on Gandalf's beard. Before they can say much to each other, the mountain begins to rumble and boom.
>
> In fear, Gandalf throws himself on the floor, flattens himself against it, puts his hands over his head, and puts a protective magic spell on himself so that nothing can hurt him. Tinkerbell, who is caught between his scratchy beard and the cave's hard floor, starts yelling to Gandalf, "Get up, it is the mountain speaking to us!" Slowly Gandalf gets up and Tinkerbell frees herself from his scratchy beard.
>
> During the rumbling and booming, the cave's walls start to glow red, and the mountain says in a deep voice, "No-talking bulldozer, talking giant parrot!" Then the cave's ceiling starts to crackle. From two different parts of the ceiling, orange pieces of stone fall to the floor. This is what the two sets of stones look like.

Exhibit 1.18

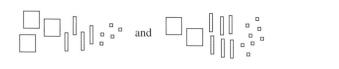

[*Doris puts these base ten blocks on a classroom table where everyone can see them. She asks her students how to say what is in each set of blocks.*]

Next the cave's floor starts to glow pink, and this magic place value chart appears on it, etched in the stone. [*Doris holds up a place value chart and then places it on the table with the base ten blocks.*]

Exhibit 1.19

hundreds	tens	ones

Then Thoughtful Mountain's rumbling and booming cease, and the lights go out. Tinkerbell and Gandalf are left in the dark. Tinkerbell fires up her magic halo of stars so that it glows brightly. Gandalf gets ready to say some magic words. [*Doris signals and magic clapping occurs.*] "Lit, flitt, latt, flight." [*more magic clapping*] Suddenly a small moon begins to glow above Gandalf's head. There, in the dim starlight and moonlight, the two wizards stand, wondering what to do.

Gandalf says, "I think we need to figure out what the mountain's words mean."

Tinkerbell agrees and repeats the words, "No-talking bulldozer, talking giant parrot!" She says, "It seems that we will need both a bulldozer that cannot talk and a talking parrot. Since I have already been a bulldozer, why don't I be the bulldozer and you be the talking parrot."

"No way," says Gandalf, "I don't want to be a bird. Parrots have fleas. No way do I want to be a feather-covered, flea-infested parrot."

"Would you rather be a rusty, old metal bulldozer?" asks Tinkerbell.

"I don't want to be that either," exclaims Gandalf.

"So then be the talking parrot," says Tinkerbell. "I'll turn you into the most beautiful parrot there ever was. I'll give you a beautiful coat of blue, red, and gold feathers that shine brilliantly. I'll make sure you have no fleas. All you will have to do is talk like a parrot in a squeaky voice!"

Gandalf agrees to be the parrot.

The two wizards now plan how they will use the pieces of stone on the cave's floor to solve the mountain's addition problem. They plan how Tinkerbell will act as a bulldozer who cannot say anything as it moves the stones. They plan how Gandalf will act as a giant parrot and verbalize the result of each of Tinkerbell's actions. As they plan, Tinkerbell sings Gandalf her "Addition Song." Let us sing it for him also.

[Doris has students get out their copies of "Tinkerbell's Addition Song" and sing (or chant) it.]

Tinkerbell and Gandalf now discuss the meaning of the song's words and how Gandalf might describe in words each of Tinkerbell's actions. Then Tinkerbell and Gandalf go into action.

Tinkerbell says the magic words [Doris signals and magic clapping occurs.] "Crack, cronk, crooky." [more magic clapping] Suddenly Gandalf turns into the most beautiful parrot there ever was, with a beautiful coat of blue, red, and gold feathers that shines brilliantly, that has no fleas, and that speaks in a squeaky voice.

[Doris pulls a multicolored wood parrot perched on a wood dowel out from her book bag and holds it up for her class to see. She found two dozen of these parrots in her custodian's storage room. They had once been used during a fundraiser.]

Tinkerbell then says some more magic words [Doris signals and magic clapping], "Brump, flump, clump." [more magic clapping] Suddenly Tinkerbell turns into a bright yellow bulldozer. [Doris holds up her yellow plastic bulldozer for her class to see.]

During the following demonstration, whenever Doris acts out Tinkerbell's actions with base ten blocks, she has a hand on her yellow bulldozer. Whenever she utters Gandalf's parrot verbalizations, she holds up the wood parrot and speaks in a squeaky voice. She performs the demonstration on the table in front of the classroom in such a way that her students can see the correspondence between her verbalizations and actions.

With a roar Tinkerbell drives over to one pile of orange stones, picks them up, and deposits them on the floor's magic place value chart, being careful to never let a stone fall into the wrong column. If she does, she might be turned into stone by the mountain. [As she speaks, Doris begins doing this.]

While Tinkerbell is moving the orange stones, Gandalf the Giant Talking Parrot says in a squeaky voice, "We take our first group of orange stones and place them on the magic place value chart so that the three flats are in the hundreds column, the four longs are in the tens column, and the five cubes are in the ones column. This makes three hundred forty-five." [While saying this Doris speaks in a squeaky voice while holding up the parrot.]

Tinkerbell then does the same for the other pile of orange stone pieces [using the bulldozer] while Gandalf the Giant Talking Parrot says in a squeaky voice, "We take our next group of stones and place them on the magic place value chart so that the two flats are in the hundreds column, the six longs are in the tens column, and the eight cubes are in the ones column. This makes two hundred sixty-eight. [*Again Doris holds up the parrot while speaking in a squeaky voice. The stones are arranged like this.*]

Exhibit 1.20

hundreds	tens	ones

Gandalf then announces, "Now we add three hundred forty-five and two hundred sixty-eight. First we add all of the cubes in the ones column." [*Again, Doris holds up the parrot when speaking in a squeaky voice.*]

Tinkerbell now roars her motors [*Doris makes "vrrroom" sounds*] and backs up so that she is above the ones column with her shovel pointing toward the column. Tinkerbell the Bulldozer now moves slowly forward pushing all of the orange stone cubes before her until they are in the shaded box near the bottom of the ones column. This box is called the thinking and trading area. Tinkerbell now has twelve stone cubes in her scoop. Gandalf the Talking Parrot calls out in a squeaky voice, "Five cubes plus seven cubes equals twelve cubes." He then squawks, "Trade ten ones for one ten." Ten of the ones disappear in a puff of smoke and a long falls out of the ceiling and into Tinkerbell's bulldozer's scoop. [*Doris acts this out in front of the class, trading 10 cubes for a long.*] Gandalf the Giant Talking Parrot squeaks, "Twelve cubes is the same as one long and two cubes." Carefully Tinkerbell drives forward a little [*Doris makes "vrrroom" sounds*] and drops the two stone cubes in her scoop into the small rectangular area at the bottom of the magic place value chart, making sure not to let the long fall into the ones column. Gandalf squeaks, "Two cubes are left in the ones column and one long gets carried to the top of the tens column." As he says this Tinkerbell backs up the ones column, and when she reaches the top where the writing is, she rotates clockwise 90 degrees and drops the stone long into the tens column on top of the word "tens"—making sure that it is entirely in the small rectangular area surrounding the word. [*Doris acts this out with the bulldozer while making "vrrroom" sounds.*] As the one stone long that was carried over to the tens column hits the magic place value chart, Gandalf squeaks, "One long has been carried over into the tens column."

Doris now repeats this demonstration for the stones in the tens and hundreds column of the place value chart. When she finishes, she continues the story.

> As Tinkerbell backs off of the magic place value chart, Gandalf the Giant Talking Parrot squeaks, "Three hundred forty-five plus two hundred sixty-eight equals six hundred thirteen."
>
> As soon as Gandalf says that, the color of the room flashes pink and purple for one full minute as the stones on the cavern's magic place value chart float up into the air and disappear by quietly exploding into glorious sprays of red, green, and blue fireworks. [*While saying this, Doris clears the place value chart of base ten blocks.*]
>
> Tinkerbell and Gandalf feel very proud of themselves. But when the lights stop flashing . . . two more sets of stones fall out of the ceiling, representing the numbers 446 and 378.

Doris asks her class which base ten blocks should be set out to represent these numbers. She calls on students to answer, and under their guidance lays out the blocks on the table next to the place value chart.

Doris tells her students that in their groups of two they must help Tinkerbell and Gandalf by acting out the second problem given by Thoughtful Mountain as though they are the wizards. One member of each group must pretend to be Tinkerbell, use the bulldozer, and move the base ten blocks. The other member of the group must pretend to be Gandalf the Giant Talking Parrot, hold up the wood parrot when speaking, and be the *verbalizer*, who describes in words all of the actions taken by the bulldozer. Doris tells her students that there will be a third problem given by the mountain and that they will switch roles for the third problem so that each person in their group will have a chance to be Tinkerbell and Gandalf.

Doris has her students choose roles as she distributes wood parrots. Next, she has her students sing "Tinkerbell's Addition Song" and reminds them of the meaning of some of its phrases. She also reminds them that they are to work cooperatively, what this means, and that if someone needs help to gently and kindly teach them what they need to know in the same way that Tinkerbell would. Doris's students then start working the problem 446 + 378. Base ten blocks are moved about by plastic bulldozers as children make "vrrroom" and "beep, beep, beep" sounds (of bulldozers going forward and backward). Parrots are raised into the air as squeaky voices verbalize the mathematics being performed by the bulldozer. Students monitor each other's behavior and discuss what to do next as they refer to "Tinkerbell's Addition Song."

Doris circulates among her students while they work, observing them, correcting their base ten blocks manipulations and their verbalizations, and reminding them (as needed) what it means to work cooperatively (by treating each other with respect as Tinkerbell would, and remembering that what is important is the success of both members of the group and not just the ability of one member to get a correct answer).

When her students complete the second problem, Doris asks them to switch roles as Tinkerbell and Gandalf and gives each group the problem 275 + 188.

As groups complete the third problem, Doris asks students to discuss in their small groups how the work they did relates to mathematics they might have learned elsewhere. (Doris's students had previously constructed "invented algorithms" for addition.) Doris reminds her students that they are helping Tinkerbell in Thoughtful Mountain, and they must be thoughtful and must share their thoughts with the other members of their group so that all members of their group can learn from their reflections. Doris's students record their thoughts as they discuss.

When small-group discussions are complete, Doris holds a whole-class discussion. During the discussion Doris relates her students' comments to "Tinkerbell's Addition Song" and her addition demonstration. Some of the issues commented on include place value, addition, regrouping, trading between columns, working column by column, and working from right to left versus left to right. A debate arises over whether it is best to do addition from right to left or left to right. The following issues are raised: Does it make a difference? Which direction requires the least backtracking of work? Which direction is most efficient? And what is our cultural convention? After the discussion, Doris continues the story.

> When Tinkerbell and Gandalf complete the third problem with your help, the cavern in Thoughtful Mountain flashes pink and purple for two full minutes as the stones on the cavern's place value chart float up into the air and disappear by quietly exploding into glorious sprays of red, green, and blue fireworks. [*While saying this Doris clears the place value chart of base ten blocks.*]
>
> Then the cavern becomes completely dark and the mountain speaks to Tinkerbell and Gandalf in a deep voice, "Very good, little Wizards. You can now either be released from me to go in peace, or have any wish that is in my power to grant."
>
> Gandalf exclaims, "Release my friend Habble!"
>
> There is a great sound of breaking stone as Habble falls out of the stone wall, fully human again. Gandalf walks over to him, gives him the secret wizard's foot-shake, and asks him why he came into Thoughtful Mountain. [*Doris demonstrates a special foot-shake to her students that includes tapping ankles together.*]
>
> Tinkerbell examines Habble's essence. She discovers that he can be trusted, that he is a lover of flowers, that he knows better than any other wizard how to speak their true speech, and that he will always be loyal to his friends. She also discovers that Habble is absentminded. He can forget to put on his shoes for days at a time or can start out to visit a friend for dinner, get distracted by a flower, sit down and talk with it, and forget that he is going to dinner. Habble tells Gandalf and Tinkerbell that he came to Thoughtful Mountain to save one of his friends, Bondo. Bondo is one of the stone wizards in the cavern's wall.
>
> Before they can say much, the mountain begins rumbling and booming, and Tinkerbell, Gandalf, and Habble get prepared for something earth-shattering.

DAY 3

During this episode of "The Wizard's Tale," Doris puts her students in groups of three, with base ten blocks, plastic bulldozers, wood parrots, place value charts, chartreuse crayons, and worksheets with four magic addition graphics on each. (See the adjacent sample sheet.) When they are in groups with the necessary materials, Doris continues the story.

Exhibit 1.21

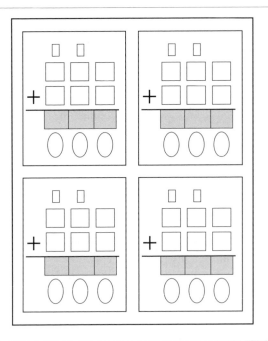

"The Wizard's Tale" ended yesterday with Tinkerbell, Gandalf, and Habble talking in Thoughtful Mountain. Before they could say very much, the mountain began to rumble and boom.

Habble falls to his knees in terror, his hair stands on end, and he starts yelling, "Mama! Mama!" Tinkerbell shouts, "Stop yelling for your mother and get up. It is the mountain speaking to us!" Habble quiets down and gets up. As the mountain continues to boom and rumble, Tinkerbell, Gandalf, and Habble stand quietly.

Suddenly, the booming and rumbling stop as the cave's walls start to glow red and the mountain [*Doris*] says in a deep voice, "No-talking bulldozer, mathematically talking giant parrot, writing gorilla!"

Then the cave's ceiling starts to crackle. From three different parts of the ceiling orange pieces of stone fall to the floor. There is a pile of cubes, a pile of longs, and a pile of flats. [*Doris places a pile of each of these types of base ten blocks on her demonstration table.*]

Next the floor of the cave starts to glow pink, and a magic place value chart appears on it, etched in the stone. [*Doris holds up a place value chart, then puts it on the table with the base ten blocks.*]

Then one of the cave's walls starts to glow violet, and loud crunching sounds can be heard as hundreds of ants appear to be eating away at it. Out of the wall gradually appears a violet-colored, magic addition graphic. Next to the magic addition graphic there also appears a small stone shelf with a chartreuse "stone pencil" on it, with these words inscribed on it, "Use me to write on the wall." This is what the magic addition graphic looks like. [*Doris hangs a large copy of the addition graphic, drawn with a violet crayon, on the wall behind the demonstration table. It is the same as the four on the student worksheet.*]

Exhibit 1.22

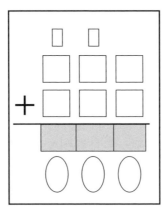

Then the lights go out, and Tinkerbell, Gandalf, and Habble are left in the dark. Tinkerbell fires up her magic halo of stars so that it glows brilliantly while Gandalf makes the small moon above his head glow brightly.

There, in the starlight and moonlight, the three wizards wait until Gandalf says, "I think we need to figure out what the mountain's words mean."

Tinkerbell agrees and repeats the words: "No-talking bulldozer, mathematically talking giant parrot, writing gorilla!" Then she says, "I think we need a bulldozer that cannot talk, a mathematically talking parrot, and a writing gorilla. Since I have already been a bulldozer and Gandalf has already been a giant talking parrot, why don't we make Habble a writing gorilla!"

The three wizards now plan how they will work together. Tinkerbell the Bulldozer will move the stones about without saying anything. Gandalf the Mathematically Talking Parrot will describe in words each action that Tinkerbell takes. And Habble the Writing Gorilla will use the chartreuse stone pencil to record on the addition graphic what Tinkerbell does and Gandalf says. Tinkerbell sings Habble her "Addition Song," they discuss the meanings of its words, and they discuss how Gandalf might verbally describe in words each of Tinkerbell's actions and how Habble might write the result on the addition graphic with the chartreuse pencil.

Doris tells her students that the wizards will benefit from their thoughts, so they must sing "Tinkerbell's Addition Song" and then discuss the same things the wizards are discussing. Afterward, they will telepathically send their thoughts to the wizards. During the discussion Doris highlights issues of how a mathematically talking parrot is different from a talking parrot; whether in mathematical language they should say "cubes" or "ones," "longs" or "tens," and "flats" or "hundreds;" how the magic addition graphic is similar to the magic place value chart (both with their columns and thinking and trading areas), and what it is that should be written on the addition graphic. Doris ends the discussion by having her class telepathically send their thoughts to the wizards by participating in the ritual of clapping three times, concentrating on the important issues of the discussion, and then clapping three more times.

> While discussing how to add, the wizards all have the same thoughts right after we telepathically send them our thoughts. As a result they decide that Gandalf the Talking Parrot should talk proper mathematical language and use the words "ones" instead of "stone cubes," "tens" instead of "stone longs," and "hundreds" instead of "stone flats." They decide that Habble should only write numbers with the chartreuse stone pencil, and that the numbers should only go in the boxes, ellipses, and thinking and trading area of the addition graphic. They also decide that each base ten block manipulation should be immediately followed by the talk and writing that go with it.
>   When the wizards finish their discussion, they go into action.
>   Gandalf gets ready to do magic. [*Doris signals and magic clapping occurs.*] "Crack, cronk, crooky," [*more clapping*] and Gandalf turns himself into a beautiful parrot that speaks in a squeaky voice. Tinkerbell gets ready to do magic. [*Clapping*] "Brump, flump, clump," [*more clapping*] and Tinkerbell turns herself into a bulldozer. Habble does not know how to do form changing magic, so Tinkerbell does magic on him. [*Clapping*] "Habble, gore, gorie, gorum," [*more clapping*] and Habble becomes a hairy gorilla with long arms and a bright pink nose.

During the following demonstration, whenever Doris acts out Tinkerbell's actions with base ten blocks, she does so with her yellow plastic bulldozer. Whenever she utters Gandalf's squeaky verbalizations, she holds up the wood parrot. Whenever she writes numbers for Habble, she uses the chartreuse marker on the addition graphic hanging on the wall. She performs the demonstration on the table in front of the classroom in such a way that her students clearly see the correspondence between her actions, verbalizations, and writing.

> As soon as the wizards change their forms, a screeching sound comes from the addition graphic on the wall and the numbers 377 and 455 appear in it, like this. [*Doris writes the numbers with her chartreuse crayon while saying this.*]

Exhibit 1.23

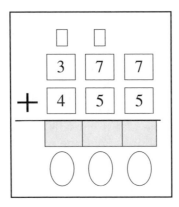

Gandalf immediately squawks that 377 is three hundred seventy-seven, which is three hundreds, seven tens, and seven ones.

With a roar of her engine [*"Vrrroom," says Doris*] Tinkerbell drives over to the pile of hundreds and picks up three, then to the tens and picks up seven, and then to the ones and picks up seven. As she does this Gandalf [*Doris*] squeaks "three hundreds" when she picks up the hundreds, "seven tens" as she picks up the tens, and "seven ones" as she picks up the ones. Habble points at each of the digits in the addition graphic as they are uttered [*as does Doris*]. Tinkerbell the Bulldozer [*accompanied by Doris's "vrooms"*] now deposits the stones in the cave's magic place value chart being careful to never let a stone fall into the wrong column. As she does this, Gandalf the Mathematically Talking Parrot squeaks, "We take our first group of stones and place them on the place value chart so that the three hundreds are in the hundreds column, the seven tens are in the tens column, and the seven ones are in the ones column. This makes three hundred seventy-seven." As this is done Habble [*Doris*] points to the corresponding digits in the addition graphic.

The wizards (and Doris) then do the same for the number 455 and base ten blocks are arranged on the demonstration table's place value chart like this.

Exhibit 1.24

hundreds	tens	ones

Gandalf then squeaks, "Now we add three hundred seventy-seven and four hundred fifty-five. First we add the ones."

Tinkerbell roars her motor, moves so her shovel points down the ones column, and moves forward collecting all of the ones until her scoop is above the shaded thinking and trading box near the bottom of the column. Tinkerbell now has twelve ones in her scoop. Gandalf squeaks, "Seven ones plus five ones equals twelve ones." As Gandalf says this, Habble writes "12" in the thinking and trading area in the ones column. Gandalf then squawks, "Trade ten ones for one ten." Ten of the ones disappear in a puff of smoke and a ten falls out of the ceiling and into Tinkerbell's bulldozer scoop. Gandalf the Mathematically Talking Parrot squeaks, "Twelve ones is the same as one ten and two ones." Carefully Tinkerbell drives forward a little and drops the two ones near the bottom of the ones column. Gandalf squeaks, "Two ones are left in the ones column, and one ten gets carried to the tens column." As Gandalf says this, Habble writes a "2" in the ellipse in the ones column to represent the two ones. Next Tinkerbell backs up the ones column [*as Doris's students make "beep, beep, beep" sounds*], and when she reaches the top where the writing is, she rotates clockwise 90 degrees and drops the stone ten into the tens column on top of the word "tens." As it hits the magic place value chart, Gandalf squeaks, "One ten has been carried over to the tens column," and Habble writes a "1" in the small box at the top of the tens column in the addition graphic to represent that ten. This is what the addition graphic now looks like:

Exhibit 1.25

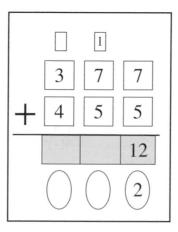

Doris now repeats this demonstration for the tens and hundreds columns. When she finishes she continues.

As Tinkerbell backs off of the magic place value chart on the floor, Gandalf squeaks, "Three hundred seventy-seven plus four hundred fifty-five equals eight hundred thirty-two," as Habble points to this in the wall's addition graphic.

Exhibit 1.26

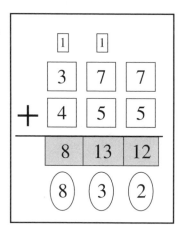

As soon as Gandalf says that, the color of the room flashes pink and purple as the stones on the place value chart float up into the air and disappear by exploding into glorious sprays of red, green, and blue fireworks and as the numbers in the wall's addition graphic disappear. [*While saying this, Doris clears the place value chart of base ten blocks and puts up a new addition graphic.*]

Tinkerbell, Gandalf, and Habble feel very proud of themselves. But when the lights stop flashing . . . the numbers 626 and 295 magically appear in the addition graphic as firecrackers explode next to it.

Doris asks her students which base ten blocks should be set out to represent these numbers. Then she asks them to show her in each of their groups on their worksheet with a chartreuse crayon what should be written in the rectangles of one of the addition graphics.

Doris tells her students that in their groups of three they must help the wizards by acting out the second problem given by Thoughtful Mountain as though they are the wizards. One member of each group must pretend to be Tinkerbell, use the bulldozer, and move the base ten blocks. Another must pretend to be Gandalf the Giant Talking Parrot, hold up the wood parrot when speaking, and be the verbalizer, who describes in words Tinkerbell's actions. The other group member must pretend to be Habble the Writing Gorilla and use a chartreuse crayon to record numbers in one of the addition graphics on the worksheet, numbers that describe Tinkerbell's actions and Gandalf's verbalizations. Doris tells her students that there will be a third and fourth problem given by the mountain and that they will switch roles for these problems so that each group member will have a chance to be Tinkerbell, Gandalf, and Habble.

Doris then has her students choose roles and get the symbol of their role: a bulldozer for Tinkerbell, the wood parrot for Gandalf, and the chartreuse crayon for Habble. Next, her students sing "Tinkerbell's Addition Song." Doris reminds them of the meaning of some of its phrases and that they are to work cooperatively and what this means.

Doris's students go right to work on the problem 626 + 295. Base ten blocks are moved about by plastic bulldozers as children make "vrrroom" and "beep" sounds, parrots are raised into the air as squeaky voices verbalize mathematics, and chartreuse crayons are carefully applied to worksheets. Students monitor each other's behavior and discuss what to do next. As before, Doris circulates among her students observing them, providing help as needed, asking questions, and reminding them what it means to work cooperatively.

As students complete the second problem, Doris asks them to switch roles as Tinkerbell, Gandalf, and Habble and gives each group the problem 255 + 366. When the third problem is solved, students again switch roles and work the problem 394 + 177.

As before, when groups complete the third problem, Doris asks students to discuss in their small groups how the work they did relates to mathematics they might have learned elsewhere and to record their conclusions. When small group discussions are complete, Doris holds a whole-class discussion during which students share their thoughts.

During the discussion Doris focuses attention on correct mathematical language. For example, she points out that for a problem like 372 + 251, when adding the 7 and 5 in the tens column, one *should not* say, "7 plus 5 equals 12, leave 2 and carry 1," but that one *should* say, "7 tens plus 5 tens equals 12 tens. Regroup 10 tens for 1 hundred so that we have 1 hundred and 2 tens. Leave the 2 tens in the tens column and carry the 1 hundred over to the hundreds column." Doris emphasizes that simply saying, "7 plus 5 is 12, leave a 2 and carry 1" is inadequate, for it does not highlight the meaning of the mathematics—which is required by Thoughtful Mountain in order to avoid being turned to stone. (Helping children relearn some of their mathematical language in a thoughtful way so that the language highlights mathematical meanings is an important part of this story.)

When the discussion is complete, Doris continues with the tale. As before, base ten blocks disappear, Thoughtful Mountain offers freedom or the granting of a wish, and Gandalf chooses that Thoughtful Mountain release Bondo. Then . . .

There is a great sound of breaking stone and Bondo falls out of the cavern's wall, fully human again. Habble runs over to her, gives her the secret wizard's foot-shake and a big hug, and asks her why she came into Thoughtful Mountain. As this takes place Tinkerbell studies Bondo's essence. She discovers that Bondo loves to have pretty things and that she loves to be the center of attention. That is probably why she has twelve rings on her fingers and eight different hair pins in her pony tail (one of which is a bee hive with real bees flying about it). She also loves puppy dogs, kittens, and mice. Bondo can be trusted, although she might act spoiled and silly at times.

While Tinkerbell is studying Bondo, Bondo tells the wizards that she came to Thoughtful Mountain to save her puppy dog Zunk, who had been turned into a witch and sent to Thoughtful Mountain by an evil wizard for bothering him while he was contemplating. Zunk is the stone witch who remains frozen in the cavern's wall.

Before they can say much, the mountain begins rumbling, and Tinkerbell, Gandalf, Habble, and Bondo get prepared for something earth-shattering.

Doris now ends this episode of the story.

DAY 4

Day 4 activity is similar to day three, but with three differences. First, base ten "stones" and the place value chart are no longer used. Second, mathematical problems begin to be related to real world situations. Third, the wizards—and Doris's students—work in groups of two as a "mathematical talker" and a "mathematical writer."

Doris begins by putting her students in groups of two and giving each group a wood parrot, a chartreuse crayon, and a copy of the worksheet containing four addition graphics.

Doris starts the story by telling her students how Tinkerbell, Gandalf, Habble, and Bondo were talking when the mountain began to rumble and boom. At the sound of the rumbling, Bondo turns herself into a lion and tries to eat Gandalf, who saves himself with some magic words that turn Bondo back into herself.

> Then the cavern's walls start to glow red, and in a booming voice the mountain says, "Two by two wizards go as mathematically talking giant parrot and mathematically writing gorilla!"
>
> Next, one of the cavern's walls starts to glow white like polished marble. Across the top half of the wall a miniature marching band appears playing musical instruments. Band members are dressed in uniforms made out of green emeralds and blue sapphires and carry musical instruments made out of gold. First there is a group of musicians in a square array lined up in ten neat rows with ten musicians in each column." That's one hundred musicians!" yells Habble. Following them is a second square of one hundred musicians. Following them is a third square of one hundred musicians. Next, there are six neat rows of musicians with ten trumpet players in each row. Finally, there are eight separate musicians, each playing a big gold drum. Then the music and the musicians stop.
>
> The wizards decide that there are three hundred sixty-eight miniature musicians in the three square arrays, six rows, and eight individuals.
>
> After about two minutes, music starts up again and across the lower half of the wall marches a second miniature marching band whose members are dressed in white opals and purple amethysts and whose musical instruments are made of silver. As before the musicians march in square arrays, rows of ten, and as individuals. First two squares, each of which has one hundred musicians, march across the wall. They are followed by three rows of musicians, each of which contains ten trombone players. Next, five musicians enter, each playing a silver xylophone.
>
> When the music and the musicians stop, the wizards discuss how many musicians there are on the lower half of the wall.

Doris asks her students to raise their right hands if they know how many musicians are on the lower half of the wall. After a pause Doris says, "On the count of three, yell out the answer all together in unison . . . one, two, three." Her students bellow, "Two hundred thirty-five." Doris responds, "You know what? The wizards also decide that there are two hundred thirty-five musicians."

"But why are they there?" asks Gandalf.

One of the other walls of the cavern now starts to glow violet. It appears to have hundreds of small green jade dragons eating away at it. Out of the wall gradually appears an addition graphic that glows violet. Next to the addition graphic appears a small stone shelf with a chartreuse "stone pencil" on it. Then, with a screeching sound, like chalk being drawn across a blackboard, numbers appear in the addition graphic, like this. [*Doris writes chartreuse numbers in an addition graphic on a large sheet of paper hanging on her wall.*]

Exhibit 1.27

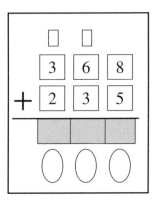

Next the lights go out and the rumbling stops, and Tinkerbell, Gandalf, Habble, and Bondo are left in the dark. Tinkerbell makes her magic halo of stars glow brilliantly while Gandalf makes the small moon above his head glow brightly. There, in the starlight and moonlight, the wizards stand quietly.

Suddenly Habble yells, "I know what to do with the marching bands! The number of musicians in each band is the same as the numbers in the wall's addition problem! The number problem on the wall represents the picture problem of the musicians. We need to add the number of musicians in the two bands! Aren't I smart!"

"That makes sense," says Tinkerbell, "and I don't have to be a bulldozer again!"

Gandalf laughs as he comments, "Well, now you can be a talking parrot or a writing gorilla! The mountain said, 'Two by two wizards go as mathematically talking giant parrot and writing gorilla!' We now have to solve problems in groups of two, with a talking parrot and a writing gorilla in each group."

Tinkerbell agrees and adds, "Gandalf, why don't you and I go first so we can show Bondo what to do. Since you have done such a good job as a mathematically talking parrot, why don't you be the parrot and I'll be the writing gorilla?"

Gandalf agrees.

Bondo says loudly, "I don't know what I am supposed to do!"

The three wizards who have already done problems now sing Bondo "Tinkerbell's Addition Song" and explain how it relates to addition.

As before, Doris tells her students that the wizards will benefit from their thoughts, so they must sing "Tinkerbell's Addition Song" and then discuss the same things the wizards are discussing. During the discussion Doris highlights issues of how a mathematically talking parrot is different from a talking parrot and what should be written in the addition graphic. Doris ends the discussion by having her class telepathically send their thoughts to the wizards by participating in the clapping, thinking, clapping ritual.

While discussing how to add, the wizards all have the same thoughts right after we telepathically send them our thoughts. As a result they tell Bondo how to add numbers in each column, column by column, from right to left. First the ones, then the tens, and then the hundreds. They describe how the columns always have to be legal with only ones in the ones column, tens in the tens column, and hundreds in the hundreds column. They describe how the thinking and trading area works, how to make ten for one trades, and how to carry the traded numbers to the next column. And they make very sure that Bondo understands that when adding two numbers in the tens column, such as in the problem 34 + 52, that she must never say, "3 plus 5," but that she must say, "3 tens plus 5 tens," because the 3 and 5 really represent 3 tens and 5 tens and not just 3 and 5. They carefully explain how the place where a digit is located in a problem tells what its value is and how a mathematically correctly speaking person has to say its value when adding.

The three wizards comment that teaching Bondo how to add helps them better understand addition.

Gandalf starts to hiss as they finish teaching Bondo addition. "The mountain is playing a trick on us!" he says as he spits out twenty-seven firecrackers that explode in mid-air.

"What do you mean?" Tinkerbell asks.

"Look at the problem: 368 + 235! Look at the tens column. If we add the 6 tens to the 3 tens we get 9 tens. But we are going to have 1 ten to carry over from the ones column. So if we add this to the 9 tens, that will give us 10 tens. If we now trade 10 tens for 1 hundred, we have no tens left. That's the trick. What do we do when we have no tens?"

"We can just write nothing," says Habble.

"No way!" says Gandalf. "We have to put something in the ellipse at the bottom of the tens column. And since we don't have any tens, we have nothing to put in it."

"Why can't we just write down nothing?" asks Tinkerbell.

"How can you write nothing and have something written down?" asks Gandalf.

"Come on, silly," says Tinkerbell, "just write down 0 and then you will have written down that there is nothing in the tens column."

"But 0 is nothing, and we have to write something!" Gandalf insists.

Doris asks her students how to help Gandalf understand what to do. After taking several answers, she continues the story.

"Gandalf, come on! There is a difference between the numeral 0 that tells you that you do not have anything and the amount that you have when you have 0 amount, which is nothing," says Habble. "If we put a 0 in the tens column, it means that we have no tens. 0 is the numeral that allows you to say that you have none. If we have the number 'two hundred three' and we write it without a 0, we would just have 2, 3 which is twenty three; if we put in the 0 to say that there are no tens, then we have 2, 0, 3, which is two hundred three."

"OK, now I've got it!" says Gandalf. "Let's just make sure that whenever we have nothing as a result of adding and making our trades, that we write down the 0 to say we have none of something."

Tinkerbell says, "Let's start solving the problem, already! Gandalf and I will start out doing the first problem, and then Bondo and Habble can do the next one." Gandalf gets ready to do magic. [*Doris signals and magic clapping occurs.*] "Crack, cronk, crooky," [*more magic clapping*] and Gandalf turns himself into a beautiful parrot that speaks in a squeaky voice. Tinkerbell gets ready to do magic. [*Clapping*] "Brump, flump, clump," [*more clapping*] and Tinkerbell turns herself into a hairy gorilla with long arms and a pink nose, who writes the results of Gandalf's verbalizations with a chartreuse stone pencil.

During the following demonstration, whenever Doris utters Gandalf's parrot's squeaky verbalizations, she holds up the wood parrot. Whenever she writes numbers for Tinkerbell, she uses the chartreuse marker on the addition graphic hanging on the wall. She does this in a way that highlights the correspondence between verbalizations and writing.

Gandalf squawks, "We are adding 368 and 235, which is three hundred sixty-eight plus two hundred thirty-five. 368 is 3 hundreds, 6 tens, and 8 ones. 235 is 2 hundreds, 3 tens, and 5 ones." As Gandalf the Mathematically Talking Parrot says this, Tinkerbell the Writing Gorilla points at each of the digits in the magic addition graphic.

Gandalf the Mathematically Talking Parrot now announces that they will first add numbers in the ones column. Tinkerbell points to them. Gandalf the Mathematically Talking Parrot squeaks, "8 ones plus 5 ones equals 13 ones. Write the 13 in the thinking and trading area in the ones column." As Gandalf says this, Tinkerbell the Writing Gorilla writes "13" in the thinking and trading area in the ones column. Gandalf then squawks, "Trade 10 ones for 1 ten. 13 ones is now the same as 1 ten and 3 ones. Write the 3 in the ones column and carry over the 1 ten and write it in the tens column." As Gandalf says this, Tinkerbell the Writing Gorilla writes a "3" in the ellipse at the bottom of the ones column to represent the 3 ones and a 1 in the small box at the top of the tens column to represent the 1 ten that is carried over to the tens column.

Exhibit 1.28

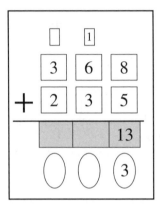

Doris now repeats this demonstration for the tens and hundreds column. When she finishes, she continues.

Gandalf the Mathematically Talking Parrot finally squeaks, "Three hundred sixty-eight plus two hundred thirty-five equals six hundred three," as Tinkerbell points to this in the wall's addition graphic.

Exhibit 1.29

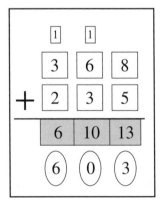

Everything is quiet for a minute as if something more needs to be done. Habble starts jumping up and down while pointing at the marble wall with the two bands of musicians. Gandalf then adds, "If a band of 368 musicians joins with a band of 235 musicians, then there will be one band with 603 musicians!"

As soon as Gandalf the Mathematically Talking Parrot says that, the color of the room flashes pink and purple for two minutes as the numbers in the addition graphic burn away to nothing in flames and as the two marching bands march together to form a single band of 603 musicians and then explode into fireworks that sparkle with 603 tiny points of bright white light.

Tinkerbell and Gandalf feel very proud of themselves as they say magic words that turn themselves back into their normal selves. They worked together cooperatively, listening to and watching each other carefully as they coordinated their talk and writing.

Next, Habble and Bondo take their turns. Or rather, you students take their turns for them, so listen carefully to what happens and keep track of any mathematical things that you might need to use when you do the problem for Habble and Bondo.

Next, the marble wall begins to glow and on the upper half of it a baker appears carrying a muffin tin filled with one hundred delicious-looking cupcakes, each of which is decorated with precious diamonds that twinkle in the dim light of the cave. The cupcakes are arranged in the muffin tin in neat rows and columns with ten rows of cupcakes and ten cupcakes in each row. Following the first baker are three more bakers carrying muffin tins each holding one hundred cupcakes. Following them is a baker carrying a muffin tin with only five rows of ten cupcakes in it. And following him is a baker carrying a tray of six individual cupcakes. When all of these bakers and cupcakes are on the upper half of the wall, a second set of bakers carrying cupcakes decorated with blue sapphires walks onto the lower half of the wall. They carry two muffin tins of one hundred cupcakes each, one muffin tin with six rows of ten cupcakes, and four individual cupcakes.

When all of the bakers are lined up and standing still, the wall's addition graphic begins to glow violet, and with a screeching sound new numbers appear in it. And what do you think the numbers are?

Doris asks her students to meet in their groups and write the numbers on a scrap of paper and then raise their hands. When hands go up she checks to see that 456 and 264 are recorded. One group makes a mistake, and she asks a group sitting next to them to help them.

Doris has now demonstrated to her students how to do one problem, carefully demonstrating Gandalf's verbalizations and Tinkerbell's writing. She has also set up a second problem.

Doris tells her students that in their groups of two they must help the wizards by acting out the second problem given by Thoughtful Mountain as though they are the wizards. One member of each group must pretend to be the giant talking parrot, hold up the wood parrot when speaking, and be the verbalizer. The other group member must pretend to be the writing gorilla and use a chartreuse crayon to record numbers in one of the addition graphics on their worksheet, numbers that describe what the gorilla says. Doris tells her students that there will be a third problem given by the mountain and that they will switch roles for this problem so that each person in their group will have a chance to be a talker and writer.

Doris has students choose roles and get the symbol of their role: a wood parrot or chartreuse crayon. Next, she has her students sing "Tinkerbell's Addition Song" and again reminds them of the meanings of some of its phrases. She also reminds them that they are to work cooperatively and what this means.

Doris's students start working the problem 456 + 264. Parrots are raised into the air as squeaky voices verbalize mathematics. Chartreuse crayons are carefully applied to worksheets. Students monitor each other's behavior and discuss what to do next. As before, Doris circulates among her students observing them and providing help as needed.

When the second problem is correctly completed, Doris asks students to switch roles as writer and talker and gives each group a third problem: 358 + 328. Over the years, Doris has embedded these problems in a variety of real-world situations: for example, Canadian geese flying in formation (a square of one hundred, a line of ten, and individual birds) or farmers carrying cartons of eggs (big square cartons of one hundred, long skinny cartons of ten, and individual eggs). The problems often relate to situations encountered in her classroom that the students recognize.

As before, when groups complete the third problem, Doris asks students to discuss in their small groups how the work they did relates to mathematics they might have learned elsewhere, and to record their conclusions. When small group discussions are complete, Doris holds a whole-class discussion during which students report their thoughts.

When the discussion is complete, Doris continues "The Wizard's Tale." As before, Thoughtful Mountain offers freedom or the granting of a wish. Bondo chooses that Thoughtful Mountain release Zunk. Then . . .

> There is the sound of breaking stone, and Zunk falls out of the stone wall. Zunk is in the form of an evil witch, the form that the wizard who was annoyed by her playfulness gave her. Zunk takes one look at Gandalf, Tinkerbell, Habble, and Bondo and starts hissing magic curses. "Gandalf, gum, gam, gibble," she says and turns Gandalf into a big squirmy worm. "Habble, gum, gam, gibble," she says and turns Habble into a big squirmy worm. Tinkerbell quickly flies out of sight and hides. "Bondo, gum, gam, gibble!" yells Zunk and turns Bondo into a worm. Then she goes over to the worm Bondo and with great delight on her face, raises her foot to prepare to squash Bondo.
>
> But Tinkerbell acts first. She gets ready to say some magic words [*Doris signals and magic clapping occurs.*], "Ding, bing, ping, swing Zunk" [*more magic clapping*]. Tinkerbell turns Zunk back into her puppy dog self. Then she turns Gandalf, Habble, and Bondo back into themselves.
>
> Zunk immediately runs over to Bondo with her tail wagging and making whining sounds of delight upon seeing her old master. Bondo picks up Zunk and gives her a hug. Zunk starts licking Bondo in the face. But before anything else can happen, the mountain begins to rumble and boom.

Doris now ends this episode of the story.

DAY 5

This is the last installment of "The Wizard's Tale" and Doris wants to get her students prepared to do multidigit addition at a symbolic level without external aids. She also wants to extend addition beyond three digit numbers, connect multidigit addition with money, and check to make sure that her students know what to do when a column sums to 0.

The first part of Day 5 functions as a review of the previous day with students working in groups of two using a sheet of paper with four new transitional addition graphics on it. The purpose of the new transitional addition graphic is to wean students away from recording numbers in the thinking and trading area. The new graphics do not contain the thinking and trading area, and while solving problems it is necessary for the wizards to imagine the invisible thinking and trading area even though it is impossible to write anything in it. As on Day 4, Thoughtful Mountain announces that, "Two by two wizards go as mathematically talking parrot and writing gorilla!" It then presents the problem 568 + 226 using a display of jewels on its cavern's wall in which dollars (that turn into square arrays of one hundred pennies) are made out of opals and emeralds, dimes (that turn into lines of ten pennies) are made out of silver and rubies, and pennies are "intricately carved pieces of jade inlaid with diamonds." This is what the new transitional addition graphic looks like.

Exhibit 1.30

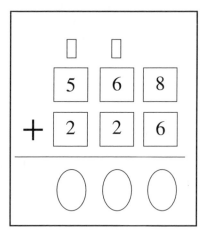

Day 5 then proceeds as did Day 4: Doris's students discuss how much money is on the wall and yell their answer in unison; the problem appears in a new addition graphic on the cave's wall; Tinkerbell and Gandalf magically light their stars and moon (with the help of magic clapping from Doris's class); Tinkerbell and Gandalf decide to be talking parrot and writing gorilla respectively; Doris's students sing "Tinkerbell's Addition Song," discuss how to do addition, and telepathically send their thoughts to the wizards; the wizards with the telepathic help of Doris's students describe to Zunk (the dog) how to do addition and then comment that each time they have to find words to help them describe how to do addition it helps them better understand the process themselves; Tinkerbell and Gandalf magically turn themselves into talking parrot and writing gorilla (with the help of Doris's students' clapping); and Doris demonstrates (while speaking in a different tone of voice to represent each wizard) how to do the problem on the wall while "imagining" the existence of a thinking and trading area (which no longer exists in the new addition graphic).

When Doris finishes reviewing the previous day's work and relating addition of money to addition of numerical symbols, she asks her students to help the wizards solve two problems in their pairs, as they did the previous day. While solving the first money problem, $177 + 277$, they pretend they are Habble and Bondo. When solving the second money problem, $389 + 151$, they pretend they are Tinkerbell and Gandalf. During the problems they practice imagining the now invisible thinking and trading area in their minds while adding numbers in each column and making trades. While solving each problem, one student acts as the writer and uses the chartreuse crayon on one of the new addition graphics on the worksheet and the other acts as the speaker and holds a wood parrot while speaking. As before, students switch roles after each problem.

When students finish their problems and everything disappears from the cavern except for the magic stone pencil, which was left on its shelf on the wall, Doris continues the story.

> Then Thoughtful Mountain gives three loud booms and says, "Tinkerbell and Gandalf, Mathematically Talking Giant Parrot and Writing Gorilla, on the wall add 345 and 456." The mountain then becomes quiet.
>
> Gandalf says, "Just as I expected, now we have to do the addition without the help of any addition graphic. Remember those numbers: 345 and 456. Tinkerbell, do you want to be the parrot or the gorilla?"
>
> Tinkerbell says, "I'll be the parrot and you can be the gorilla. But what do we do?"
>
> "Yes," joined in Bondo and Habble, "what do we do when there is no addition graphic?"
>
> "Easy," said Gandalf, "just pretend that the addition graphic is there and put numerals in its invisible boxes and ellipses! It's a cinch! Just look at the wall. Can't you see where the addition graphic is? . . . See it there? . . . There are the two little boxes up top, the six bigger boxes in the middle. . . . The line and the addition sign is under them, the thinking and trading area under that, and on the bottom are the three ellipses. And everything is arranged in nice neat columns so that as the song says, we can add
>
> Column by column
> Column by column.
>
> "Just remember 'Tinkerbell's Addition Song' and imagine the addition graphic in your mind."

With the help of clapping from Doris's class, Tinkerbell and Gandalf now magically turn themselves into a talking parrot and writing gorilla so that Doris can demonstrate how to do this new problem without an addition graphic. In what follows she records the addition on her blackboard.

Tinkerbell then speaks up, "We are going to add 345 and 456, so we must first write down these numbers, one above the other with ones above ones, tens above tens, and hundreds above hundreds."

When this is said, Gandalf the Writing Gorilla [*Doris*] writes the problem on the wall with his magic pencil.

Then Tinkerbell the Mathematically Talking Giant Parrot says, "Draw a line below the numbers we are going to add that separates the problem from its answer and put an addition sign to the left of the lower number." Gandalf [*Doris*] does this, and the wizards are ready to begin adding.

Exhibit 1.31

$$
\begin{array}{r}
3\ 4\ 5 \\
+\ 4\ 5\ 6 \\
\hline
\end{array}
$$

Feathery Tinkerbell then says, "First we add the ones. 5 ones plus 6 ones equals 11 ones. Next the 11 ones are traded for 1 ten and 1 one in the invisible thinking and trading box. 1 ten and 1 one are now legal. So we write a 1 at the bottom of the ones column, move the ten over to the tens column where it belongs, and record it at the top of the column." While she says this, Gandalf [*Doris*] is at work writing on the wall of the cavern everything she says.

Exhibit 1.32

$$
\begin{array}{r}
\overset{1}{}\ \ \ \ \\
3\ 4\ 5 \\
+\ 4\ 5\ 6 \\
\hline
1 \\
\end{array}
$$

Doris continues working the problem in this manner until it is complete, and this is what is on the wall.

Exhibit 1.33

$$
\begin{array}{r}
{\scriptstyle 1 \quad\;\; 1} \\
3\;\;4\;\;5 \\
+\;\;4\;\;5\;\;6 \\
\hline
8\;\;0\;\;1
\end{array}
$$

Next Habble and Bondo will have to take their turn, or rather you children will take their turn for them.

Doris has now both discussed and demonstrated how to do Thoughtful Mountain's latest problem with her students. She has both provided a cognitive map of the addition process and modeled the desired behaviors in such a way that her students can see how the writing takes place, hear how the mathematical thought processes are verbalized, and understand the correspondences between writing and verbalizations.

Doris gives her students the next two problems orally. They are 484 + 217 and 284 + 247. Her students work in pairs, as before, with one child acting as a writer and the other as a talker and switching roles between problems. This time, however, they write on a blank sheet of paper.

When her students finish adding, Doris continues the story.

> Then Thoughtful Mountain gives three loud booms and says, "One last problem for you little wizards, 567 + 678. Each of you work it alone, compare your work, and tell me the answer." There is a sudden screeching sound, and out of the floor of the cavern grow four stone desks, one in front of each wizard. On each desk is a stone slate and a magic stone pencil. There is a sudden sound of trumpets from within each stone desk. And then the mountain becomes quiet.
>
> Gandalf says, "I guess we each have to do the problem ourselves. Probably to prove to the mountain that we can each do addition. To the task wizards, and we will compare our answers when we are done! Remember the problem, 567 + 678. It is a tricky one, but I am sure that we can each do it. Just remember, if you start doing something, keep going in the same way until you finish."

Doris has now presented her students with a problem designed to help generalize the addition algorithm by extending addition beyond the hundreds place. Each student must now solve the problem individually, on a plain sheet of paper, speaking to himself or herself as they write. When they finish, they are to check their written work, verbalizations, and answers with their previous partner and help their partner if necessary. Doris monitors her students' work.

(Laura McBride says that some of her third graders do not know what to do after adding in the hundreds column—even though they have previously worked with base ten block ones, tens, hundreds, and thousands—and that this stimulates wonderful class discussions.)

When groups finish their work, Doris's students telepathically send their thoughts to the wizards in Thoughtful Mountain (using the clapping process). First, they send the problem's answer (1,245) by yelling it in unison. Then, after sitting quietly and thinking about what they have done, they quietly send their thoughts about addition.

Then, as on previous days, Doris has small groups discuss and record how the work they did today relates to mathematics they might have learned elsewhere. This is followed by a whole-class discussion.

After the discussion, Doris continues the story.

As soon as the problem is complete and all of the wizards agree on its answer, the color of the room flashes from gold to silver to purple over and over again for several minutes as all of the desks, pencils, and slates in the cavern disappear in great fountains of sparkles. Then Thoughtful Mountain gives three loud booms and says, "Very good, little wizards. You can now either be released from me to go in peace or have any wish that is in my power to grant."

Gandalf replies, "Release us from your cavern to go in peace!"

As soon as he says that, Thoughtful Mountain starts to make the sounds of a volcano beginning to erupt. All of the wizards move together in a fearful cluster, and Zunk jumps into Bondo's arms. Below their feet, the floor of the cavern turns to molten lava that burbles like a caldron of liquid red stone. For some magical reason, however, it does not burn their feet or roast them. Then suddenly the roof of the cavern opens up in the shape of a volcano's crater and blue sky shows up above. Gradually the molten lava below their feet bubbles up through the core of the mountain and the wizards are carried to the top of the volcano's rim. Then, all of a sudden, the wizards are shot up into the sky like cannonballs shot from cannons as Thoughtful Mountain erupts and spews smoke, lava, and them into the sky.

As soon as they are thrown into the sky, Gandalf and Tinkerbell turn themselves into giant eagles with the magic words [*Doris signals and magic clapping occurs.*] "Eagle, agle, oggle, ungle" [*more magic clapping*]. Gandalf flies under Habble, who lands on his back. Tinkerbell swoops under Bondo, who is still holding Zunk, and the two of them land on her back. Then the two wizardly eagles with their cargoes fly away from Thoughtful Mountain as its volcanic eruption subsides and it closes its volcanic crater so that it looks like it has never been a volcano.

Gandalf squawks to Tinkerbell in an eagle's voice, "Follow me to my home. It is closer than yours!" And the two eagles fly off to Gandalf's home.

When they reach Gandalf's house, the eagles put down their cargoes and turn themselves back into their normal forms of Gandalf and Tinkerbell. Zunk barks loudly to let everyone know that she is hungry. All of the others agree. They go into Gandalf's dining room, and Gandalf creates a wonderful dinner for them by turning dust into food. There is plenty of food because there is lots of dust in Gandalf's house. And what a wonderful meal it is, with heaps of meat and vegetables, but the best part is the desserts. There are three wonderful ice cream desserts, each of which has fireworks exploding over it and music coming from within it.

When the meal is finished, the three wizards and the puppy dog leave Gandalf's house, each to return to their own homes.

And this is where the story ends.

This is not where Doris's instruction on multidigit addition ends, however. Following the story Doris's students play numerous homemade academic skill development games to maintain and further develop their mathematical skills and understanding of addition. Doris makes the games out of such things as egg cartons, wood cubes, poster board, tongue depressors, and printer's cards. Doris also introduces her class to computer games that require multidigit addition.

Later in the year, Gandalf sends Doris's class letters addressed to Tinkerbell that describe different methods of doing addition that he discovers while traveling around the world. These alternative algorithms introduce Doris's students to ways in which other cultures do addition and help students clarify and deepen their understanding of the way in which they were taught the operation. A copy of one letter follows.

Exhibit 1.34

Dear Tinkerbell,

The Museum of Ancient Wizardry has asked me to search throughout the entire world for outstanding portraits of wizards. I am traveling everywhere looking for pictures. I am now in Italy.

While here I discovered an interesting method of doing addition. I was told that it was invented over 400 years ago in Italy. This is how it works.

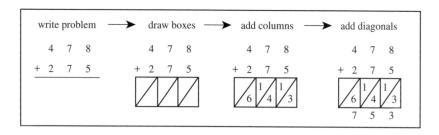

Can you figure out how this addition method works?

Do you think that this old Italian method of addition always gives the same answer to addition problems as the addition method that we used in Thoughtful Mountain?

I think that this method is similar to ours in some ways, and I also think that it is different in some ways. Will you explore how this method is similar to and different from the method we used?

My magical regards,
Gandalf

Chapter 2

MATHEMATICAL EPIC ORAL STORYTELLING

Underlying Assumptions

One might wonder, "Was Doris's storytelling endeavor really a mathematics lesson?" When we think of mathematics instruction, we usually think of different types of things occurring in a classroom.

In the (perhaps overly vilified) traditional method of teaching mathematics, teachers instruct children differently than Doris. Usually a teacher will write an addition problem on a chalkboard, describe to students how to work the problem while demonstrating how to do so, and then assign to students twenty or so number problems from a mathematics textbook, workbook, or worksheet to complete independently by themselves with paper and pencil before the next class session. The teacher will then give students a chance to start their mathematics work during class so they can ask questions of the teacher if they have difficulties with the work. Problems not completed in class become homework, which will be reviewed at the beginning of the next mathematics class.

In one of the more modern methods of teaching mathematics, a teacher might write an addition problem on a chalkboard, put students into small groups, give them base ten blocks, ask them to use the blocks to invent a method of combining the two numbers written on the chalkboard, and then ask them to discuss the addition methods they invent.

In another of the more modern methods of teaching, we might find a teacher at a chalkboard writing addition problems for students to solve, students independently doing the calculations mentally "in their heads," students telling the teacher their answers to the problem, and then students having a debate over which answer to the problem is correct (Kamii, 1987).

In each of these three types of classrooms, serious objective mathematical reasoning is at the center of the instructional process, and there is little room for fantasy, emotion, and playfulness during instruction. Most (although not all) current methods of mathematics instruction tend to remove the "story" from mathematics and present mathematics in a decontextualized objective manner in small atomized units, each of which stands alone and involves one day's worth of activity.

This, however, is not what is occurring in Doris's classroom. In Doris's classroom we find the teacher orally presenting a mathematical fantasy that she creates using her imagination, a fantasy that is wrapped around a mathematics skill that she wants her students to learn. It is a fantasy in which her students become intellectually, emotionally, and physically involved as their mathematical endeavors help a heroine (Tinkerbell) save the lives of her friends. In Doris's classroom we find students clapping to make magic occur and the teacher using intonation, gestures, and physical movements to stimulate her students' imagination. In Doris's classroom students drive bulldozers, make "vrrroom" and "beep" sounds, sing songs, and help each other learn (rather than work quietly and independently).

What Doris is doing is not uncommon: she is teaching her students the multidigit addition algorithm popularized by our twentieth-century Western educational establishment. But within Doris's classroom serious decontextualized objective mathematical reasoning is not at the center of the instructional process. Instead, Doris is using oral epic mathematical fantasies that tap into both the learner's and teacher's subjective consciousness in an attempt to personalize and contextualize mathematics. Fantasy, imagination, intuition, emotion, and playfulness are at the center of the instructional process, as well as the mathematical processes that Doris wants her students to learn.

What is occurring in this classroom? And why might some educators believe that orally delivered epic fantasies have potential to increase students' ability to do, understand, and appreciate mathematics?

This book is about helping children learn mathematics through oral storytelling, in particular through the use of narrative fantasy tales that take several days to complete. As presented in this book, mathematical epic oral stories are multistage adventures in which a hero or heroine (or group of heroes or heroines) encounters multiple adventures during a major quest, expedition, or journey. The stories are orally delivered from memory (even if they are written down so that a storyteller can remember them or share them with other storytellers). The storyteller's intonation, gestures, body movements, and eye contact with listeners are important parts of the storytelling experience. Also important is the rich use of descriptive language that paints a vivid picture of the epic's characters, adventures, and places they visit. These stories also involve the use of mathematical manipulatives, imagery, symbols, diagrams, or algorithms by both the storyteller (who models behavior for the audience) and the audience (who responds like a chorus, frequently with variations on the behavior modeled by the storyteller). Crucial to a story's oral presentation is the audience's ability to "listen in" to the mathematical thought processes of the storyteller and hear (and see with the use of mathematical manipulatives, diagrams, or algorithms) the story's characters think though mathematical problems.

In presenting mathematics in the context of oral epic fantasies, five things are important: that mathematics is presented through the medium of a story; that the story is orally presented; that the story is a fantasy; that the story contextually situates mathematics in ways that are interesting, involving, and relevant to the reader; and that the story takes several days to present. Each of these aspects of mathematical oral storytelling will now be examined.

THE IMPORTANCE OF STORY

During most of the twentieth century, mathematics educators have believed that stories, primarily in the form of the *word problem,* are important. In fact, during the last decades of the twentieth century, they became increasingly interested in the power of stories—primarily in the form of children's trade books (or storybooks) that can provide a jumping-off point for mathematical explorations—to help children learn mathematics. However, these conceptions of the possible use of stories just scratch the surface of what is known about the power of stories in the lives of individuals and cultures.

Stories as Word Problems

During most of the twentieth century, stories were an important part of mathematics instruction. They were found at the end of problem sets in mathematics textbooks and were known as word problems or *story problems.* Their importance derived from educators' conceptions of what mathematics was most worthy of being taught and how to teach it.

In general, it was believed that the essence of school mathematics was the decontextualized, abstract, objectifiable facts, algorithms, and processes that could be written down in an impersonal, symbolic, theoretical format. Mathematics instruction tended to remove the *story* from mathematics, the story that described the historical origins of mathematics, the story of mathematicians' practical achievements, and the story of how people have imagined mathematics might be used in the real everyday world and in their dream and fantasy worlds.

This mathematics was generally presented in a lesson that progressed from the mathematics deemed to be most important to that deemed to be least important. First there was an objective, impersonal, symbolic, theoretical, and decontextualized presentation of mathematical facts, algorithms, or processes. This was followed by sample problems that demonstrated to children how they were to solve the type of problem under consideration. Next came many *number* problems for children to solve that provided them with the practice needed to *learn* the specific mathematics being presented. Finally, at the end of the number problems were the word problems or story problems. These short story problems were needed in order to demonstrate to children how the important mathematics they had just learned could be applied to real-world situations and to give children practice applying that mathematics to the real world.

Unfortunately, these mathematical "stories" found at the ends of problem sets tended not to have a powerful influence on children, for several reasons. They were considered to be of secondary importance because they came at the end of the really important mathematical work—the theoretical number work. Children were often exhausted and bored with the many number problems before they got to the stories. Children rarely took any of the stories seriously because they usually had to solve numerous different story problems that related to entirely disjointed story lines, one after another. And most importantly, the stories were so brief, had so little life to them—had so little character development and plot to them—that they could hardly be called stories.

As a result, the mathematical stories presented during most of the twentieth century were generally considered to be impotent, painful exercises rather than powerful, exciting glimpses into rich human endeavors. More could be expected of mathematical stories.

Children's Trade Books as Springboards
for Mathematical Explorations

During the last decades of the twentieth century, new conceptions of school mathematics and ways of teaching mathematics became popular. Educators were inspired by the 1989 statement of the National Council of Teachers of Mathematics (NCTM) *Curriculum and Evaluation Standards for School Mathematics,* the *whole language* approach to reading, *literature based* language arts, *reading across the disciplines,* developmental psychology, and *constructivism.*

Their view of what was important in school mathematics shifted. It now included a conception in which children could become powerful problem solvers, users, and communicators of mathematics who were excited by the subject and who constructed their own mathematical meanings.

Inspired by this new view of school mathematics, educators searched for ways of teaching mathematics that would make it interesting, powerful, and meaningful to children. To their delight they discovered children's trade books that contained mathematics, many of which were of interest to children. They discovered children's trade books such as *The Doorbell Rang* (Hutchins, 1986), *Anno's Mysterious Multiplying Jar* (Anno & Anno, 1983), *The Toothpaste Millionaire* (Merrill, 1972), and *How Much Is a Million?* (Schwartz, 1985). They experimented with different ways of using children's trade books to enhance mathematics instruction and then wrote books about how to use children's storybooks during mathematics instruction. They wrote books such as *Read Any Good Math Lately?* (Whitin & Wilde, 1992), *How to Use Children's Literature to Teach Mathematics* (Welchman-Tischler, 1992), *Math and Literature* (Burns, 1992), and *It's the Story That Counts* (Whitin & Wilde, 1995).

Children's trade books, it was proclaimed, were wonderful jumping-off points for beginning new mathematical topics of study or introducing mathematical problems to children. Many reasons have been cited for linking mathematics and children's literature during instruction: to help children learn mathematical concepts and skills; to provide children with a meaningful context for learning mathematics; to facilitate children's development and use of mathematical language and communication; to help children learn mathematical problem solving, reasoning, and thinking; to provide children with a richer view of the nature of mathematics; to provide children with improved attitudes toward mathematics; to motivate and interest children in mathematics; to help children integrate mathematics with life and other school disciplines; and to help educators teach mathematics (Schiro, 1997).

Unfortunately, there was a noteworthy limitation to the twentieth-century movement to use children's trade books to enrich mathematics instruction. Most (although not all) educators viewed children's storybooks as springboards for beginning an exploration of a mathematical topic or problem (Kliman, 1993, p. 320; Welchman-Tischler, 1992, p. 1). They viewed children's literature as a jumping-off point for introducing a new topic to be studied, as a way of introducing a problem that needed to be solved, or as a way of providing an example of how mathematics could be contextualized in a real- or fantasy-world setting. Literature was used to propel children into mathematical explorations in such a way that once the children were engaged in the mathematics, the literature was abandoned and children never seriously returned to it. There is nothing wrong with using children's literature in this instrumental way—as a springboard into mathematics—but doing so limits the power that mathematical stories can have in children's lives.

It is possible to integrate children's stories and mathematics so that the two become inseparable, to stay focused on both the story and the mathematics for the duration of the learning experience, and to value, *equally,* both children's literary *and* mathematical experience during instruction. It is possible to combine mathematics and stories in such a way that the benefits of mathematical stories, like *The Doorbell Rang* and the others mentioned above, can be reaped while at the same time the stories can be far more powerful experiences for children than if stories are simply used as springboards into mathematics and then left behind. To understand the power of mathematical stories, the importance of stories in people's lives must be examined.

The Importance of Stories in People's Lives

Stories are important to both cultures and the individuals who live within them. When viewed from a cultural perspective, stories are one of the major ways in which cultures pass on to succeeding generations their way of viewing the world and making meaning out of cultural and natural occurrences. When viewed from an individualistic perspective, storytelling is a *primal act of mind.* It is one of the major ways in which individuals construct meaning out of their encounters with their world and give meaning to their lives.

Cultural Perspective

Throughout historical times (and certainly up until the use of the printing press during the fifteenth century) oral stories offered cultures—and the masses of humanity who comprised them—a way of understanding their world and passing on their understanding to succeeding generations. The teacher, the priest, the artisan, and the parent were all cultural agents who used oral stories to pass on their traditions. The professional storyteller served as a historian, a bringer of news, a religious and moral teacher, or an educator, as well as an entertainer (Pellowski, 1990). In the broadest sense, the early oral storyteller was the medium through which a society passed on its culture to its preliterate or illiterate (and often its literate) population. Telling stories about people, events, the heavens, geological structures, the gods, animals, and how honorable and dishonorable people responded to them was one of the main ways in which society passed on its culture to the next generation, while at the same time providing entertainment. (Stories were not the only way of passing on culture, for such media as painting, sculpture, basketry, weaving, song, dance, poetry, and drama were also ways of passing on a society's culture.)

Viewed from a sociocultural perspective, stories—whether oral or written—are one of the primary means by which every society attempts to introduce its members to its way of viewing the world. As Frank Smith (1990, p. 63) puts it, "In fact, it might be said that a major function of cultures is to provide and perpetuate the stories that individuals need in order to make sense of the world in which they find themselves. . . . Cultures teach us the stories by which we will live." According to Smith, the stories told within a culture teach its members that culture's interpretation of who is a hero or villain, "right and wrong, good and bad, aims and obstacles, collaboration and conflict, power and prohibition, causes and consequences."

Stories—and particularly narrative fantasies—were, and still are, a powerful cultural communication medium. They offer mankind a well-known and easily understood way of exploring their world and articulating its meaning to themselves within a social context, as well as a safe, familiar way of making coherent meaning out of the feelings and thoughts that their world arouses within them (Bettelheim, 1976, p. 24).

Individual Perspective

Narrative stories are also important to individuals. What is important about narrative stories—be they stories in which imbalances are resolved, growth takes place, obstacles are navigated, treasures are sought after, or thoughts are revealed—is that fictional narrative shares much

> with that inner and outer storytelling that plays a major role in our sleeping and waking lives. For we dream in narrative, remember, anticipate, hope, despair, believe, doubt, plan, revise, criticize, construct, gossip, learn, hate, and love by narrative. In order really to live, we make up stories about ourselves and others, about the personal as well as the social past and future. (Hardy, 1977, p. 13)

It has even been argued that storytelling is a primal act of mind: that as well as being the conscious and deliberate activity of a storyteller, it is also "not a conscious and deliberate activity, but the way in which the mind itself works" (Wells, 1986, p. 197). As Whitin and Wilde suggest, "Stories are the fundamental way of making meaning" (1995, p. x) that people use in their endeavor to make sense of their lives and their world. Frank Smith elaborates when he writes that

> thought flows in terms of stories—stories about events, stories about people, and stories about intentions and achievements. . . . We learn in the form of stories. We construct stories to make sense of events. Our prevailing propensity to impose story structures on all experience, real or imagined, is the ultimate governor on the imagination. . . . The brain is a story-seeking, story-creating instrument.
>
> We cannot help thinking in terms of stories, whether we are recalling the past, contemplating the present, or anticipating the future. . . . When we say we cannot make sense of something, we mean that we cannot find the story in it or make up a story about it. We look at life in terms of stories, even when there is no story to be told. That is the way we make sense of life: by making stories. It is the way we remember events: in terms of stories. (1990, pp. 62-64)

What is particularly important here is that the

> stories that we construct are not a special way of perceiving the world or of making sense of everything we hear or read. It is the *only* way we can make sense of the world, of literature, and of art; it is also the way our fantasies make sense to us. Stories are our way of perceiving, of conceiving, of creating; they are the way the imagination works. . . . No one has to tell us, or teach a child, to perceive life in terms of stories; it is what everyone does. . . .

[Our] stories are the vantage points from which we perceive the world and the people in it. We anthropomorphize, invest with human personalities, not only animals, but toys, cars, ships, and computers. We give them names, characters, and motives—we see them behaving. We see nations as characters in global dramas. . . . We fictionalize "the people," "the government," even "the gods"—and give them roles, often dominant ones, in the stories of our lives. (1990, pp. 64-65)

Children tell stories to themselves in these ways whenever they project themselves—in their imagination—into the role of hero or heroine of a movie recently viewed. Children tell stories to themselves in these ways whenever they project themselves—in their imagination—into the persona of the hero or heroine in a computer simulation in which they must role-play the simulation's hero or heroine. (Just watch children play *GoldenEye 007* (Nintendo), the James Bond computer simulation, to see how they project themselves into a story's characters and live that character's adventures. Then wonder about what would happen if the maze they negotiate in the James Bond simulation was a mathematical algorithm or a problem-solving strategy we might want to teach them to navigate in school.)

Stories and storytelling have a far more important function within the lives of individuals and cultures than simply as springboards that propel children into mathematical endeavors, illustrations that contextualize theoretical mathematics, or entertainment. *Outer storytelling,* when viewed as an "essential transmitter of culture," is one of the major ways in which cultures pass on to succeeding generations their way of viewing the world and their way of making meaning out of cultural and natural occurrences in that world. *Inner storytelling,* when viewed as a primal act of mind, is one of the major ways in which individuals construct meaning out of their encounters with their world and give meaning to their lives.

Mathematical Applications

How might mathematical oral storytelling relate to the comments just presented about the importance of stories in peoples' lives? Let us consider this by reflecting on how children might react to "The Wizard's Tale."

While the story is being told, children might imagine themselves to be Tinkerbell by projecting themselves into her person and might experience (in their imagination) what Tinkerbell experienced in the story. Tinkerbell's questions might become the children's questions, Tinkerbell's problems might become their problems, Tinkerbell's song might become their song, and Tinkerbell's mathematical actions might be viewed as their actions.

After the story is told, children might relive the story in their imaginations while riding home in a bus, waiting for dinner, taking a bath, or falling asleep. As children relive the story they might fantasize about solving a problem, roaring around like a bulldozer, or singing the "Addition Song." Children might retell the story to themselves, facing critical decision points and deciding what to do next in a personally unique way, with all of the hope, doubt, anticipation, and planning of Tinkerbell.

In so doing, children would construct and repeatedly reconstruct for themselves the story line, their own view of themselves as mathematicians (or mathematical wizards), and their own view of themselves (as a bulldozer) embodying a set of mathematical procedures needed to solve a problem. In doing so the children would themselves become storytellers who create their own stories (that closely parallel the one told to them and that anticipate the tale's next episode) and would themselves become learners who construct and reconstruct their own personal mathematical meaning that parallels Tinkerbell's mathematical actions. And children would do this not because it was assigned to them but because of a primal act of mind that drives them, as story creating creatures, to relive the experiences of Tinkerbell by retelling those experiences to themselves—retelling them repeatedly as they try to figure out the meaning of those experiences, experiences that they relive by projecting themselves into the persona of Tinkerbell.

Anyone visiting Laura McBride's third grade class while she told "The Wizard's Tale" could see these things. Laura's mathematics time was in the morning, and that is when she told the story. Each afternoon Laura's students had a quiet time when they could write, draw, read, or just think. During the afternoon quiet time, after hearing the story in the morning, many children drew or painted pictures on their own initiative about the story—pictures of their own choosing. After the first session of the story, they drew pictures of Tinkerbell in the hammock, as a hawk flying to Thoughtful Mountain, seeing the wizards frozen in stone, and being a bulldozer driving up and down the columns of the addition problem. The pictures showed children being storytellers as they retold to themselves parts of the story through their art. And children had verbal stories for each of their pictures, stories that they shared with their friends and teacher. For the observer of the children as they drew, one of the most natural questions to ask was, "Who are these pictures about, Tinkerbell or the children who are creating the drawings?"

From a slightly different perspective, the power of stories goes beyond just offering understanding, for one of the appeals of the narrative story lies in the ways it stimulates the emotions. It allows children to step into someone else's shoes and acquire a taste for their enjoyment of doing mathematics and their feeling of pride and power after successfully doing mathematics. It allows mathematical endeavors to be tied to the human emotions, wonderings, and hopes that generate mathematical endeavors in the first place (Egan, 1986; Griffiths & Clyne, 1991). Thus the observer of Doris's and Laura's classrooms during the telling of "The Wizard's Tale" is not surprised when children joyfully raise their hands with a victory sign when they (or is it Tinkerbell?) complete a problem correctly.

From a cultural perspective, the effect of "The Wizard's Tale" goes far beyond its use as an instructional medium for passing on to children our culturally approved addition algorithm. It is also designed to pass on more subtle cultural messages. Compare it to the story of Little Red Ridinghood. Little Red Ridinghood is not just about the events that a girl encounters as she travels to visit her grandmother. It is also about girls dressing up in beautiful clothes, girls taking care of their elders, wolves being bad, and the killing of wolves being a manly act. Similarly, "The Wizards Tale" is about children's ability to be competent powerful doers of mathematics (just like Tinkerbell) who can understand and use mathematics in their lives (just like Tinkerbell), about friendship and caring for one another, about teaching and learning from one another, and about doing the right thing (even if it involves confronting dangers such as Thoughtful Mountain). Important here is that "The Wizard's Tale" can counteract other powerful stories that most U.S. children have heard from peers and parents about their dislike of mathematics, feelings of impotence as mathematicians, and beliefs that they cannot understand the subject and that it is irrelevant to their lives.

From still another cultural perspective, stories allow the storyteller to speak to children (while passing on cultural information, attitudes, and values) in a way and on a level that is uniquely suited to children's way of making meaning. Many developmental psychologists have commented on the ways in which children understand differently from adults. Piagetians, for example, have described elementary school–aged children as being at the concrete operational stage of intellectual development. Put simply, concrete operational children understand mathematics best when given *concrete* examples—examples involving specific situations, actions, or physical objects—upon which they can either directly act or envision themselves or another person acting (or *operating*). Part of what this means is that children are best capable of understanding in the context of specific narrative situations (or stories) where the mathematics to be learned is related to concrete actions of an identifiable person and their explanations of those actions. Thus, what most children will understand best are not the generalized, logical, deductive, and abstract explanations of adults (characteristic of Piaget's next stage of development), but rather narrative stories that describe how recognizable people (or other anthropomorphic creatures) do or understand things in terms of a series of specific concrete actions. "The Wizard's Tale" provides an example of such a concrete action-oriented narrative: it allows children to see the mathematics they are learning in the context of specific real-world adventures; it allows them to *do* mathematics by personally doing such concrete things as acting like a bulldozer, talking like a parrot, and writing like a gorilla; and it allows children to *think* mathematically by using (or operating on) base ten blocks.

One of the things missing from most of the mathematical explanations given to children today are excellent stories—stories that allow children to project themselves into the problem-solving endeavors of the stories' characters so that they can relive (or retell to themselves) those problem-solving scenarios; stories that deeply stir children's emotions, intellect, imagination, and curiosity while mathematics is being taught; and stories that show children how problems can be solved through specific concrete actions in a real or fantasy world. Providing children with such stories is one of the intentions of mathematical epic oral storytelling.

ORALLY PRESENTED STORIES

The major literary storytelling media used in mathematics classrooms for instructional purposes during the twentieth century were children's trade books. Doris Lawson used children's trade books in her classroom prior to using oral storytelling and continues to use them. She also used other storytelling media. She used *Journey to the Other Side* (Sherrill, 1994), a chapter book about problem solving that a teacher reads and during which children sing songs. She used *The Wonderful Problems of Fizz and Martina* (Snyder, 1991), a video about the adventures of two anthropomorphic creatures who are aided in their mathematical endeavors by the students watching the video. She also continues to use mathematical computer simulations. However, children's storybooks and oral storytelling are the two instructional media that she prefers. Comparing these two media helps demonstrate their differences.

While children's trade books share much in common with oral storytelling, the very nature of the oral delivery of a story from within the storyteller's consciousness is what differentiates it in significant ways from a story that is read either by a teacher to a group of children or by children themselves.

Sarah Cone Bryant commented on this difference in 1905 in the first book on storytelling published in the United States: "With few exceptions, children listen twice as eagerly to a story told as to one read. . . . And there are sound reasons for their preference" (p. xvi). Four reasons deserve mention.

First, the orally delivered story is different from the read book because the storyteller is free from any text. In contrast, the reader of a book is intellectually, visually, and physically tied to a book that is being read. As Sarah Cone Bryant comments,

> The great difference . . . between telling and reading is that the teller is free; the reader is bound. The book in hand, or the wording of it in mind, binds the reader. The story-teller is bound by nothing; he stands or sits, free to watch his audience, free to follow or lead every changing mood, free to use body, eyes, voice, as aids in expression. Even his mind is unbound, because he lets the story come in the words of the moment, being so full of what he has to say. For this reason, a story told is more spontaneous than one read, however well read. And consequently, the connection with the audience is closer, more electric, than is possible when the book or its wording intervenes. (1905, p. xvi)

Second, the orally delivered story is different from the read story because of the different roles of the *storyteller* and the *reader.* The reader of a children's book transforms a book's written words into oral form, but no matter how the reader of the book adds emotion to the words through his or her voice, the reader must remain true to the words in the book, and those words originate from within the book and not within the reader. In comparison, the oral story comes from within the personal consciousness of the storyteller where (in most storytelling traditions) they have the freedom to change their stories based on their unique interactions with each of their audiences. (Oral storytellers frequently speak of playing their audiences by elaborating certain parts of their story and engaging their audiences in different parts of their story based on the unique relationship they develop with their audiences.) In other words, an oral story comes from within the storyteller and becomes intimately connected with the storyteller's personal expression, while a children's book that is read is separate and distinct from the reader.

Critical to this difference is that oral storytellers share a part of themselves with the reader through their story. Oral storytellers let listeners into their personal space as part of an intimate sharing of thoughts and feelings. This does not occur when a children's book is read aloud to children, for even though readers may add emotion to the words they are reading, they are *sharing* the message of another person (the author) who is not present. Sarah Cone Bryant tries to get at this difference when she says that part of what differentiates telling from reading a story

> is the added charm of the personal element in story-telling . . . . Everybody has something of the curiosity of the primitive man concerning his neighbor. What another has in his own person felt and done has an especial hold on each one of us. The most cultured of audiences will listen to the personal reminiscences of an explorer with a different tingle of interest from that which it feels for a scientific lecture on the results of the exploration. The longing for the personal in experience is a very human longing. And this instinct or

longing is especially strong in children. It finds expression in their delight in tales of what father or mother did when they were little, of what happened to grandmother when she went on a journey, and so on, but it also extends to stories which are not in themselves personal: which take their personal savor merely from the fact that they flow from the lips in spontaneous, homely phrases, with an appreciative gusto which suggests participation. (1905, pp. xvi-xvii)

Third, the told story is different from the read story because of the ability of oral storytellers to include their audiences in the story and to tailor their stories to the unique interactions that occur between themselves and their audiences. An example of how storytellers can include their audience in their story is found in "The Wizard's Tale" when Doris's students take an active role in the story in ways that make a difference within the story by doing such things as helping magic occur by clapping and telepathically sending important thoughts to the wizards. An example of how storytellers can tailor their stories to the unique interactions that occur between themselves and their audiences by doing such things as using the name, a piece of clothing, a gesture, or an utterance of an audience member is provided by the way in which Doris included in "The Wizard's Tale" the "beep, beep, beep" sound that her students invented for a bulldozer moving backward. This ability to include an audience in a story is simply not available to the reader of a children's book, who must be true to the words within a written text—a text written by an author who is not capable of personally interacting with his or her audience and changing the text accordingly.

Fourth, and related to the above reasons, is the ability of the storyteller to craft a story to his or her own unique needs. This is one of the important reasons why Doris prefers oral storytelling to the reading of storybooks. It is frequently easier for her to craft her own story to teach a specific topic the way she desires than it is to locate a children's book that deals with the topic in the manner she desires. Being free of any predesigned text allows Doris to craft a story to meet her instructional goals in precisely the way she wants. Being free of any predesigned text allows Doris to include the students in her classroom and the members of her family in the stories she tells, which immensely adds to the interest of the stories for her students (they love her stories about her son and daughter). And being free of any predesigned text allows Doris, when she discovers that her students need help with a topic, to spontaneously and immediately create and tell an oral story that deals with that topic. Being able to spontaneously invent a story and tell it immediately, a story that addresses student needs she had not anticipated, is a real advantage for Doris of oral storytelling over reading children's trade books. Granted, it took Doris a while to become a sufficiently accomplished and confident oral storyteller, able to spontaneously create and tell stories that fit a specific academic need, but once she did and was free of any predesigned text her teaching job became easier.

Two differences between the oral story delivered to a group of children and the written story that children read to themselves by themselves deserve mention. First, the oral story is different because it is told to a social group that can—in the right circumstances—facilitate the formation of a shared collective understanding (a collective intersubjective consciousness), while the children's book that is read by individuals tends to set individuals apart from each other. Second, the orally delivered story is different because the human voice is a very different medium from the written word. As Marshall McLuhan has powerfully argued, "the medium is the message," and the medium of the human voice is more personal, individual, and immediate.

Perhaps unfairly overlooking advantages of the *read* story, Sarah Cone Bryant sums up the advantages of the told story over the read story in this way:

> The greater ease in holding the attention of children is, for teachers, a sufficient practical reason for telling stories rather than reading them. It is incomparably easier to make the necessary exertion of "magnetism," or whatever it may be called, when nothing else distracts the attention. One's eyes meet the children's gaze naturally and constantly, one's expression responds to and initiates theirs without effort, the connection is immediate. For the ease of the teacher, then, no less than for the joy of the children, may the art of storytelling be urged as preeminent over the art of reading. (1905, pp. xvii-xviii)

FANTASY STORIES

Many different types of stories exist: romances, tragedies, comedies, and satires; stories about people, objects, animals, and gods; stories about real life events and fantasies about imaginary events; secular and religious stories. The type of story used to carry a mathematical message is not as important as the story's ability to capture children's interest, its ability to contextually locate mathematics in children's lives in ways that are relevant to them, and its ability to encourage children to project themselves into its characters' roles so that they can engage in the mathematical endeavors of those characters.

"The Wizard's Tale" is a fairy tale about two mythical wizards confronting the mysterious forces of nature. Many other types of stories have been successfully used during mathematical oral storytelling. Rainy tells a science fiction story about her son and daughter to help students learn subtraction. Laura tells her third graders a Greek tragedy to help them learn their multiplication facts. Sheila and Theresa tell their preschoolers an adventure story about small mammals to help them learn geometry. Mary tells her eighth graders a romance about real children who use mapping skills to save their friends.

These are all fantasies that ask listeners to suspend their belief in how the objective world *really* works in order to enter an imaginary world where things are a little (or sometimes very) different from their everyday world. They are all fantasies that excite listeners' imaginations and tap into their fantasy lives in such a way that the story and its embedded mathematics become part of their subjective and objective reality. In doing so, a story can become as real to the listener and as intellectually challenging and involving as everyday events—and the mathematics within it can become as interesting, involving, and relevant as mathematics arising from the listener's everyday world. This does not mean that listeners cannot distinguish between the fantasy of the story and the objective world in which they live, but rather that both can—each in its own way—excite children's feelings of interest, involvement, and relevance.

Using fantasy to teach mathematics is not new. We have textbooks that follow the daily lives of Burrits (creatures similar to fairies) through the year (Coombs, Harcourt, Travis, & Wannamaker, 1987), units that ask children to enter the world of *Gulliver's Travels* (Kleiman & Bjork, 1991), videos that ask children to believe in humorous, otherworldly creatures

(Snyder, 1991), read-aloud science fiction novels accompanied by taped music to teach problem solving (Sherrill, 1994), and websites that involve children in fantasy adventures of people, animals, and gnomes (www.uwinnipeg.ca/~jameis). However, using fantasy to teach mathematics is the exception, rather than the norm.

In fact, most people think that mathematical activity has little to do with fantasy. The picture that school mathematics presents to children, and that the discipline of Western mathematics presents to society, is one in which mathematical activity is portrayed as devoid of intuition, feeling, imagination, emotion, and all of those aspects of human intelligence that have to do with fantasy and people's "non-logical" intelligences. Most people think that mathematics is a purely logical discipline primarily involving analytical proof. How incorrect they are.

There are really at least three very different aspects of mathematical activity: the act of discovering problems and their solutions; the endeavor of proving one's findings and communicating them to others; and the application of mathematics to everyday problems.

The act of discovering problems and their solutions has more to do with insight and intuition than logic. It involves gut feelings, emotions, imaginative play, visual imaging, and muscular activity. In other words, the creative act of bringing into existence new ideas that have not been previously conceptualized (by either their original discoverers or individuals who later rediscover them for themselves) involves intuitive and imaginative acts of invention and discovery. Insight is born from blending imaginative and intuitive feeling with intellect.

Once a mathematical idea has been discovered, the creator of the idea then faces the task of finding ways of communicating its reasonableness to others, usually by offering logical mathematical proofs. As Henri Poincaré, the great nineteenth-century mathematician, said, "It is by logic that we prove, but by intuition that we discover" (Poincaré, 1913/1946).

Applying mathematics to real-world situations frequently involves a combination of the endeavors of discovery and proof: of having insight into how to fit a mathematical structure to a real-world situation, of logically working out the details of the fit between mathematical possibility and real-world limitations, and then logically carrying out mathematical processes and checking their plausibility.

Mathematical endeavors involve both intuition and proof, both fantasy and reality, both subjective and objective thinking. And it is often the ability to deal with both that produces an effective mathematical exploration. Fantasy, intuition, and imagination suggest what might be, while logic, analysis, and proof allow one to clearly deal with the restrictions of objective reality. Fantasy has a very real role to play in mathematical endeavors (Hadamard, 1945; Root-Bernstein & Root-Bernstein, 1999).

Not only does fantasy have a role to play in mathematical endeavors, but it also has an important role to play during mathematics instruction in helping children learn mathematics in ways that make the subject personally meaningful to themselves.

For example, when Doris Lawson tells her students "The Wizard's Tale" she integrates a fantasy about wizards with instruction in how to use the multidigit addition algorithm. At one level the fantasy story is designed to excite children's interest so that they are enthusiastic about learning mathematics. Stimulating children's interest in and enthusiasm for mathematics is an important component of mathematics instruction.

At another level the fantasy associated with "The Wizard's Tale" is designed to allow children to project themselves into the roles of its characters so that they can act in ways demonstrated by those characters. Demonstrations are an important teaching tool, but they must be followed by children projecting themselves into the role of the demonstrator and replicating the behavior demonstrated. And it is fantasy, and the ability of people to fantasize and use their imagination, that allows them to project themselves into another person's endeavors, to suspend their grasp on the regularities of their own everyday reality for a time while experiencing another person's reality. The endeavor of helping children use their imagination in such a way that they can step into another's role and enthusiastically reenact that person's mathematical endeavors is an extremely important function of mathematics instruction.

But the power of fantasy in enabling children to project themselves into the roles of actors in imaginary stories goes beyond just replicating behaviors, for fantasy can also allow children to experience what it feels like to be a particular character in a story: to feel success upon learning mathematics, to feel powerful while doing mathematics, to feel effective after using mathematics to solve problems so that lives can be saved, or perhaps to feel influential after having taught someone mathematics. Fantasy plays an important role in mathematics instruction when it allows children to experiment with feelings of mathematical power and success.

At still another level the fantasy associated with "The Wizard's Tale" is designed to present mathematics in such a way that children see it as relevant to their lives. The story is sufficiently different from the real everyday lives of children that they can suspend their beliefs about the limitations of their everyday world and dream of a different world in which mathematics gives them the power to make a difference in people's lives. Fantasy and imagination allow the child to enter a world in which the mathematics being learned is of personal importance to them and of critical importance to the circumstances in which they find themselves as they live the lives of the story's characters. And when children feel that their endeavors are of critical importance—as in "The Wizard's Tale" where they are of life or death importance—they are more likely to bring to bear all of their intellectual powers to help them master the mathematics needed to succeed in their adventures. Fantasy can play an important role in mathematics instruction if it can help children see that their mathematical endeavors are of critical significance in their lives and if it can help them mobilize their intellectual powers to master mathematics.

STORIES THAT PLACE MATHEMATICS IN CONTEXT

During the last half century mathematics educators have come to believe that one of the ways that they can make mathematics interesting, involving, and relevant to children is by placing it in a meaningful context (or "contextualizing" it). One of the difficulties that they face is determining just what exactly is a "meaningful context."

In the past, many mathematics educators, and particularly those who produce textbooks, have assumed that the way to contextualize mathematics for children is by closely associating it with their real, objective, everyday lives.

In contrast, when Doris uses "The Wizard's Tale" to teach the multidigit addition algorithm, she is contextualizing mathematics for children by weaving it into a fantasy story that becomes "part of an ongoing web of intrigue" that forms and gives meaning to her students' lives (Snyder, 1991, p. 7).

This ongoing web of intrigue can consist of either real or imaginary events in children's lives that catch their attention, arouse their feelings, stir their interest, stimulate their intellect, excite their imagination, inspire their intuition, or encourage their active participation in life. It can be grounded in objective reality or subjective reality—in the real everyday events children encounter or in the real fantasies that stimulate children's intellects.

Many educators have difficulty with the practice of *only* contextualizing mathematics in objective reality—with the belief that the *only* way of contextualizing mathematics is by associating it with those things that might arise within a child's real everyday world, particularly if one insists on crafting one's mathematical problems around the ordinary events that children might encounter in their everyday lives. To highlight their concerns, and particularly their concern that mathematics should never be contextualized for children in fantasy stories, let us examine two sets of problems with respect to issues of contextualizing mathematics.

First, let us compare a number problem and a word problem, both of which might be found in a mathematics textbook among numerous other number and word problems:

Number problem: 2.67 + 3.50 =

Word problem: Mary found $2.67 on the way to school. She found $3.50 on the way home. What is the total amount of money that Mary found on the way to school and the way home?

The number problem is physically located in the real context of a textbook that most children know well. It is surrounded by neighbors (other problems) that look just like it in a textbook that presents many similar problems, and in a book that is probably used at the same times and locations every day (mathematics class and homework time). Such problems could be said to be contextually located in children's real everyday life. But simply locating a problem in a child's life is not what is really meant by placing mathematics in context.

The word problem could be located in the child's life in the same way as the number problem: in a textbook that is a regular part of the child's life at school. In contrast to the number problem, however, the word problem puts mathematics in the context of a pleasant real-world situation that a child might confront: finding money at two different times during the day and wondering how much was found in all. Important questions, however, must be asked about the word problem when wondering how it contextually locates mathematics: Will children confronted by the problem in the context of the textbook identify with Mary and her predicament? Are there enough dramatic elements in the problem—plot, character development, suspense—to make the problem come alive for children in such a way that they will become intellectually involved in the mathematical situation confronting Mary? and Will children, after doing 20 number problems and six other similar word problems about different people in different settings, be able to step into the problem described by this new real-world setting and live this problem as Mary might in the context of her real life, with the enthusiasm that Mary might have upon finding the money? True, the word problem is contextually located in the real world of a person's life—but is it located in the lives of the children who must solve it as part of an assignment? And is it located in their lives in such a way that it will come intellectually and imaginatively alive for them?

Second, let us compare two problems related to tangrams:

For the first tangram problem imagine a teacher standing in front of a class of students, each of whom is sitting at his or her individual desk. The teacher places a set of seven tangram pieces in front of each child and then says, "Put these seven tangram pieces together to make a square and then you can go to recess."

Exhibit 2.1   Tangram Puzzle and Solution

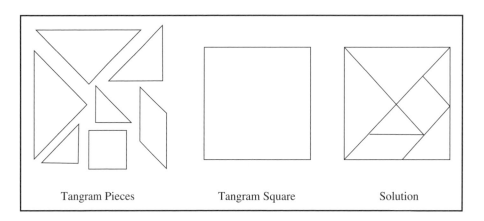

Tangram Pieces   Tangram Square   Solution

For the second tangram problem imagine a teacher standing in front of a class of students orally telling the following (supposedly) ancient Chinese story about a poor pottery maker named Tan:

> Tan was a poor potter in ancient China. He was so poor that he had only one set of clothes, could afford only one meal a day, and could not afford the dowry he needed to marry the woman he loved. However, Tan was well known for his ability to make beautiful floor tiles.
>
> One day the Emperor of China asked Tan to make him a beautiful square floor tile. Tan did so while thinking about how his fame and fortune would be secured if the Emperor liked his tile. If the Emperor liked Tan's tile, then he might be able to afford more than one shirt, more than one meal a day, and the dowry to marry the woman he loved.
>
> On his way to deliver his square tile to the Emperor, the tile fell from Tan's hands, landed on the ground, and broke into seven pieces. Tan was very distressed, for it seemed as though his fame and fortune had just slipped through his fingers. He looked at the broken tile pieces and noticed that they had broken into triangles, squares, and parallelograms. Tan wondered if the tile could be reassembled. He sat down on the ground and tried to put the seven pieces back into a square. He was delighted when he could. He decided to bring the Emperor his broken square tile and to tell him that it was a special square tile puzzle, for he had heard that the Emperor liked puzzles.
>
> On the way to the Emperor, Tan wondered if he could make the seven pieces into something other than a square. He wondered if the tile pieces could be assembled into a triangle, a rectangle, or a parallelogram. He wondered if the seven pieces could be made into a fish, a cat, or a boat. When he showed the Emperor of China his tile puzzle, the Emperor was delighted with it because he loved puzzles.

The Emperor told Tan that he would pay him for each new recognizable shape that Tan could make out of the seven-piece puzzle. The Emperor named the puzzle a tangram in honor of Tan, and the Emperor said that he would create a book called *Tangram Puzzles* that contained each recognizable shape that Tan could make out of the seven tangram pieces. Tan's fame and fortune would be made if he could create many new puzzle shapes for the Emperor (and others) to solve.

We as a class are going to see if we can help Tan invent new shapes into which the puzzle can be made. I am going to give you each a tangram puzzle that contains seven pieces.

First, see if you can put the seven tangram pieces together to make a square, as Tan did. Is there more than one way to do this? Compare your solutions with each other.

After you have made the square, see if you remember how the pieces fit together, then mix the pieces up and see if you can reassemble them into a square with your eyes closed. The Emperor could. Work in pairs if you need to do so.

Next, see if you can put the seven pieces together to make a triangle, rectangle, and parallelogram. If you can do so and someone sitting near you needs help, give them a hint but do not show them how to make the shape.

If you can make a triangle, rectangle, and parallelogram out of the seven tangram pieces, see what other puzzles you can invent that Tan might have created for the Emperor, puzzles such as a cat, fish, or boat. If we can help Tan invent many new puzzles, we will help him obtain fame and fortune. This will allow Tan to be able to afford more than one shirt and pair of pants, more than one meal a day, and the dowry to marry the woman he loves.

I am now going to give you each a tangram puzzle. [*The teacher now puts seven tangram pieces in front of each child in the class.*] Start your work now, and draw a picture of how you put the pieces together to make each new shape you construct. [*The teacher now demonstrates how to draw the solution to a tangram construction.*] Continue your explorations for homework tonight and we will share what you have created in class tomorrow and begin to construct our own classroom tangram puzzle book. Tomorrow I will tell you more about Tan and his puzzle. As you work, share your constructions and thoughts with each other.

The first tangram problem could be said to contextualize mathematics. This is because physical manipulatives often are believed to provide a real-world context for mathematics problems—because children perform *real* actions on *real* mathematics manipulatives. This is also because the child will receive a very tangible reward upon solving the problem (the ability to go to recess). This tangram problem is situated in the child's everyday life; the child is likely to become interested and involved in solving it; and it is certainly relevant to the child's ability to go to recess. However, the problem is disjointed from any "ongoing web of intrigue" that forms the child's intellectual life.

There are several ways in which the second tangram problem (situated in the fantasy story) is different from the first tangram problem in locating mathematics in a real-world context.

62 FOUNDATIONS OF MATHEMATICAL EPIC ORAL STORYTELLING

First, the second tangram problem and its accompanying story take several days to complete while the first tangram problem will likely be completed in one sitting. During the more lengthy process of completing the second problem, children will be better able to dream about, discuss, imagine, share ideas about, and fantasize about what will happen to Tan and different ways of putting together the tangram pieces. Second, in the second tangram problem there are real dramatic elements that enter into the problem that tie it to children's ongoing web of intrigue that forms about their lives, elements such as what will happen to Tan in the next installment of the story, how many different tangram constructions can be invented, what types of surprise constructions they and their peers will invent, and how their efforts will aid Tan in his quest for fame and fortune. Third, in the second tangram problem children share their work with each other and help each other, while in the first tangram problem they work alone. By working together and sharing their work, children are involved in a social construction of meaning as well as an individual construction of meaning. The social construction of meaning connects them to an intellectual endeavor and knowledge base larger than their own and adds connectedness and comradeship to the ongoing web of intrigue that forms about their lives. This is especially the case when the class as a whole constructs a tangram puzzle book to which all members of the class contribute. Fourth, in the second tangram problem children do their mathematical work in the context of a fantasy story in which they are going to be helping Tan, whereas in the first tangram problem they are simply trying to construct a square to achieve a reward (a task that is disconnected from the reward). The second story connects the mathematics to children's fantasy lives and allows the children to imagine themselves in Tan's predicament, and by doing so weaves the geometry problem into the ongoing web of intrigue that forms about their lives. Fifth, the second tangram problem allows for more creative thinking than the first. In allowing for more creative thinking (by inventing new shapes that can be constructed versus replicating a single preconceived shape), the second problem has the potential to provide children with greater intellectual stimulation, both in terms of the subjective fantasies they have about the shapes they might create (a sailboat floating down a river), and in terms of the objective mathematics skills they might develop (such as part-whole skills, skills in rotating and sliding geometric shapes in their imagination, skills of holding geometric images in their minds, and skills of drawing geometric constructions).

Both tangram problems are real-world problems because they require that the child become actively involved with the manipulation of mathematical materials in the search for a solution to a geometric problem, but the second problem takes on its life not *just* because it is a real-world problem, but also because it taps into children's fantasy lives, allows them to make decisions that have consequences on the lives of (imaginary) others, allows them to be participants in the construction of social as well as individual meanings, and because it has the possibility for dramatic elements such as plot, character development, and surprise to enter into the problem.

The problem of finding ways to place mathematics in a meaningful context for children is an important one for educators. In the past it has been assumed by many educators that the best way of contextualizing mathematics is by locating it in objective reality and by associating it with those things that might arise within children's ordinary everyday life. This assumption is problematic. It is problematic because it cannot be assumed that the objective reality surrounding children directly corresponds to the subjective reality within their minds.

The problem of contextualizing mathematics is not one of simply positioning mathematics in the environment where children are physically located. Simply doing so will not make it any more meaningful to a child than an unopened, unread book sitting in the same room with the child. Rather, the problem of contextualizing mathematics is one of situating mathematics within children's consciousness in such a way that it catches their attention, stirs their interest, arouses their feelings, stimulates their intellect, and propels them to actively engage that mathematics. It is one of finding how to locate mathematics in children's minds in such a way that it comes alive to *them,* is meaningful to *them,* and has an impact on *their* view of what is important in their lives.

One of the goals of orally delivered mathematical stories, such as "The Wizard's Tale," is to make mathematics meaningful to children in this way. Oral fantasy stories are but one of numerous ways of doing so, albeit an important one that has been overlooked or avoided by most educators in the past partially because of their assumptions about mathematical contextualization.

THE EPIC STORY

Stories can take very different lengths of time to present. Most jokes—which are one form of story—take only a few seconds to tell. Other stories, such as the *Iliad* (Homer/Murray trans., 1999) or the *Ramayana* (Valmiki trans., 1927), are normally told over lengthy periods of time.

Doris usually takes 5 to 8 days to tell "The Wizard's Tale," depending on how quickly her students work, the amount of remedial help her students need, and how many language arts classes she combines with her mathematics class. In contrast, the typical story located in a mathematics text book—the word problem—takes only a few seconds to read.

Tellers of oral mathematical epic stories are not the first to locate mathematics in fantasy stories that take an extended time period to tell. *Journey to the Other Side* (Sherrill, 1994) is a fantasy involving problem solving that is designed to be read to middle school children by a teacher over twenty-seven class sessions. *Algebra the Easy Way* (Downing, 1989) is a mystery with twenty chapters that contain problems that the reader solves while reviewing Algebra I. *Explorations 2* (Coombs, Harcourt, Travis, & Wannamaker, 1987) is a second grade textbook that presents the story of how a group of Burrits build their society through the use of mathematics. It contains twelve fantasy episodes that are read at the beginning of each of its units.

Doris, and other tellers of epic stories, report that there is something special about epic stories—stories that last for two or more class sessions. They report that after hearing only part of a story their students frequently come to the next class asking, "What is going to happen in math today?" They say that their students often report having dreamt about mathematics between story episodes. They report that good epics often have the power to capture their students' intellects, emotions, memories, curiosities, and imaginations in a way that goes far beyond that of shorter mathematical stories. One teacher obtained from me at a conference the first two of four sessions of an epic about superheroes using fractions and decided to try them out with her students. Before long, e-mails were sent requesting the next two sessions, for the teacher's students were desperate to know what happened next in the story.

When an oral story that captures children's interest extends over several days, there are frequently unexpected benefits that occur.

One benefit is that children often think about the story and its mathematics between story-telling sessions and in doing so increasingly invest themselves in the story and its mathematics. Between sessions children often discuss the story with their peers: they retell and act out for each other parts of the story they have heard; they discuss more efficient or better ways of doing the mathematics in the story; they caution each other about errors that might be made in the mathematics necessary to help the hero; and they speculate about what is going to happen next in the story. Between sessions children also frequently reflect on the story as individuals: they might draw pictures about events in the story, retell parts of the story to themselves, and dream about the story. In the process children become increasingly invested in the story and its mathematics as both become progressively more alive in their fantasy lives. Some results of this seem to be that children put increasingly large amounts of intellectual energy into endeavors related to the story and its mathematics, that the story's mathematics appears to be learned faster and remembered longer, that the story's mathematics becomes associated with events in the story in such a way that when children forget some of the mathematics they can more easily recall it by recalling the associated story events, and that when children fondly remember the story they associate those positive feelings with its mathematics. Give a good epic and its mathematics time to percolate in a child's imagination and they often come alive to the child in a way that a story told (or read) in one sitting infrequently does.

Another benefit of epics over short stories is that epics that take several days (or weeks) to tell provide the necessary time for literary elements such as character portrayal, plot, and suspense to be developed. Stories with their dramatic elements more fully developed can provide richer learning experiences for children than stories that take less time to develop their dramatic elements. Richer stories often more easily allow their mathematics to come alive for children and more easily allow children to project themselves into the mathematical endeavors of their characters.

Another benefit of epics is that they allow teachers to locate a set of related facts or an algorithm in a single story in such a way that children can be given sufficient experience and practice with the mathematics in the story's context. This helps children learn and remember the mathematics; and if it is forgotten, its association with a powerful story allows it to be more easily reconstructed. "The Wizard's Tale" illustrates how Doris Lawson built repetition into a story so that she could provide her students with the repetition she believed they needed.

Another benefit of epics relates to the sequencing of increasingly complex mathematical experiences over time. The careful sequencing of an epic's adventures and its related mathematics allows the storyteller to gradually increase the level of complexity of the mathematical problems being presented, move the reader from concrete toward abstract mathematical representations, present a complicated sequence of interconnected algorithms, or present a global process (or complex body of content) that consists of multiple substrategies (or unitary concepts) that might need to be learned individually before being assembled together. The ability of epics to introduce children to a story and a mathematical model and then gradually move them through a series of adventures that progressively build a complex mathematical understanding or capability is one thing that differentiates mathematical epics from short stories and story problems. Exhibit 2.2 presents a brief overview of some of the dynamics

Exhibit 2.2   Overview of the Pedagogical Components of "The Wizard's Tale"

Day	Story Goal	Children's Major Expressive Modes	Children's Role	Pedagogical Supports	Language Level	Place Value Imagery	Grouping	Comprehension Level
1	set the stage for the story; intuitively present addition using manipulatives	simultaneous enacting and verbalizing; singing; reflection → talk → listen → discuss	imitate storyteller and monitor each other; reflect on current and past beliefs	bulldozer, base ten blocks, and place value chart	concrete representational ("longs")	continuous structural manipulative (flat, long, and cube)	large-group listening; pairs act and reflect; large-group discussion	intuitive; procedural
2	distinguish writing from verbalizing and clarify each	separate enacting and verbalizing; singing; reflection → talk → listen → discuss	imitate storyteller and monitor each other; reflect on beliefs about addition	bulldozer, base ten blocks, and place value chart	concrete representational ("longs")	continuous structural manipulative (flat, long, and cube)	pairs listen, act, and reflect; large-group discussion	intuitive; procedural; intuitive; conceptual
3	introduce writing during addition	enacting, writing and verbalizing; singing; reflection → talk → listen → discuss	imitate storyteller and monitor each other; teach each other; reflect on beliefs about addition	bulldozer, base ten blocks, place value chart, and writing template	concrete mathematical ("tens")	continuous structural manipulative; verbal and written numerical	groups of three listen, act, and reflect; large-group discussion	verbalizable; procedural; intuitive; conceptual; intuitive; relational
4	separate writing and speaking from intuitive actions; relate to real-world events	verbalizing and writing; singing; reflection → talk → listen → discuss	imitate storyteller and monitor each other; teach each other; reflect on beliefs about addition	writing template and real-world graphics	symbolic	discrete visual structural; verbal and written numerical	pairs listen, act, and reflect; large-group discussion	verbalizable; procedural; verbalizable; conceptual; verbalizable; relational
5	generalize how addition works	verbalizing and writing →; writing only; singing; reflection → talk → listen → discuss	imitate storyteller and monitor each other; teach each other; reflect on beliefs about addition	writing template and real-world graphics → no supports	symbolic	discrete visual structural; discrete visual nonproportional; numerical	pairs listen and act → individuals; act → multi-size group discussion	verbalizable; procedural; verbalizable; conceptual; verbalizable; relational

underlying the daily presentation of "The Wizard's Tale." Note how goals, language levels, place value imagery, and comprehension level all develop as the story progresses. (These components will be discussed in a later chapter.)

Mathematical epic oral stories, as well other mathematical activities that last for extended periods of time, seriously challenge the currently popular assumption that mathematics lessons should be self-contained entities that run no longer than one sitting.

In summary, this chapter has examined several elements central to mathematical epic oral storytelling, including the importance of story in children's lives, the power of orally presented stories, the role of fantasy in stories and children's lives, the way in which stories contextualize mathematics, and the benefits of multiday mathematics learning experiences.

Chapter 3

MATHEMATICAL EPIC ORAL STORYTELLING

Structural Relationships Among Teachers, Children, and Mathematics

Let us observe a fourth grade classroom on two consecutive days.

On Monday when we observe at 10:00, the teacher is standing in front of the class presenting a mathematics lesson using an instructional format that might be described as lecture while calling on children to answer questions. The class is quiet and orderly, but over half of the students in it are disengaged. Several students are daydreaming, off in another world of their own. Several are poking at each other with some private joke. Several are following what the teacher has to say from a slouched position at their desks. Several others are attending to the teacher while sitting stiffly upright. The classroom seems to have little coherence that binds its members together.

On Tuesday when we observe the same classroom at 10:00, the teacher is again standing in front of the class presenting a mathematics lesson. But this time the teacher is telling an oral story. All of the students have their eyes riveted on the teacher while they lean alertly forward in their desks. As the teacher moves to one side of the classroom the entire class sways in that direction as a single entity. As the teacher moves back toward the center of the classroom, the entire class seems to shift their bodies toward the center of the room. The teacher and students are so engrossed in the lesson that they seem to be a single organism moving together.

These two classroom observations of one teacher and twenty-five children portray two very different views of how teachers, children, and mathematics can be structurally related to each other during instruction. This chapter will explore the nature of these relationships during epic oral storytelling. It will partially do so by comparing more traditional instruction with mathematical oral storytelling.

In more traditional American classrooms the instructional model that defines the way teachers, children, and mathematics interact can be characterized as transmission of abstract, generalized, objective mathematical truths by a knowledgeable teacher from a textbook to a student. In this model mathematical knowledge is seen to exist outside the learner and teacher in an impersonal, logically organized, objective form that is usually stored in a book. The teacher is seen as acting primarily as a transmitter of these impersonal truths, be it as a conveyer of truths to the child's intellect or as a trainer of the child's mind to perform mathematics skills. The teacher's stance is that of an agent disconnected from both the mathematics and the child in any intimate way.

Let us now examine how the relationships among teachers, children, and mathematical content function during epic oral storytelling.

THE TEACHER-STUDENT RELATIONSHIP

The intersubjective sharing of meanings between teacher and student during the collective endeavors of telling and listening to an oral story are very different from the transmission of objective information from a teacher to a student that takes place during more traditional mathematics instruction. The resulting relationships between teacher and student are also different.

While telling an oral story such as "The Wizard's Tale," storytellers take their students into their confidence as they share a personal fantasy that is laden with both subjective and objective meanings, with both affective and cognitive messages. They share the story in the way a person might share a piece of good news or a secret. They share both the content of a message and their personal feelings about that message.

Both the storyteller and the listener stand on the same side of an oral story as they travel through its adventures together. They interact together more as leader and followers on an adventure than as transmitter and receivers of information. For example, Doris and her students accompany each other as companions—with Doris leading the way—as they project themselves into "The Wizard's Tale" and help Tinkerbell and her friends on their adventures.

Both storytellers and listeners have complementary roles to play as they construct a story. Storytellers construct a story from within themselves and share it with listeners. Listeners take what a storyteller offers and reconstruct the fantasy within their own conscious and subconscious minds for themselves as they join the storyteller in the story's adventures. Storyteller and listeners suspend a certain amount of worldly belief as they enter a fantasy world together.

During an oral story, listeners are not passive receivers of information from a storyteller. Not only do listeners reconstruct the story for themselves in their minds in order to give it meaning, but they also help the storyteller tell the story by doing such things as magic clapping, singing songs, answering questions, and taking on roles such as bulldozer, parrot, and gorilla. In addition to joining in the construction of a story, listeners join the story's characters on their adventure as they project themselves (in their fantasies) into a story. During the adventure the teacher, students, and story's characters share many subjective and objective meanings as they get to know each other, have adventures together, and learn from and teach each other. In doing so a closeness and trust develops between teacher and students, between a more experienced leader and less experienced followers.

In comparison, a more formal impersonal relationship exists between teacher and students during traditional mathematics instruction. The more formal impersonal relationship exists for at least three reasons: First, the knowledge transferred from teacher to student is primarily impersonal, logical, objective information in which neither teacher nor students have a personal vested interest. Second, their relationship is between a superior person who has the knowledge and an inferior person who lacks the knowledge. Teacher and students are not pursuing an adventure together with danger before both of them; rather the teacher has a desirable item—knowledge—that needs to be transferred to students who lack that item. The relationship is between a giver and a taker who are on opposite sides of information, rather than between two helpers who are both on the same side of the adventure. Third, the instructional medium of lecture and examination that connects them places the teacher and student on opposite sides of instructional endeavors rather than on the same side of an adventure encountered together.

The more personal relationship that develops between teacher and student during oral storytelling, in comparison to what exists between teacher and student during more traditional instruction, might be partly described as an *I-thou* relationship in comparison to an *I-you* relationship. The difference between an I-thou relationship and an I-you relationship can be partly described in terms of how the more personal, familiar, and affectionate French pronoun *tu* is used in comparison to *vous*. Persons having an I-thou relationship share emotions, thoughts, and awareness in a more personal manner than persons in an I-you relationship, in which objective information is the major item passed between them. In I-thou relationships there is a joining or meeting of people's minds and feelings, whereas in I-you relationships there is a more formal transmission of intellectual capital from one individual to another.

This intersubjective sharing of meanings between teacher and students takes place both while the teacher is telling the story and while the teacher is circulating among, monitoring, and helping students as they solve (mathematical and social) problems in their small groups.

THE STUDENT-STUDENT RELATIONSHIP

Students do not listen to stories alone. They listen as members of a collaborative group. This raises the question, "How is a group of students collaboratively listening to an oral story different from the following types of groups found within more traditional mathematics classrooms: a group of students listening, as individuals, to a lecture (in which a teacher delivers a monologue that is received by many separate individuals); a group participating in a discussion (involving multiple individual exchanges between students and a teacher who acts as a moderator); a group doing worksheets (during which students work alone); or even a group listening to a children's book being read (in which a teacher delivers a monologue replicating text that is received by many separate individuals)?"

One difference is that together students are collaboratively constructing the story's meaning, jointly acting within the story, and sharing subjective and objective meanings with each other. The "togetherness-as-a-group-of-colleagues" on a joint adventure, is very different from the "one-among-many-separate-individuals" working alone through a task. Two issues will be examined to illustrate how the relationships among these groupings of students are different. The first issue relates to how oral storytelling facilitates the building of unique mathematical cultures in classrooms. The second issue relates to how the collaborative learning environments in which oral storytelling takes place help students acquire knowledge and construct meaning.

Culture Building

Every classroom in which mathematics is taught has a set of rules and regulations, instructional rhythms, roles for students and teachers, myths, traditions, values, expectations of students and teachers, and modes of communication. Together these make up the classroom's mathematical culture. The mathematical cultures of most more traditional classrooms are fairly uniform, and the casual observer could step from a third grade Massachusetts classroom into a third grade California classroom and hardly notice a difference.

One of the unexpected things that occurs during epic oral storytelling is that groups of children (under the guidance of a teacher) build distinct mathematical cultures in their classrooms that are very different from one classroom to another. These cultures are likely to include such things as unique special languages, heroes, myths, traditions, knowledge, symbols, values, and modes of communication. Surprisingly, these distinct cultures can be fairly quickly established and can have an enormous influence on how students interact with each other and learn.

As an example let us look at some of the unique elements of Doris Lawson's fourth grade that came into existence and remained in existence in her classroom for the duration of the school year as a result of "The Wizard's Tale." By the time "The Wizard's Tale" was complete, all of Doris's students acquired the habit of uttering the sounds "beep, beep, beep" during addition. Everyone knew that this simultaneously meant a bulldozer backing up and the process of "carrying" a ten, hundred, or thousand to the next column once a "trade" was made during addition. This "beep, beep, beep" sound continued to be quietly uttered by students throughout the year, and everyone accepted it and knew exactly what it meant, just as they would know what it meant if students raised their hands after a teacher asked a question.

In Doris's classroom students occasionally said to each other, "You are going to turn to stone." Everyone understood what this phrase meant. It was a warning that someone was making a mathematical error. Similarly, everyone in Doris's classroom also knew what was being requested of them if they were asked to talk like a parrot (using a particular type of mathematical language) or write like a gorilla (using specific types of mathematical symbols). And if Doris asked, "Would Tinkerbell do that?" or if one of her students asked, "Help me the way Tinkerbell would," everyone knew what this meant, for everyone knew Tinkerbell's values and her standards for kind and helpful behavior. These expressions were classroom regularities just as much as the ringing of the school bell to signal the end of the school day is a classroom regularity.

If, however, uninitiated visitors stepped into Doris's mathematics class for the first time, they would not know what lay behind all of these unique cultural elements because they are regularities only within Doris's classroom.

During epic oral storytelling children (under the guidance of their teacher) seem to quickly build unique, powerful mathematical cultures within their classrooms. Part of the reason for this is that oral storytellers, such as Doris, view their stories as microworlds that they and their classes temporarily live within, microworlds that have their own unique rules for causality and their own unique systems of expectations for social interactions. When children listen to a mathematical epic oral story they have to learn how to act within it in ways that are consistent with its story and its underlying social structure. They have to both understand (at either the conscious or subconscious level) the story's culture and adapt their behavior so that it is consistent with that culture. They have to suspend acceptance of their own everyday classroom culture and enter a new culture and behave in accordance with its special linguistic elements, heroes, myths, traditions, symbols, values, knowledge and meanings, rules and regulations, instructional rhythms, roles for students and teachers, expectations of students and teachers, and modes of communication.

There are two aspects of oral storytelling that facilitate children entering a story's microworld and then transforming elements of their regular classroom culture to correspond to the story's culture. Both have been previously discussed. They include (1) the ability of listeners to take an active role in a story and act within it in ways that make a difference in the story, and (2) the ability of oral storytellers to tailor their stories to the unique interactions that occur between themselves and their audiences (such as when the oral storyteller uses the name, piece of clothing, gesture, or utterance of a member of the audience in a story).

During an oral fantasy, students do not simply sit and hear the story. They actively engage in, listen to, and act within the story. It is the active engaging in, listening to, and learning to act within the fantasy's culture that helps students learn to behave (or *live*) in accordance with its cultural traditions and values and then later to transfer selective components of the fantasy's culture into the normal everyday culture of their classroom. Also, as a result of learning to successfully act in a fantasy's mathematical culture in ways that make a difference in that culture, children have an incentive to carry their success within the story into their classroom. They use the mathematical modes of behavior learned within the story in their classroom because it allows them to feel—and be—powerful mathematical actors. And when many children collectively bring behavior learned in the context of a story into their classroom, with strong motives to behave in accordance with the story's culture because it makes them feel powerful, then (under the guidance of their teacher) they have the ability to transform their previously existing classroom's mathematical culture into a new one. If students only passively observed the story, rather than actively engaging it, they would not get to practice new behaviors that they could then use during their normal mathematics time.

The ability of storytellers to tailor their stories to the unique interactions that occur between themselves and their audiences also facilitates the creation of unique classroom cultures. Typical ways of drawing part of a classroom's culture into a mathematical fantasy include naming a story's characters after students and incorporating into the fantasy memorable classroom events. By connecting classroom events with occurrences in an oral fantasy, aspects of the fantasy become part of a class's collective cultural memory. By having a flexible interplay between the culture underlying the oral fantasy and the culture underlying normal mathematical class time, transfer of the culture underlying the fantasy to the culture of the classroom is also facilitated. It is facilitated as a result of associating and connecting aspects of the two cultures in students' collective mathematical memory. The transference of the fantasy's culture to the normal classroom culture is further reinforced because the memories of the story are in the children's collective consciousness, and any class member's reference to an element in an oral story during normal classroom time reinforces all class members' memory and association with the mathematical culture underlying the story. The unique collaborative experiences children share while experiencing a story also provide a bond that ties them to the story's underlying cultural elements and in doing so helps them mold and sustain a new mathematical culture outside of the story within their classroom.

Two examples illustrate how elements can transfer between a normal classroom culture and a story's culture. Laura McBride tells "The Wizard's Tale" and other mathematical oral stories in ways that connect her third grade class's cumulative memory during stories with that of their normal classroom time. One day the teacher from the classroom next to Laura's ran into her classroom very upset because she had a tick on her. Laura calmed the teacher down, removed the tick, and disposed of it in front of her class while talking about what to do if you get a tick on yourself. Soon afterward the teacher's behavior and the tick showed up in an oral epic tale; and yes, it could only be removed when a particular mathematics problem was solved. What is important here is that all of Laura's students associated the story's tick with the adjacent classroom teacher's tick, and this mental connection enriched the story and the class's cumulative memory. In an oral tale about multiplication that was set in ancient Greece, Laura named a mathematical wizard after one of the girls in her class who had very little confidence in herself as a mathematician. During the story the girl's namesake was spoken of as someone who was a marvelous mathematician, and the children in Laura's classroom (including the girl) associated the wizard with the girl. During the story the girl gained increased confidence in her ability to do mathematics as a result of the association. In addition, other students in Laura's class associated the girl with the wizard with the same name and began to treat the girl as particularly competent in mathematics. As a result, the girl's mathematical self-esteem, skills, and understanding increased greatly as elements of the story's culture flowed into Laura's normal classroom culture.

Collaborative Learning Environments

In "The Wizard's Tale" students learn in small and large (whole-class) collaborative groups. Examining the dynamics of the groups will provide insight into the structural regularities of collaborative groups and how collaborative learning environments can help students acquire mathematical knowledge and construct mathematical meanings. To do so, three issues need to be explored: role differentiation, collaborative social interactions, and collaborative learning.

Role Differentiation

When Doris puts students into small groups during "The Wizard's Tale," she does not just tell them to work together. Rather, she very clearly defines the roles in which students are to function. These functional roles represent different types of mathematical endeavors. They also define the ways in which she wants her students to think about mathematics and learn mathematics.

The major roles Doris assigns students are those of mute bulldozer (Tinkerbell), talking parrot (Gandalf), and writing gorilla (Habble). All students also have two other (seemingly hidden) roles that they must always function in: listeners to what each other says and watchers of what each other does.

When Doris's students are the bulldozer, they are a *doer* and physically demonstrate how to do addition with base ten blocks using *bodily-kinesthetic* actions. These actions provide the learner with an intuitive subverbal action-oriented understanding of the meaning of addition.

When they are the talking parrot, they are a *talker* and *verbally articulate* the mathematical processes occurring as the base ten blocks are manipulated by the doer. The role of talker forces students to clarify their understanding of addition by using verbal language to bring to a fully conscious level their intuitive understanding of addition.

When they are the writing gorilla, they are a *writer* and *record using mathematical symbols* the actions demonstrated by the doer and verbalizations articulated by the talker. Each recording of a number is contextualized by its correspondence to a physical action and a verbal articulation that fits it into the overall algorithm.

All group members must constantly listen to what each other says and *aurally interpret* the meaning of verbal articulations. Both the doer and writer must listen carefully so they can follow the instructions of the talker. All group members must listen to each other so that they can constructively participate in group discussions.

Actions with blocks also provide all group members with a series of *visual images,* each relating to a stage in the addition algorithm. The images provide a series of pictorial storyboards that illustrate how the base ten blocks are physically arranged at each stage of the addition process and that visually guide learners through the addition process.

These five roles define both how students are to act in small groups and how students need to think about and learn mathematics. Every student must learn how to function in each of the five roles. This is because Doris believes that if a student can experience the meaning of mathematics from each of these different perspectives, and intellectually coordinate their understanding from all of these perspectives, then the coordinated relational understanding that they construct will be of greater depth and provide them with greater conceptual flexibility than if they can think about mathematics in only one way.

Collaborative Social Interactions

During "The Wizard's Tale" Doris structures the social interactions among students in their small groups around four principles. The first is *mutual independence* (Johnson, Johnson, & Holubec, 1991). This refers to structuring groups so that group members see themselves as linked together in such a way that no one in the group can succeed unless all members of the group succeed, and if the group as a whole succeeds then all members of it have succeeded. Within small groups (and the story) children (and wizards) are indispensable members of their group and must carefully coordinate their endeavors with those of other group members.

The second principle underlying group behavior is *clear role accountability* (Johnson, Johnson, & Holubec, 1991) for both the group as a whole and individuals in the group. This involves clear specification of the group's goals and the role each student is to perform in their group. In "The Wizard's Tale" the group goals and the group member roles (as doer, talker, and writer) are clearly defined.

The third principle is *mutual peer tutorial interaction.* In essence, mutual peer tutorial interaction means that children take responsibility to help each other learn, as needed, by being each other's peer tutors. This involves children assessing each other's endeavors, providing each other with constructive feedback, teaching and learning from each other as necessary, and discussing the nature of the learning being jointly experienced. Doris emphasizes the importance of this principle during the story when she says, "The characters comment on how explaining a concept to someone else helps the one who is explaining it understand it better themselves."

The fourth principle guiding groups is *group reflective processing.* This involves establishing an environment where students reflect on their experiences and share their insights and thoughts with each other. Group reflective processing is distinguished from the phrase *group processing* in the sense that the former primarily involves reflections on content issues while the latter primarily involves reflections on how the group is working together as a dynamic social entity. In "The Wizard's Tale" group reflective processing takes place as group members monitor each other's behavior, discuss what they learn each day, and share, as groups, their reflections with the whole class.

The five roles within which students function and the four principles guiding social interactions do not just happen by accident. Doris actively promotes them, both while telling the story and while circulating among, monitoring, and helping students as they solve problems in their small groups.

Collaborative Learning

The five roles for students and the four principles for group interactions are important because they define the structure of the social interactions in Doris's class during "The Wizard's Tale."

They are also important because they define the structure of the intellectual environment of small groups that governs how mathematical knowledge and meanings are exchanged among group members (through teaching and learning). These exchanges of knowledge and meaning between group members will be called *interintellectual* exchanges—or intellectual exchanges *between* people.

In addition, they are important because they define the structure of the intellectual environment in which individuals speak to themselves, teach themselves, and learn from themselves. These intellectual exchanges within individuals, through which they construct meaning, will be called *intraintellectual* exchanges—intellectual exchanges *within* a single person.

What is significant here is that the principles that guide how people socially interact and the roles within which they function provide a structural model that governs how they exchange ideas, teach each other, and learn from each other (interintellectual exchanges). In addition, these rules and roles that determine how people physically interact with each other also provide a structural model that governs how individuals construct meaning within themselves (intraintellectual exchanges).

This models current learning theory that suggests that intellectual development cannot be separated from the social contexts in which it occurs and that the intellectual communication of knowledge and meaning between people and within a single individual are greatly affected by the social context in which they occur (Albert, 2000). Vygotsky suggests this when he says that "[all] the higher [level intellectual] functions originate as social relations between [people]" (1978, p. 57).

It also goes beyond current learning theory, however, to suggest that as educators we can intentionally construct social environments in classrooms where the rules and roles for social interactions that we insist children work within provide the intellectual model for how they exchange ideas between each other (interintellectual exchanges) and within themselves (intraintellectual exchanges).

In fact, this is what Doris attempts to do in her classroom when she tells "The Wizard's Tale" and sets up a social structure that designates how students are to act and interact, a social structure that in turn determines how learning takes place between individuals and within individuals. Two examples help explain this.

Let us first examine interintellectual exchanges among three students working in a collaborative group as doer, talker, and writer in Doris's classroom during "The Wizard's Tale." Assume the writer erroneously records a trade of ten ones for one ten. Several things might happen. First, the talker or doer might make a comment that what was done by the writer is incorrect. (This follows the principle of mutual interdependence.) This might be followed by an explanation of the correct behavior by reference to the actions of the doer and verbalizations of the talker. (This follows the principle of role accountability.) The doer might now demonstrate to the writer the actions that parallel the correct recordings and point out the discrepancy between those actions and the writer's erroneous recordings. The talker might now describe in words to the writer what the doer demonstrated and again point out the discrepancy between the verbal description he or she offered and the erroneous written symbols. (This follows the principle of mutual peer tutorial interaction.) These cross-modality discrepancies (between action and recording and between talking and recording) are what pressures the writer to rethink how the writing should take place, and either re-perform the recording correctly or ask for more clarification in order to better understand what to do. (This follows the principles of mutual peer tutorial interaction and group reflective processing.) Finally, the doer and talker will ask the writer to explain in words and recordings what should be recorded and why those recordings should be made. (This follows the principle of group reflective processing.) When everyone is satisfied that the writer knows what to do, and why to do it, the members of the group continue their work. (This follows the principle of mutual interdependence.)

Let us now examine a hypothetical example of an intraintellectual exchange by viewing what might occur within one of Doris's male students when that individual thinks or speaks to himself during "The Wizard's Tale." Imagine the student working an addition problem all by himself while using only recordings. The student progresses satisfactorily until making a mistake. Assume the error involves a trade of ten ones for one ten. The student is monitoring his own behavior and stops himself. You can see the troubled look on his face. The student says to himself, "There is something wrong here." Now the student reconstructs in his mind what underlies the recording by reference to actions he imagines in his mind (using visual images) that he would perform as a doer and by making subverbalizations to himself during which he recounts to himself what he would say to himself as the talker as he describes his imaginary actions. You can see the child doing this. His hands are moving above his paper as though he is pushing base ten blocks around (he is doing the real pushing of images in his imagination), and his lips are moving as he imitates the speech of the parrot (as he speaks quietly to himself). While rethinking to himself the actions and talk that accompany the erroneous recordings, the student discovers the discrepancies between what was recorded and the actions and talk that underlie those recordings. You can see that the child has discovered something because of the "Aha!" look on his face. The cross-modality discrepancies (between action and writing and between talking and writing) clarify for the student what is wrong and how to correct it. The need to eliminate the cross-modality discrepancies (or the cognitive dissonance) is what pressures the student to reconstruct for himself (as a result of assimilation and accommodation to preexisting intellectual constructs) new cognitive structures that do not contain the discrepancy. In the process the student reconstructs for himself a new conception of how to do multidigit addition and why things work as they do during addition. (This is called learning.) The student then continues working on the problem.

Several things are important here. First, there are principles of social interaction that underlie the interpersonal dynamics of social groups, knowledge exchanges among members of a social group (interintellectual knowledge exchanges), and knowledge construction within an individual (intraintellectual knowledge construction). The principles discussed above are *mutual interdependence, clear role accountability, mutual peer tutorial interaction,* and *group reflective processing.* These are not the only principles that exist, and oral storytellers, including Doris, do structure groups differently. Principles such as these do not just emerge in a classroom by themselves. They are modeled and described by teachers as they tell a story and reinforced by teachers as they circulate among, monitor, and help students as they work in small groups.

Second, these principles can parallel each other at the level of group social dynamics, interpersonal knowledge exchanges, and intrapersonal knowledge construction.

Third, there are mathematical roles that group members can be given by a teacher that pressure them to act in a specific manner. The roles presented thus far are those of doer, talker, writer, visualizer, and listener. These roles are some of the major vehicles through which knowledge and meaning can be taught and learned in social settings. These are not the only roles available to oral storytellers. (For example, Doris has experimented with adding a fourth student to groups to function as a group coordinator.)

Fourth, the physical roles that students can be asked to assume within a group can parallel, provide models for, and shape interintellectual exchanges of knowledge between individuals and intraintellectual knowledge construction within an individual. When a person speaks to others (during interintellectual knowledge exchanges) or to him or herself (during intraintellectual knowledge construction) using the voices (or roles) of doer, talker, writer, visualizer, and listener, that person is using some of the major modes of mathematical communication and knowledge construction.

Fifth, learning can result when students working in a cooperative group take on distinct roles (such as doer, talker, and writer) and then notice and comment on discrepancies between their behaviors. Similarly, when a person speaks to himself or herself using different voices (such as those of doer, talker, and writer), this cross-voice speaking, along with natural impulses to minimize cognitive dissonance, offers a powerful way of clarifying meaning, generating knowledge, and constructing understanding.

Sixth, teachers can design the social structure of instructional groups and specify the cognitive roles that students must assume as they interact in groups. These social structures and roles can provide a model for both interintellectual knowledge exchanges and intraintellectual knowledge exchanges. The social context in which children learn, and the actions, talk, and writing that are expected of them as they work in groups, can provide a model for how they learn by communicating with others and with themselves.

This is what Doris attempts to do in her classroom when she tells "The Wizard's Tale," both while telling the story and while circulating among, monitoring, and helping students as they work on mathematical problems and social interactions in small groups. She sets up a social structure that designates how students are to act and interact that in turn shapes the intellectual structures that dictate how communication and learning take place between individuals and within individuals.

In fact, every teacher (including those teaching mathematics in more traditional ways) determines how children learn (through both interintellectual and intraintellectual knowledge exchanges) by the way in which they structure the social environment of their classrooms, the roles they and their students are forced to assume, and the principles of social interaction. A question that each teacher must ask is, "Have I carefully thought about the social structure of my classroom and its effects on children's learning?"

THE RELATIONSHIP OF CHILDREN TO MATHEMATICS

The relationships between children and mathematics during oral storytelling are different from those during more traditional instruction. They are not different in the way *red* is different from *not red,* but in the way *red* is different from *red and not red.*

Underlying the relationship between mathematics and children during oral storytelling is a view of two different ways that the child can think about mathematics. One way is associated with children's natural childlike way of conceptualizing, thinking about, and speaking about their world. The other way is associated with adults' professional mathematical way of conceptualizing, thinking about, and speaking about their world. Oral stories introduce children to mathematics using children's concepts, thinking, and language and then systematically move children as far as possible toward the adults' conception of professional mathematics. In contrast, more traditional mathematics instruction attempts to present to children as pure a view as possible of adult professional mathematics. Several distinctions highlight the differences.

Logical Versus Logical and Imaginative Thinking

More traditional mathematics instruction tends to view mathematics as abstract, generalized, logical, objective truth that is free and separate from the influence of the person who created it, who transmits it, or who possesses it, and free from the influence of any specific social, cognitive, affective, or physical context within which it might exist, arise, or be used.

In more traditional classrooms during the process of learning mathematics, children are conceptualized as rational cognitive minds that are capable of acquiring knowledge and developing the ability to use algorithms, deductively solve problems, and reason logically. In many of the newer models of more traditional mathematics instruction, children are also recognized as social, physical, and affective beings having connections to their real physical and social worlds. But even so, while children are in the process of learning mathematics they usually continue to be conceived of as primarily rational minds capable of acquiring objective truth by using a variety of logical and rational modes of thinking that might employ symbolic, physical, graphical, or pictorial mathematical representations.

From the perspective of oral storytelling, children's minds contain more than just rational and logical capabilities. One of the most powerful parts of children's intellectual life is their imaginative and fantasizing capability.

Epic oral storytelling views the child as containing both imaginative and fantasy capabilities and rational and logical capabilities. When these two types of intellectual capabilities are simultaneously drawn upon during instruction, it is believed to be possible to intellectually touch a child more deeply than if only the child's rational and logical capabilities are drawn on. In general, oral storytellers attempt to *start where the child is* and move toward where we would like the child to be as an adult. At the very least, they attempt to facilitate children's understanding through the use of their rational and logical capabilities as a result of employing the energy and motivation inherent in their imaginative and fantasy capabilities. The valuing of both types of capabilities can be seen in the way in which Doris asks children to use their rational and logical capabilities to understand and do mathematics while at the same time imagining themselves as mathematical actors in the fantasy world of "The Wizard's Tale."

Formalized Versus Formalized and Personalized Mathematics

Setting mathematics in a fantasy story that requires children to use both their rational and logical and imaginative and fantasizing capabilities transforms mathematics into something different from what it is if it is only viewed as a subject in which children use their rational and logical capabilities.

As previously mentioned, more traditional instruction views mathematics as abstract, generalized, logical, objective truth that is free and separate from the influence of the person who created it, who transmits it, or who possesses it, and free from any specific and particular social, cognitive, affective, or physical context within which it might exist, arise, or be used. During oral storytelling mathematics is also viewed as personalized, particularized, temporalized, socialized, concretized, physicalized, contextualized, and made intuitive as it is given both subjective and objective meaning through the child's actions in the child's cognitive, affective, physical, and social consciousness. The word *also* is very important here, for in oral storytelling mathematics has associated with it both objective truth and personalized meaning, as well as both dimensions of all the dualities mentioned above.

Crucial here is that oral fantasy stories broaden our conception of school mathematics, mathematics instruction, and the nature of the child as a mathematician. In so doing they transform our conception of mathematics and the way in which children and mathematics relate during instruction. For example, because children use both their logical and imaginative capabilities while doing mathematics during oral storytelling, oral storytelling in turn imbues mathematics with both imaginative and fantasy and rational and logical dimensions, with both objective truth and personalized meaning.

To elaborate on what this means, "The Wizard's Tale" will be examined to illustrate eight dimensions of this broader view of mathematics.

Personalized

When Doris tells "The Wizard's Tale," the mathematics that her students encounter originates from within her. It is Doris's personal creative interpretation of the fantasy (that I wrote) and its mathematics that is shared with her students in such a way that Doris is sharing a part of herself. By doing so, Doris personalizes the story's mathematics.

She also personalizes mathematics in other ways. One way is by associating it with the endeavors of the story's characters. When Tinkerbell becomes a bulldozer that acts out the addition algorithm, addition is personalized by being embedded in her persona. Another way is by asking children to pretend to be a character in the story and to do mathematics the way that character would. When children are asked during "The Wizard's Tale" to pretend to be a bulldozer, talking parrot, or writing gorilla, they are being asked to project themselves into the role of story characters and imitate their mathematical actions—and in so doing they embody and personalize that mathematics within themselves.

Once mathematics has been learned in a personalized context, the storyteller systematically proceeds to begin to generalize that mathematics in such a way that it can float free from the particular individuals associated with it. Through this process mathematics learned in a very personal way also becomes understood in its more objective, abstract, symbolic form. By the end of "The Wizard's Tale"—after the bulldozer and parrot are stripped from the story—students do addition using only numerical symbols.

Particularized

In "The Wizard's Tale" mathematics is first presented in the context of very specific situations and problems that arise as Tinkerbell moves about two particular sets of base ten blocks. It is particularized in such a way that it has meaning only with respect to one problem and one specific set of actions. Later, once the algorithm has been mastered and understood in very specific contexts, it is generalized so that students can apply it to a wide range of mathematical situations. Eventually, generalized mathematical understandings will be built upon a foundation of particularized mathematical experiences.

Concretized and physicalized through the child's actions

When Doris tells "The Wizard's Tale," she first gives her students very concrete physical ways of thinking about mathematics (that are consistent with Piaget's concrete operational stage of development). She does so in two ways.

One involves using concrete models of abstract mathematical ideas by having specific (concrete) characters in the story actively (and concretely) do mathematics by manipulating physical materials. Here we see Tinkerbell the Bulldozer acting out mathematical operations (with concrete actions) using "stone" base ten blocks (concrete representations of numbers) on a magic place value symbol (a concrete representation of our place value number system meant to embody attributes such as different columns for a number's differently valued digits). The other involves having children give meaning to this concrete mathematics by physically acting out the mathematics *themselves* using physical manipulatives. Here children use their own real, concrete bodily actions to act out mathematical operations. As a result, mathematics becomes something inherent in children's own concrete way of behaving and not a formal construction separate from their physical selves.

After mathematics has been concretized and physicalized through the child's actions, an attempt is made to generalize it and make it abstract in such a way that it stands free from individuals' specific concrete behaviors. This transition takes place during the last two episodes of "The Wizard's Tale." Moving from the use of base ten blocks to numbers is moving from a concrete, physical, and enacted conception of mathematics toward a more abstract, generalized, and objective form of mathematics. In the story, telling another person how to do something mathematical is one step removed from only knowing how to do it oneself.

Socialized

In "The Wizard's Tale" the addition algorithm is given meaning in four very specific social contexts: through the social interactions of Doris (the storyteller) and her students; through the social interactions among the story's characters (Tinkerbell, Gandalf, etc); when

Doris's students help the story's characters (teaching each new wizard liberated from stone how to do addition); and when students work together in small social groups to learn mathematics. Doing so involves cooperatively explaining and acting out the algorithm, coordinating clearly defined roles (such as acting bulldozer, talking parrot, and writing gorilla), monitoring and assessing each other's behavior, and teaching and learning from each other as necessary.

Important here is that mathematics is not presented separate from social contexts. The learning of mathematics originates in actual social interactions that take place between human beings. Of course, by the end of the story Doris's students must do mathematics by themselves.

Contextualized and temporalized

When Doris Lawson tells "The Wizard's Tale," she places mathematics in a very specific story context and time frame. In addition, she attempts to tell the story in such a way that her students project themselves into the story and see themselves as accompanying its characters on their adventures. This gives mathematics meaning by connecting it in numerous ways to the children's real and fantasy lives in ways that are consistent with Piaget's concrete operational stage of development (when children are believed to best understand new knowledge by relating it to very concrete situations in which they act or visualize themselves acting).

This is in contrast to the way in which more traditional instruction presents mathematics in a decontextualized, abstract, and generalized form. Of course, by the end of "The Wizard's Tale," children are asked to begin to build more decontextualized, abstract, and generalized mathematical ideas, but those ideas are based on their contextualized and temporalized concepts.

Made intuitive

One of the difficulties faced by many mathematics teachers is finding a way to help children transform the abstract, generalized, objective truths of mathematics into personal meanings that become part of their intuitive way of acting within their world. One of the reasons why Doris tells oral stories is to help children understand mathematics on the intuitive level where they "know it in their bones." She wants children to act mathematically as though it was "second nature." She wants to help children know mathematics as well as they know how to walk. Once they have an intuitive understanding of and feel for mathematics, they can then move on to understand it at a more abstract, generalized, objective level.

As it is given both subjective and objective meaning

When Doris tells "The Wizard's Tale," she attempts to intertwine both subjective meanings and objective knowledge, and to link them to each other in order to give subjective meanings increased objectivity and to give objective meanings increased intuitive meaning. During the story mathematics is constantly placed in a context that is rich with fantasy, imagination, and specific personalized idiosyncratic meaning. At the same time, however, Doris presents objective mathematical algorithms, and she regularly asks her students to meet in social groups where they must perform a variety of mathematical roles that are constantly assessed against a standard rooted in objective mathematics. Doris believes that to make mathematics come alive for children in meaningful ways educators must nurture both subjective and objective mathematical understanding.

In the child's cognitive, affective, physical, and social consciousness

Oral storytellers see children as cognitive, affective, physical, and social beings. They attempt to teach mathematics to the *whole child.* The physical, cognitive, and social dimensions of Doris's endeavors have already been commented on above.

Doris is also concerned with her students' affective stance toward mathematics. Her concern for her students' feelings about mathematics and their feelings about themselves as mathematicians is part of the reason why she places mathematics in the context of an exciting fantasy where its characters enjoy doing mathematics and where successfully doing mathematics enables its characters to thrive within their social and physical environment. Doris believes that when her students project themselves into the roles of the story's characters (as bulldozer, parrot, and gorilla), they also try on those characters' positive attitudes toward mathematics, see how they feel, and often accept those feelings as their own. As previously mentioned, Laura McBride reports surprising success in naming characters in her stories after students in her class with the result that her students take on the positive attitudes toward mathematics of the characters that were named after them.

Telling stories that involve the whole child in learning mathematics (cognitively, affectively, physically, and socially) broadens the more traditional conception of mathematics as primarily a body of logical objective truths that can be cognitively understood.

Dualities

If children are to grow to be creative mathematicians, they will need to be able to handle the creative tension between the abstract and the concrete, the formal and the personalized, the general and the particular, the deductive and the intuitive, the logical and the imaginative, the objective and the subjective, the cognitive and the affective, and the social and the individual. Inherent here is not just a view of children learning two forms of mathematics and how to transition between them, but also a view of children learning how to use different types of mathematical intelligence: their more rational and logical and their more imaginative and fantasizing intellectual capabilities. If children are to become mathematicians—either as creators of new mathematics or appliers of mathematics already understood—they will eventually need to experience both of these modes of thinking, understand how to move between them, be able to bring both to bear separately and simultaneously while doing mathematics, and know how to handle the creative tension between them (Kline, 1980, p. 298).

Underlying these dualities might be an assumption that the extremes are distinct from each other with a no-man's-land in between. These dualities might be seen as similar to the Western construction of the mind versus body duality or the subjective versus objective duality, with everything being one or another and nothing being both. This is the way more traditional instruction views mathematics, with the assumption that only the rational and logical extreme is of value. This is not, however, the assumption underlying oral storytelling, in which mathematical activity is viewed as a mixture of both of these dualities—like the interaction of the yin and the yang that the Chinese believe comprise everything rather than like Western dualities.

THE RELATIONSHIP OF TEACHERS TO MATHEMATICS

Most of what needs to be said about the relationship between teachers and mathematics has already been presented. One point, however, needs elaboration. The relationship of teachers to mathematics during oral storytelling is quite different from that within more traditional instruction. More traditional mathematics instruction tends to depend on lecture, recitation, and seatwork (that extends into homework). When teachers lecture, by and large, they act as instruments whose job it is to deliver to students objective truth, the origins of which lie entirely outside themselves (usually in textbooks or curriculum guides). During recitation teachers stand outside of the re-presentation process and act as coordinators and evaluators of children's activity. When children do seatwork (or homework), teachers are supervisors or evaluators of children engaging in mathematical endeavors, and they stand separate from the mathematical endeavors in which children are engaged. In most traditional instruction, teachers stand separate from mathematics and have little vested interest in it or personal involvement with it, except to the extent that they are invested in helping children learn it.

During oral storytelling, teachers present mathematics and mathematical stories from within themselves. The telling of each story is a very personal affair in which teachers present their fantasies and mathematical meanings to groups of children in such a way that feelings and thoughts, affect and ideas, and subjective and objective meanings are mixed together in a fantasy story line. In presenting mathematics in this way, teachers become personally invested in the mathematics, for teachers are presenting parts of themselves and not simply transmitting objective information that originates outside and separate from themselves. Doris Lawson says that when telling an oral story she presents much more of herself—in the sense of exposing her personal thoughts, feelings, hopes, joys, humor, and fears—than she ever did when teaching from a textbook.

During more traditional instruction, the mathematics being transmitted originates outside the teacher, and the teacher is simply an instrument through which that impersonal mathematics is communicated. During oral storytelling, the mathematics and story presented come from within a teacher, and that mathematics is intimately tied into a teacher's persona. When Doris tells "The Wizard's Tale," the mathematics and story are mixed together and come from within Doris in such a way that Doris is telling her students about herself, her fantasies, and her mathematical meanings. When telling an oral story, teachers tell their students something about themselves. In taking mathematics into themselves in this way, teachers transform both themselves and mathematics. They transform mathematics from an impersonal decontextualized subject to a very personal contextualized one, from an abstract generalizable subject to a very concrete and contextually specific one. And they transform themselves from an instrument, whose job it is to deliver objective truth, into a person who is presenting to an audience his or her own personal beliefs, meanings, feelings, and fantasies.

For children the difference in these roles is enormous. It is similar to the difference between reading an impersonal historical account of a military battle and hearing a soldier who was in the battle tell about his or her own personal experiences during the battle with all of that soldier's excitement, fears, horrors, and triumphs mixed in with the telling. The personal investment of the storyteller in the story and its mathematics transforms the way in which listeners view the story and its mathematics.

For teachers the difference in these roles is also enormous. One of the most tragic elements of more traditional American mathematics instruction today is that so many teachers hate teaching the subject and are so uninvested in the subject that they develop little real understanding or appreciation of it (Ma, 1999). Part of the problem is that most teachers teach mathematics by teaching a textbook in which they have no real personal interest, they convey to children something outside of and disconnected from themselves, and they transmit a subject in which they are not personally involved.

When teachers tell an oral story, something very different happens, for the story and its mathematics must come from within themselves, and they offer to their students a little bit of themselves with the story and its mathematics. This has a transforming effect on many teachers and the mathematics they teach. It can help teachers embrace mathematics and make it more meaningful to themselves, and it can help teachers begin to have fun and enjoy teaching mathematics—because they are teaching a part of themselves.

Chapter 4

MATHEMATICAL EPIC ORAL STORYTELLING

Pedagogical Issues

There are a number of pedagogical practices built into "The Wizard's Tale" that deserve mention. They are designed to make it a powerful mathematical experience for children. They can easily be built into most epic oral stories. Their interrelationships and sequencing over time are presented in Exhibit 2.2.

MULTIPLE MODES OF LEARNING AND UNDERSTANDING

Doris Lawson believes that students should be able to use the "learning" or "thinking" style that works best for them when engaging in mathematics. As a result she tries to build different ways of learning and thinking into many of her stories. This practice is common among creators and tellers of oral stories, who believe that one of the problems with more traditional instructional methods is that they restrict children to one or two ways of thinking about and learning mathematics.

For many years educators and psychologists have spoken about the different ways in which people learn, think, perceive, problem solve, remember, or understand. For example, at the beginning of this century, L. S. Vygotsky noted the difference between visual thinking and linguistic thinking (1978, p. 33). More recently, researchers have spoken about the ability of the mind to process and remember thought using primarily either a visual-spatial sketchpad or an articulatory loop (Baddeley, 1986). Doris makes both of these ways of thinking (visual and verbal) available to her students in "The Wizard's Tale." Both are easily inserted into oral stories if the storyteller uses oral language in coordination with diagrammatic pictures or physical manipulatives. Storytellers since ancient times have done so in India, China, and Japan, often telling stories while pointing to a painted or woven storyboard that pictorially presented the highlights of their story (Pellowski, 1990).

Educators have described many different thinking or learning styles. Gardner (1993) has identified eight different types of intelligence: linguistic, logical-mathematical, naturalistic, musical, spatial, bodily-kinesthetic, interpersonal, and intrapersonal. He believes everyone has all eight "intelligences," but that the amount or strength of each that people have may differ and that this affects the way in which people learn, think, perceive, problem solve, remember, and understand. Gregoric (1979) speaks of concrete/abstract versus random/sequential learning styles. Others speak about oral, aural, reading, writing, diagrammatic, kinesthetic, visual, and tactile learning styles.

What is important for oral storytelling is to take into account that different children do seem to have different preferred ways of interacting with and perceiving their environment and different preferred ways of learning, thinking, problem solving, remembering, or understanding within their world.

Underlying the attempt in "The Wizard's Tale" to accommodate children's different learning and thinking styles are three related beliefs: first, that children think and learn mathematics in a variety of ways; second, that each child has a preferred type of mathematical learning style, thinking style, or intelligence from among the variety that exist (either because of nature, nurture, or a combination of the two); and third, that different ways of learning and thinking should be made available to children during mathematics instruction.

In "The Wizard's Tale" it is useful to view students as engaging in eight different ways of making mathematical meaning. All can be incorporated into other oral stories and instructional methods.

*[1] Each child gets a chance to act out addition with base ten blocks using **bodily-kinesthetic** actions.* These actions provide the foundation for the concrete-operational learner's way of understanding mathematics. They also provide the learner with an intuitive subverbal understanding of addition.

*[2] Actions with the blocks provide children with a series of **visual images**, each relating to a stage in the addition algorithm.* The images are both temporal in nature (indicating what comes when in a sequence of actions) and spatial in nature (indicating how the base ten blocks are physically arranged) at each stage of the addition algorithm. The visual images guide learners in imaging (or thinking) their way through addition.

*[3] Each child has the experience of recording the essence of the mathematical process using **symbolic written language**.* Each recording of a number is contextualized by its correspondence to a physical action and verbal articulation. These recordings push the learner to generalize addition by going beyond a purely intuitive understanding of addition.

*[4] Every child constructs **verbal articulations**, understandable to themselves and classmates, which explain both the addition process and the relationship between actions taken with base ten blocks and numerical recordings.* Articulations push children to clarify their understanding by choreographing bodily-kinesthetic behavior (of the doer) and symbolic written language (of the writer). Articulations also force children to bring their intuitive understandings to a more fully conscious (objectifiable) level.

*[5] Children attend to what the teacher and classmates say and **aurally interpret** the meaning of their verbal articulations.* In their small groups children follow choreographed instructions of the talker and listen to make sure that each other's articulations are accurate.

*[6] When students sing, chant, or rap "Tinkerbell's Addition Song," the **musical articulations** set to rhythm provide a metacognitive structure that children can refer back to at any time to put their actions, writing, and articulations in perspective.* Articulations set to rhythm seem to hold meanings in memory in a very different way from nonmusical articulations.

*[7] Through **interpersonal group interactions** children construct meaning together as members of small groups and a whole class.* There is a social construction of shared meanings through the sharing of language and experiences.

*[8] After working in groups, students solve problems alone as they integrate what they learned by engaging in **intrapersonal reflection**.* While working alone, they must integrate the different roles they have performed into a single coordinated endeavor, test the adequacy of their own independent mental construction, and reinforce for themselves their own learning.

Providing learners with multiple ways of constructing meaning is important for three reasons.

First, allowing children to use their preferred learning or thinking style while constructing mathematical meanings should make it easier for them to learn, use, and understand mathematics. This is important given recent research that seems to indicate that most males may rely more on visual styles while most females may rely more on verbal styles (Casey, Nuttall, Pezaris, & Benbow, 1995). It may also be the case that children from family cultures that are primarily oral in nature may have different preferred styles than children from family cultures that are highly literate in nature (Nunes, Schliemann, & Carraher, 1993). Children of both sexes and from all types of families deserve equal access to mathematics.

Second, it is important to provide children with experiences that help them understand mathematics from a variety of different perspectives, so that they can conceptualize mathematical meanings in more than one way. Using multiple intelligences while learning a mathematical topic should provide children with a multidimensional understanding of that topic rather than a unidimensional understanding of it. The assumption here is that if children understand a mathematical experience from several perspectives—for example, from both a spatial and a verbal perspective—then they will have greater depth of understanding, greater longevity of memory, and greater flexibility of thinking about the experience than if they comprehend it in only one way.

Third, it is important to help children develop facility with different ways of thinking mathematically. Doing so may help them understand the ways in which others think about mathematics. Would not children's ability to think about, understand, appreciate, and use mathematics be greatly enriched if they could think about, appreciate, and use—to the best of their ability—the major modes of thinking about mathematics used by the other sex and a variety of other cultures?

LINGUISTIC LEVELS OF MATHEMATICAL ABSTRACTION

Having an awareness of the different linguistic levels at which children think and communicate is important to the mathematical oral storyteller. It helps the storyteller meet children where they are in order to either facilitate their learning at their current linguistic level or facilitate their growth by taking them on an adventure in which they are systematically asked to learn and use language at an increasingly abstract level.

Doris controls the type of language that she uses, and asks her students to use, by matching language to different levels of mathematical abstraction. During "The Wizard's Tale" Doris matches language to four different linguistic levels from a continuum of levels of mathematical abstraction. In doing so she attempts to match language with thought and to progressively sequence the evolution of both.

Natural language level. Children's everyday language is used to describe and think about mathematical situations or problems in the same manner as when referring to everyday events.

Concrete representational level. Children's everyday language is used to describe and think about mathematical situations or problems while referring to physical manipulatives, embodiments, or materials that represent them.

Concrete mathematical level. Mathematical language (terms, symbols, equations, or representational systems such as place value diagrams) is used to describe and think about situations or problems while referring to physical manipulatives or visual images that represent them.

Symbolic level. Mathematical language is used to describe and think about mathematical situations or problems in abstract generalizable terms.

Doris systematically sequences all four of these levels of mathematical language during "The Wizard's Tale." She also asks her students to use different levels of mathematical language at different times during the story. At the beginning of "The Wizard's Tale," she allows students to speak in their natural everyday language. Later, with the introduction of the talking parrot, children are asked to speak in concrete representational language as they manipulate base ten blocks. When the parrot becomes a mathematically talking parrot, students are asked to use concrete mathematical language. By the end of "The Wizard's Tale," Doris's students are speaking and writing using mathematical symbols. Doris moves her students through these linguistic levels by first carefully modeling for her students the language and behavior she wants them to use and then asking them to imitate her language and behavior.

Metacognitive level. Storytellers use language at a metacognitive level to let their audiences see them think about their own thoughts and cognitive processes. In addition, storytellers can ask their audiences to use language at a metacognitive level in order to help them think about their own thoughts and cognitive processes. When storytellers or audiences use language to gain insight into their own and other's thoughts and thinking processes, the sharing of ideas that results has the potential to help audiences better see, understand, access, regulate, monitor, and orchestrate their own mathematical knowledge, skills, meanings, thinking processes, behaviors, attitudes, and feelings. Metacognition is further facilitated when storytellers give audiences feedback about their own and others' thoughts and thought processes so they can reflect on them.

Metacognition is used in "The Wizard's Tale" in several ways. Each day Doris asks her students to reflect on (and then discuss) the relationship between what they learned that day and what they previously learned (their preexisting knowledge base). Doris's students also reflect metacognitively when they sing "Tinkerbell's Addition Song," comment on the meaning of the song's phrases, and describe to each newly freed wizard how to add.

COGNITIVE, PHYSICAL, EMOTIONAL, AND SOCIAL INVOLVEMENT

Cognitively, physically, emotionally, and socially involving an audience in a story is one of the techniques of oral storytellers. In doing so, storytellers help their audiences invest themselves at many levels in a story and its mathematics. This helps the story and its mathematics come alive for audiences in a way that can both compel them to construct deep literary and mathematical meanings and motivate them to frame a story as a sufficiently memorable experience that facilitates their use of and memory of its mathematics.

Doris involves her students cognitively in the mathematics of "The Wizard's Tale" by asking them to help Tinkerbell and her friends to do addition. Doris involves her students physically in "The Wizard's Tale" by asking them to do such things as help Tinkerbell do magic by clapping their hands and manipulating base ten blocks while adding. Doris involves her students emotionally by asking them help Tinkerbell while she is on a dangerous journey in such a way that they become involved with the impact of their actions on her survival. Students also become emotionally involved when they help Tinkerbell do magic and share with her visually memorable events (such as a bejeweled marching band). Doris involves her students socially in "The Wizard's Tale" by asking them to work closely together in small groups where they must carefully coordinate their thoughts and actions while acting out addition problems, and by asking them to share their thoughts and feelings about the story and its mathematics with each other as they help each other learn together during small- and large-group activities.

INDIVIDUALIZING AND PERSONALIZING MATHEMATICS

One of the archetypal goals of education is to design instruction so that it is harmonious and compatible with the nature of each individual child. This is often called individualizing instruction. Unfortunately there are many views of what individualized instruction means. From one perspective it means allowing different children to progress through a single fixed curriculum at their own rate. From a different perspective it means allowing children to have different instructional experiences as they pursue different goals that are idiosyncratic to themselves.

Since oral storytelling is a group process, it needs to be asked if there are ways of individualizing it without grouping children according to ability or interest. It also needs to be asked if there are ways of personalizing oral storytelling without grouping children according to ability or interest.

Important distinctions are being made between individualizing instruction and personalizing instruction. *Individualizing* instruction is here taken to mean adjusting instruction to the differing abilities and interests of children. *Personalizing* instruction is here taken to mean adjusting instruction so that each child sees himself or herself as personally being a crucial and central actor in the instructional process.

Among other things, individualizing involves matching instruction to children's learning styles. As previously discussed, one way in which Doris provides individualized instruction during "The Wizard's Tale" is by providing students a chance to learn in ways that are consistent with their different learning profiles.

Personalizing instruction involves, among other things, teaching in such a way that children see it directly relating to their own unique selves as individuals and their own unique class as a social group. For example, at one level instruction can be personalized by creating addition problems for students to solve that are about themselves, members of their family, members of their class, or people in their school. Laura McBride does this by naming characters in her stories after her students. At another level instruction can be personalized by giving students roles to play during instruction that are crucial to the story in such a way that they become personally invested in the instructional process. Doris does this during "The Wizard's Tale" by having students clap to help Tinkerbell do her magic, sing and discuss "Tinkerbell's Addition Song" to help wizards understand addition, and play the roles of bulldozer, talking parrot, and writing gorilla. Other ways in which oral stories personalize mathematics were presented in the previous chapter. Two additional issues related to personalized instruction need to be raised, however.

First, the elocutionary style that teachers use while presenting mathematics can have a profound effect on the way in which children become personally involved with, identify with, and understand mathematics. More traditional instruction primarily uses an elocution style based in axiomatic modes of argumentation and deductive cannons of justification (modeled on Euclidean geometric proofs) that tend to communicate to children that mathematics is something for adults and not children. This style of speaking subtly says to children that mathematics is not something that is personally relevant or involving to them in the context of their own lives. In contrast, the hidden messages embedded in the elocutionary style of mathematical oral fantasies deliver a very different message because of the personal way in which storytellers use figurative and transformative language that makes rich use of fantasy, analogy, imagination, metaphor, and intersubjective sharing of meanings and feelings. This language tends to communicate to children that mathematics is something personally meaningful to them, something that they can identify with, something that they can see themselves doing and wanting to do.

Second, underlying issues related to personalizing instruction are questions about how to adjust instruction to the nature of children by taking into account their differing cultural and socioeconomic backgrounds. On the surface level, cultural issues can be easily dealt with by altering the setting or characters within a story. For example, the talking parrot could be replaced by a raven (a folktale character from the plains of the American Southwest), Anansi the spider (from African folklore), or Coquil the peeper (from Puerto Rican folklore). At a deeper level cultural and socioeconomic issues can have more profound influences on learning than those residing in the names of a story's characters. One might wonder, for example, how to take into account the relatively strong role that oral language plays in urban African American and Hispanic cultures as compared to written language. This is in contrast to the relatively strong role that written language, as compared to oral language, plays in Caucasian suburban culture. Such questions raise critical political issues related to cultural dominance and equal access to education. These issues will be dealt with later.

LEARNING THE CULTURE OF MATHEMATICS

Questions about the nature of mathematics must be asked if one is concerned with teaching the subject to children. Is it a subject that is purely cerebral in nature? Is it simply a set of facts, figures, algorithms, and deductive and axiomatic ways of thinking and proving things? Or is it a cultural orientation shared by those persons who call themselves mathematicians? Does it include mathematicians' love for their subject, their obsession with its beauty, and their way of daydreaming about its power? Does the subject we teach to children encompass mathematicians' ways of physically building models as they work, drawing pictures about problems they are engaged with, and diagramming and doodling as they think? Does it include mathematicians' ways of socializing, sharing their endeavors, and presenting their research findings?

Here the view is taken that mathematics is a culture, and that subjective elements of the culture of mathematics must be communicated as well as the objective artifacts of the culture. In the past we have been primarily concerned with conveying the objective truths of mathematics: its facts, concepts, algorithms, and ways of problem solving. When Doris tells "The Wizard's Tale," she attempts to teach one of the conventional objective truths of mathematics: the standard addition algorithm.

However, Doris also attempts to teach her students subjective aspects of the culture of mathematics. She teaches that mathematics can be fun (her students enjoy participating in the story). She teaches that we can understand mathematics by working with our hands as well as with our minds (her students work with base ten blocks). She teaches that mathematics allows us to better understand and control the world in which we live (Tinkerbell uses mathematics in Thoughtful Mountain, and Doris's students help Tinkerbell by also using mathematics). She teaches that we can use our imagination and fantasy to help us think about mathematics (as her students do when thinking about manipulating, speaking, and writing mathematics from the perspectives of a bulldozer, parrot, and gorilla). She teaches that there is beauty in mathematics, and it helps us see beauty in our world (as children discover when seeing addition in bejeweled marching bands). She teaches that we can learn and do mathematics in social groups as well as individually, particularly if we break down complicated processes and work on different parts in a coordinated manner (perhaps as bulldozer, parrot, and gorilla coordinating their endeavors during addition). She teaches that mathematics is teachable to others, and that by teaching mathematics to others and communicating with others about mathematics we come to better understand it ourselves (as students do in the story while acting in accordance with the principles of mutual interdependence, mutual peer tutorial interaction, and group reflective processing). She teaches that there is a wide range of objective and subjective ways of thinking about mathematics (including through metaphor, physical manipulatives, different thinking and learning styles, and symbolic writing, all of which are used in the story).

Part of what is important here is that mathematics content is not taught separately from other dimensions of the culture of mathematics, such as its values, attitudes, and beliefs. Tinkerbell models cultural beliefs and social values at the same time she demonstrates mathematical algorithms. As a result children learn a wide range of cultural aspects of mathematics at the same time they are learning mathematical concepts and skills, and mathematics becomes associated with the subjective meanings, affective feelings, and values of mathematics as well as its objective concepts and skills. As discussed in the previous chapter, the cultural aspects of mathematics presented during an oral story can become connected to all mathematical activity within a classroom and contribute to the formation of its mathematical culture.

To communicate the cultural dimensions of mathematics when telling "The Wizard's Tale," Doris does not *tell* her students *about* the culture of mathematics. Doris's students do not *study* the culture of mathematics as a separate subject unto itself. Rather Doris *involves* her students in some of the dimensions of the culture of mathematics that she wants them to learn, and she embodies within the characters in the story (with whom her students identify) some of the cognitive, emotional, and social attributes of the culture of mathematics that she wants her students to learn.

Here the social medium of epic oral storytelling acts as a carrier of the culture of mathematics as well as a carrier of its organized body of objective knowledge.

MODELING MATHEMATICAL THINKING

Three different participatory levels at which children are asked to engage the mathematics in stories have been identified (Schiro, 1997).

Level 1. The listener observes the results of mathematical endeavors, without being told how the mathematics is done.

Level 2. The listener listens in to a character's or the author's thought processes while mathematics is being done in such a way that the listener is shown how to do the mathematics; the listener, however, is not required to do the mathematics in order to understand or appreciate the story.

Level 3. The listener is required to do mathematics in the story in order to meaningfully understand the story and follow its action.

Children's trade books often ask children to engage the literary dimensions of stories at all three of these levels. However, they rarely ask them to engage the mathematics in their stories beyond Level 1. For example, in *The Doorbell Rang* (Hutchins, 1986) readers see the result of repeatedly dividing twelve cookies among 2, 4, 6, and 12 children. However, the reader is never told how the correct number of cookies for each child is determined.

In contrast, in "The Wizard's Tale," Doris presents mathematics at Levels 2 and 3. An example of Level 2 presentation of mathematics occurs on Day 1 when Doris's students listen in to the talking bulldozer (Tinkerbell) think through addition out loud step by step. Shortly after this Doris proceeds to a Level 3 presentation of mathematics when she asks her students to imitate Tinkerbell's behavior and actually do addition in the same way she did.

One of the important elements of "The Wizard's Tale" is that it repeatedly asks students to engage its mathematics at Levels 2 and 3, usually by first modeling a mathematical endeavor for students at Level 2 and then systematically moving on to ask students to do that mathematics at Level 3. This can be seen in the structure of each day's episode that usually proceeds as follows: First, part of the story is told. Then a discussion among the story's characters of the mathematics thus far learned takes place as wizards who have already successfully encountered addition in Thoughtful Mountain teach the newly freed wizards how to do it. Next "Tinkerbell's Addition Song" is sung. More of the oral story is then told in a way that includes a demonstration of how to do addition (Level 2 activity). Students are then put into small groups in which they actually replicate the mathematical activities just demonstrated (Level 3 activity). Students next discuss how the mathematical work they just did relates to mathematics they learned previously. Finally, some more of the oral story is told, and the story ends for that day. Inherent here is a model of instruction that includes careful demonstrations of mathematics followed by student replication of the mathematics demonstrated.

Doris conceptualizes what she is doing in "The Wizard's Tale" to be a constructivist approach to learning that is set within the context of Brian Cambourne's approach to whole language theory (Lawson, 1995). According to Cambourne (1988), eight interrelated events occur as children learn language: *immersion, demonstration,* and *engagement* within a context of *expectation* and *responsibility* where children *respond to, approximate,* and *use* language. Doris interprets what this means to her, in terms of her endeavors as a mathematical epic oral storyteller, in the following way.

Doris's students are *immersed* in a story that *immerses* them in mathematical endeavors. By the very nature of oral storytelling they are cognitively, emotionally, physically and socially surrounded by "The Wizard's Tale" and its mathematics.

The mathematical endeavors that Doris's students are expected to learn are *demonstrated* to them: that is, they are shown *how* to do the mathematics rather than being told *about* the mathematics or its rules. In "The Wizard's Tale" Doris's students see the bulldozer move the base ten blocks, listen to the parrot think through addition, and see the gorilla write in carefully prescribed ways.

In order for immersion and demonstration to be effective, students must *engage* in the mathematics they are to learn. *Engagement* takes place as students work in small groups while pretending to be a bulldozer, talking parrot, and writing gorilla in ways that replicate the demonstration of addition.

Within "The Wizard's Tale," immersion, demonstration, and engagement take place in a context of expectation and responsibility. Because of the way Doris presents the story, her students *expect* to be able to participate in the story and do its mathematics. In addition, because of the way in which her students become emotionally involved in the story, they take *responsibility* for learning the mathematics needed to save the wizards trapped in Thoughtful Mountain. They also take *responsibility* for learning the mathematics because of Doris's rules for working in groups, in which they must take responsibility for helping each other learn.

As Doris's students learn mathematics within "The Wizard's Tale," they do so by *using* the mathematics they are learning, by learning by *approximation* where they do not have to exhibit final perfected behavior and understanding on the first try, and by receiving *responses* to their correct and incorrect behaviors and understandings from peers and Doris. During each day of the story, Doris's students are asked to *use* the behaviors she demonstrates to them. They are not asked to exhibit final perfect behavior or understanding at the beginning of the story. They learn them by successively *approximating* those behaviors and understandings over a period of 5 days. Important here is that children receive *responses* to their approximate behaviors and understandings both from classmates and Doris that help them make ever better approximations of the desired behaviors and understandings.

USE OF MANIPULATIVES, SONGS, AND MAGIC OBJECTS

While telling "The Wizard's Tale," Doris Lawson associates many things with mathematics that are not normally associated with the subject. In the story children help do magic by clapping their hands three times, they learn about magic graphic symbols written in stone, they use a chartreuse stone pencil, they have word problems presented to them in the form of bejeweled marching armies, and they use base ten blocks to act out algorithms. In the story they also associate mathematics with singing "Tinkerbell's Addition Song," emulating the values of a mathematical superhero (Tinkerbell), and doing mathematics by pretending to be a mute bulldozer, talking parrot, and writing gorilla.

Using devices such as these while telling a story is not new to storytellers. Bardic storytellers in Brittany made use of songs and poetry. Homer and ancient Sanskrit scriptures make references to the use of songs by oral storytellers. The use of audience involvement in stories (by doing such things as clapping to make magic happen or by asking members of an audience to pretend to be characters in a story) is a traditional part of the craft of oral storytellers. The use of magic drawings, picture cards, and pictures during storytelling is described as a part of Hindu storytelling 2,000 years ago, and their use has been recently popular among traditional Japanese storytellers and Hmong storytellers in refugee camps in Thailand. The use of magic graphic symbols while telling stories is popular among the indigenous peoples of Australia (who draw in the sand while telling stories) and Eskimo groups in southwest Alaska (who construct special magical knives of bone or ivory that are given to children for the purpose of drawing pictures in the snow as stories are recited). Dolls are used by Panamanian storytellers, fans by Japanese storytellers, masks by Russian storytellers, spears by Ugandan storytellers, and Chinese storytellers use bamboo clappers and blocks of wood as props during storytelling. And superheroes are found in oral stories the world round. Their adventures are what ancient oral stories such as the *Ramayana* are all about (Pellowski, 1990).

Physical manipulatives, songs, superheroes, playacting, magic actions, objects, graphic symbols and other such devices do not appear in mathematical oral epic stories just by accident. They all exist for one or more of the following five purposes: to capture audience attention and promote audience involvement in the story, to help children do and understand mathematics, to help children remember mathematics, to help children acquire desirable attitudes toward mathematics, or to help children learn and create desired social values and cultural norms in their classroom.

To capture audience attention and promote audience involvement in the story, Doris has her students do such things as help Tinkerbell do magic by clapping their hands three times and singing "Tinkerbell's Addition Song." Oral storytellers have used such techniques for centuries to entertain audiences and pass on a culture's traditions.

To help children do and understand mathematics, Doris herself models and asks students to perform the roles of a mute bulldozer, talking parrot, and writing gorilla. Acting in the roles one must perform often helps a person understand those roles. Using mathematics manipulatives (such as base ten blocks) and group discussions (of how new learnings relate to previous learnings) are learning aids recommended by the *Curriculum and Evaluation Standards for School Mathematics* (National Council of Teachers of Mathematics [NCTM], 1989).

To help children remember mathematics that they learn within the story, Doris has her students make sounds such as "vrroom, vrroom, vrroom" or "beep, beep, beep" and has them act like a bulldozer, parrot, or gorilla. This is because she feels that mathematical actions and thoughts that are associated with vivid images are more easily remembered than mathematics that is not associated with such learning aids. And if a student does not remember, perhaps one of the sounds or roles will help a student recall or reconstruct forgotten meanings.

To help children acquire desirable attitudes toward mathematics, oral storytellers often have them learn songs or magic poetry. For example, in one oral story children learn two short pieces of magic poetry derived from *The Little Engine That Could* (Piper, 1990). Before beginning a problem children always have to sit quietly for a few seconds and then say,

> *I think I can.*
> *I think I can.*
> *I think I can.*

Then after solving a problem, children have to say,

> *I knew I could.*
> *I knew I could.*
> *I knew I could.*

These two short sets of magic words are specifically designed to help children develop the attitude that they can do mathematics both by preparing themselves before beginning an activity and by congratulating themselves upon completing an activity.

To help children learn social values and cultural norms that are useful during mathematics instruction, Doris has her students do such things as sing "Tinkerbell's Addition Song" (this group action helps build a group spirit), work together in small groups where the success of the group is dependent upon all of its members cooperatively working together and supporting each other's endeavors (this helps establish the value of mutual interdependence in Doris's classroom), and pretend to be mathematical superheroes such as Tinkerbell (who are sufficiently likable and powerful that children look up to them and want to imitate their social values). Not only is mathematics presented during a story, but classroom social values and cultural norms are modeled at the same time as the mathematics is introduced.

The manipulatives, songs, magic objects, and magic actions that Doris uses in "The Wizard's Tale" are not the only audience involvement and learning devices used by mathematical oral storytellers. Oral storytellers also make use of such varied things as storyboards (that they post on a wall and point to as they tell their stories), puppets, plays (that their audience must participate in), poetry, academic games, dance, and choral responses. We shall see how many of these can be used in later chapters when "The Egypt Story" is presented.

Partially as a result of associating mathematics with such things as physical manipulatives, songs, puppets, poetry, superheroes, playacting, and magic actions, children who learn mathematics through oral stories view it differently from children who learn mathematics through more traditional instruction. The difference can have a profound effect on children's understanding of mathematics, their feelings about mathematics, and their feelings about themselves as budding mathematicians.

Chapter 5

TO TEACH OR NOT TO TEACH MATHEMATICAL ALGORITHMS

During the twentieth century, educators waged a number of battles over how to teach mathematics. During the middle of the century, educators argued over whether it was more important for children to *understand* mathematics or to be able to *do* mathematics—whether conceptual or procedural knowledge was paramount. Eventually educators decided that both were important and that it was also imperative for children to understand the relationship *between* their conceptual and procedural knowledge.

By the last decades of the twentieth century, another battle had commenced. The new battle arose because mathematics educators discovered a philosophy called "constructivism" and a new type of knowledge called "meanings." With the publication of *Curriculum and Evaluation Standards for School Mathematics* (NCTM, 1989), educators increasingly demanded that instruction focus on helping children construct their own personal meanings about mathematics—in contrast to helping them learn the accumulated knowledge created by mathematicians over the centuries.

With the gradual introduction of mathematical meanings into the school curriculum, the battles intensified about the types of knowledge children should learn in school. Should children *understand* mathematics, be able to *do* the mathematics needed to function productively in society, or construct their own personal mathematical *meanings*? The battle over *procedural* knowledge (skills) versus *constructivist* knowledge (meanings) was most visibly fought in California in the last few years of the twentieth century. In that conflict *whole math* and *whole language* were pitted against a *skills* approach to mathematics and a *phonics* approach to reading. Traces of that battle can be found at Web sites such as www.mathematicallycorrect.com. The battle between conceptual knowledge (understandings) and constructivist knowledge (meanings) was fought for over a decade under the motto "back to basics." Traces of that conflict can be found at Web sites such as www.wgquirk.com.

These battles continue to be fought today. There are those in the constructivist movement who condemn any direct teaching of skills as harmful to children. Similarly, there are those in the skills movement and the understanding movement who condemn constructivist teaching as destructive to society.

In presenting an oral story that teaches the multidigit addition algorithm, this book steps into the middle of the battle over whether understandings, skills, or meanings should be the primary type of mathematical knowledge taught in schools. In suggesting that the algorithm can be meaningfully taught, it directly confronts a pedagogical position that is currently fashionable among a number of mathematics educators who have written about the harmful effects of teaching children arithmetic algorithms and who have suggested that we stop teaching algorithms in our schools and instead allow children to invent their own methods of solving problems (Kamii & Dominick, 1998; Burns, 1994; Madell, 1985). While the reasons given for the harmful effects of algorithms are problematic in and of themselves, it is equally distressing that the challenge to those of us who do believe that algorithms can be meaningfully taught to children has not been met and debated openly in the professional literature.

This book confronts the claim that the teaching of algorithms in schools is harmful to children. It does so by providing a counter example to the claim that algorithms cannot be taught in a meaningful and enjoyable way by presenting and discussing "The Wizard's Tale." "The Wizard's Tale" demonstrates one way—and by no means the only way—of meaningfully teaching addition.

This chapter also confronts the assertion that algorithms should not be taught in schools by claiming that the teaching of algorithms is a complex task that requires the acquisition of understandings, skills, and meanings and, in addition, that it is important for children to meaningfully construct for themselves the relationship between their skills, understandings, and meanings. The teaching of algorithms is not a simple task that requires drawing on only one dimension of our multidimensional mathematical knowledge base. It is a delicate balancing act in which the teaching of understandings, skills, meanings, and values must be carefully coordinated, sequenced, and synchronized. In so doing, this book implicitly takes the position that we do not need to choose between teachers teaching algorithms and children inventing their own algorithms, but that these two activities can complement and enrich each other.

Educators' assertions about the harmful effects of teaching algorithms might be justified if they were aimed at direct teaching that promotes rote mechanistic learning of decontextualized rules (for example, in division "estimate, multiply, subtract, . . ."). The attack, however, seems to be aimed at *all* methods of teaching algorithms and is thus deemed inappropriate. Also inappropriate is the solution to the problem of how to help children learn algorithms, which seems to be to discourage teachers from teaching algorithms.

To provide children with only rote, mechanistic, decontextualized direct instruction, and no time to construct mathematical meanings on their own, is problematic, given what we know about how children construct mathematical meanings over an extended period of time based on multiple experiences. But to withhold from children algorithms that have been culturally constructed and refined through centuries of mathematical endeavors, and to prohibit teachers from providing children with meaningful direct instruction, is also problematic, for it withholds from children their cultural heritage.

We need to provide children with an appropriate mix of both meaningful direct instruction and student discovery. In the case of multidigit addition (which is featured in "The Wizard's Tale"), as well as other operations, instruction should contain at least three types of experiences that children repeatedly encounter.

One type of experience involves introducing children to the meaning of multidigit addition by extending beginning addition concepts to multidigit numbers and connecting them to place value concepts. Children should work with a variety of real-world and fantasy situations in which they are encouraged to invent their own algorithms, share them with classmates, and compare such things as the accuracy, ease of comprehension, and efficiency of their inventions. They should work a wide range of problems using discrete materials (such as apples) and continuous quantities (such as distance). They should work with real-world materials (such as pennies), physical representations (such as unifix cubes), pictorial representations, and numerical symbols. Place value concepts should be introduced using a variety of manipulatives: materials that children themselves assemble into groups of ones, tens, and hundreds (such as multilink cubes); structured materials already assembled to graphically represent ones, tens, and hundreds (such as base ten blocks); and nonproportional materials (such as money). Children should use these materials to invent ways of acting out problems, such as packaging factory inventory in groups of ones, tens, and hundreds or buying and selling groups of items from a classroom store. Problems should be worked on and off of place value mats and should be drawn from a variety of sources, including real-world situations, children's literature, teacher-generated problems, oral stories created by teachers, and written and oral stories invented by children. Children should solve problems, represent solution strategies, and communicate their ideas by doing such things as role-playing with manipulatives, orally describing their inventions, drawing pictures of their endeavors (sometimes using ink stamps and ink pads), and writing descriptions of their procedures.

A second type of experience involves teacher-directed presentation of one or more standard multidigit addition algorithms. These might arise in the context of real-world or fantasy situations. One way to do this is by telling children oral fantasy stories in which the traditional algorithm is introduced in a meaningful context in such a way that the mathematical structure and meaning of the algorithm is clearly presented. "The Wizard's Tale" is one example of such a story. It lasts several days and involves careful building of the routines that children need to learn. In addition, children participate in the story by playing roles in which they are recorders of actions with paper and pencil (the gorilla), physical manipulators of place value manipulatives (the bulldozer), and verbal narrators that describe the actions and recordings taking place (the parrot).

A third type of experience involves helping children to meaningfully generalize their understandings and skills and to see the underlying structure of mathematics by comparing addition solution strategies when using such diverse things as mental calculations, alternative algorithms (such as those presented in Exhibit 5.1), 0 to 99 number charts, calculators, and the standard algorithm. While engaging in this type of activity, children should be encouraged to explain, compare, and relate different solution procedures (including their invented algorithms, alternative algorithms, and the standard algorithm). Being able to reconcile the differences between these solution strategies and comprehend and explain how all of them accomplish the same task in a roughly similar manner is an important part of understanding multidigit addition.

These three types of experiences should be encountered repeatedly by children, nudging them to meaningfully construct increasingly greater understanding of addition and addition skills with each experience. Taken together, the three types of experiences (and possibly others) would infuse increased meaning into the addition process. They could do so by helping children construct a rich understanding of addition through many different types of

Exhibit 5.1

A	B	C	D	E
¹ 5 8	5 8	5 8	5 8	5 8
+ 7 5	+ 7 5	+ 7 5	+ 7 5	+ 7 5
1 3 3	1 3	1 2 0	~1 2~	_/₂_/₃ (¹/ ¹/)
	1 2 0	1 3	1 3 3	1 3 3
	1 3 3	1 3 3		

Addition Algorithms

A is the "currently traditional" right to left algorithm.
B is a variation on A that uses partial sums.
C is a version of B that is worked from left to right.
D is a left to right version of C in which partial sums are updated during addition.
E formats recording so that "trades" between columns are usually unnecessary.

experiences, encouraging children to invent their own algorithms in an environment in which they have to explain the underlying mathematics of their creations to their peers and teachers, helping them learn the standard algorithm, helping them acquire skills in performing addition, and cumulatively connecting new learnings to previous ones in meaningful ways. They would encourage children to think deeply about mathematics as they construct their own meanings and compare different algorithms in order to help them understand the underlying structure of mathematics and build important mathematical skills. And many different instructional techniques—including mathematical oral storytelling—would be embraced to help children with a variety of learning profiles, rather than relying only on one method that must work for all children. In so doing, meaningful teacher-directed instruction and instruction that encourages children to create their own invented algorithms would work together to help children construct a rich, multidimensional understanding of the standard algorithm or whichever algorithm is deemed appropriate for children to learn.

Chapter 6

TEACHING "THE WIZARD'S TALE" TO FOURTH GRADERS

DORIS P. LAWSON

After teaching fourth grade at a small parochial school in southern New England for 10 years, I was introduced to a wonderful way to help children learn new mathematics and better understand concepts they thought they already knew. Most of my fourth graders felt comfortable with such concepts as multidigit addition. They knew the procedure, thought they understood the concept, but used the algorithm with little understanding. Because I found it difficult to help children think conceptually about a procedure they had already learned by rote, I decided to tell my fourth graders "The Wizard's Tale" to help them gain a better conceptual understanding of the addition algorithm. Weaving an epic tale around mathematical abstractions and allowing the children to participate in the story in an atmosphere of enthusiasm resulted in a wonderful experience for them. This is the story of what happened during 3 years that I told "The Wizard's Tale."

THE FIRST YEAR, 1993–1994

The Class

The first class to hear "The Wizard's Tale" had seventeen boys and eleven girls. They were a fun, lively, imaginative group. At times they were a challenge, as some of the children occasionally indulged in mischievous behavior, such as poking at each other.

Before the Story

In my experience, children in the concrete operational stage of development learn best when they have many hands-on experiences. As a result, I use many physical manipulatives, such as base ten blocks, to help children learn mathematics. When I first started thinking of using base ten blocks to teach multidigit addition, Michael Schiro suggested that my children could pretend they were bulldozers and make bulldozer noises when they pushed base ten blocks together while learning addition.

As I considered Michael's suggestion, I thought why stop with pretending to be bulldozers? Why not use real (toy) bulldozers? The bulldozers would help children slow down and think about the concept of addition. This would help the visual learners see the materials being moved about. The auditory learners would hear the bulldozer noises as well as the clunking and clattering of the materials. The tactile learners would feel the movement of the bulldozer as it moved about the materials. Therefore, in the fall of 1993, I bought seven toy bulldozers.

The children were thrilled with the bulldozers. I made the following notes in my teaching journal on October 4, 1993:

> The biggest excitement of the day came when I introduced the bulldozers. The children outdid themselves sounding like bulldozers, including the "beep-beep" sound when they back up. . . . There was a bonus to this lesson, which had not occurred to me. When the children trade 10 little ones cubes for 1 tens long, they literally "carry" the long to the top of the tens column with the bulldozer.

The Story

Michael wrote "The Wizard's Tale" during the winter of 1993–1994. When I first read the story, I was not sure I should tell it to my children because I had already covered addition at the beginning of the year. But I decided it would be a great way to reinforce addition.

The first time I told my class the story, in March of 1994, I *read* the story word for word. The following is my journal entry of March 21:

> I love the idea of doing the math in the context of a story. The problem with this is that I should have put the story on tape and modeled the first bulldozer part myself. In this case the bulldozer part was pretty easy because the children had experience with them. I can't imagine how I would do it if I had to read the story as well as demonstrate the movement of the materials and the bulldozer. Maybe I should tape the story, even videotape it.

That first year it didn't even occur to me that I could just *tell* the story, mainly because I didn't *know* it. It was not that I felt uncomfortable telling stories; I was uncomfortable telling someone else's stories and forgetting parts of them or getting some facts wrong. I did tell short stories to illustrate a point, but these stories tended to be based on fact. This is the entry in my teaching journal on March 25:

> Wouldn't it be nice if I could help the children understand all math concepts through the use of stories like "The Wizard's Tale"? Maybe I can. Maybe I can write a story about some characters who have to solve problems in order to get out of predicaments. It's a thought.

The first version of "The Wizard's Tale" that I used did not include "Tinkerbell's Addition Song," the character of the mathematically talking parrot, or the use of the violet magic chart.

In spite of these missing pieces, the story was rich enough to excite my children and help them construct a richer understanding of multidigit addition.

THE SECOND YEAR, 1994–1995

The Class

The second class to hear "The Wizard's Tale" had eleven boys and sixteen girls. The intellectual range was more diverse than the previous class so the challenge was to provide a variety of experiences in which everyone could participate and from which everyone could benefit.

The Manipulatives

This class was familiar with base ten blocks because they used them during third grade. I let the children use the materials the day before I started the story. I felt if they were sufficiently reacquainted with the materials, they would focus more on the mathematics.

The success I had using the bulldozers the first year convinced me that the story would be more meaningful to children if they had more concrete experiences. I thought that if they could identify more with the characters and the action of the story, they would better understand addition. This prompted me to look for more materials like the bulldozer. While rummaging around in the school supply closet, I found several colorful wood parrots about five inches long mounted on a dowel. I immediately decided to use them to represent talking giant parrots. When children acted out the story, they could now become parrots as well as bulldozers.

To add further to the story, I had the children use green markers as their chartreuse magic pens and mimeographed copies of an elongated version of the base ten till on an old purple ditto machine to represent the violet magic chart. My children were familiar with purple dittos, but they had never played the part of a writing gorilla using a green marking crayon to record a bulldozer's actions as described by a mathematically talking giant parrot on a purple ditto (the magic place value chart). My children loved the way in which the objects fit in with the story. There is a light that comes on in learners' eyes when they understand a concept. The eyes of the children illuminated my classroom as they worked and had fun with the bulldozers, parrots, and purple dittos. Imagine! Having fun with a purple ditto!

I thought about getting Halloween gorilla masks for children to wear when acting as the writing gorilla but decided against it. The masks were uncomfortable and difficult to see through. Also there is the danger of overdoing a good thing. The main focus of the story was the underlying algorithm, about which the children were constructing meaning. I worried that if children had masks in addition to the other materials, the focus would shift toward the materials and away from the mathematics.

The Story

Because my previous year's class loved "The Wizard's Tale," I decided to begin the year with this positive, exciting experience. I introduced it on September 16. It has been my observation that most children like math in first, second, and even third grade. Some second grade children begin to change their minds about liking math when they encounter regrouping. Even more children become disillusioned in the third grade when they have to memorize multiplication tables. By the time they come to me in fourth grade, many children no longer like math. I felt if I could begin the year with a fun, meaning-making mathematical activity some children might think math isn't so bad after all.

The second year I still read the story, but only parts of it. If I put the manuscript down somewhere and wanted to continue the story I could, without frantically looking for it. This never would have happened the first year when I not only didn't put the manuscript down, I clutched it firmly at all times. I still didn't tell the story because it was not mine. I thought of memorizing it, but felt it would not be genuine, and I hate to memorize.

Michael rewrote "The Wizard's Tale" during the summer of 1994. The most significant change in the story for me was the inclusion of "Tinkerbell's Addition Song." The first year I told the story there was no song. Michael had written the words of the song, but not the music. In my opinion, a song includes music. I cannot read or write music. But I can sing, so I decided to borrow a tune from another song and make it fit. That didn't work, so I made up a tune, which almost fit. To make it fit, I had to repeat the line "down each column we go" at the end of the chorus. Next, I needed to save the tune so I wouldn't forget it, since I couldn't write it. I sang it over and over to myself to get it right and then made an audio tape recording of it. I taught the song to the children. They loved it and sang it so loud that the third graders across the hall heard it and also learned it. As a result, the following year when I told "The Wizard's Tale" for the third time, my class was already familiar with "Tinkerbell's Addition Song" and this added to the excitement of the story.

THE THIRD YEAR, 1995–1996

The Class

This class had twenty-four children, eighteen boys and six girls. Although they were mathematically more capable than the other two groups, I had to work hard to draw them out and elicit responses from them.

The Manipulatives

This class was familiar with the base ten blocks from the third grade. I continued to use them with this group all through the year but did not bring out the bulldozers until I told "The Wizard's Tale" in the spring. When I brought out the base ten blocks along with the bulldozers, a seemingly unmathematical manipulative, the excitement in the room was more than tangible; it had its own essence. The children were so excited to use the bulldozers, I had to just let them play for about half the math period; otherwise I'm sure they would not have been able to concentrate on the story.

The Story

NCTM (1989) advocates mathematical communication. Writing about mathematics is part of communicating mathematically. Writing helps children reflect on concepts they experience. This reflection helps them learn mathematical concepts. As a result, I had my fourth graders keep a daily math journal. They wrote letters to Michael about their impressions of the story and journal entries explaining why they thought Michael invented the talking parrot, and they made drawings of their favorite parts of the story and what they thought its characters looked like. In previous years, however, my fourth graders found it difficult to reflect on concepts that they thought they had already learned.

I wondered what would happen if I began the year with unfamiliar concepts like probability or geometry. Would the children become more reflective in their writing? If they did, would this ability carry over to more familiar concepts, especially those that they had already memorized? For this reason I decided to introduce concepts in a different order this year. I began the year with units on probability, statistics, and geometry and ended the year with a review of the four operations. As a result I did not introduce "The Wizard's Tale" until March 1. The results were as I had hoped. This class was more reflective all year long.

The third year I read the whole manuscript over before beginning the story. Then every day I would reread the next part of the story before math class began. This way I was familiar with the story and would only read the more imaginative parts, which made the story so fascinating for the children. I had decided that Michael is a better storyteller than I am. He has a wonderful imagination and had already written the story, so why not take advantage of his talents. As for the parts of the story that repeated the algorithm, I didn't *read* the story, I *told* it.

The main difference between *reading* and *telling* the story was one of dynamics. There seemed to be a different energy in the room when I *told* the story orally. It was as though the children and I were somehow drawn together in a common experience. Michael was "in the room," but it was my voice the children heard and to which they responded. When I *read* the more imaginative parts, they were still very much engaged and energy was there, but it was not as intimate because it was, in a sense, Michael's voice they heard, not mine. It's as though he had physically come between the children and me.

CHANGES IN PRESENTATION

As I became more confident in my ability to tell oral stories, I changed the way in which I told "The Wizard's Tale." It was fortunate that the first year I told the story the children were familiar with the base ten blocks and bulldozers. I don't think I would have been able to both read the story and monitor children as they figured out how to use the materials.

It was also fortunate that the second year I told the story my fourth graders were very open to new experiences. Singing in math class and pretending to be a talking parrot or a writing gorilla were new mathematical experiences. The children's willingness to try something different tremendously increased my confidence in my ability as a storyteller. If the children had been inhibited and I had to stop to urge them to pretend to be the various characters, my concentration would have been affected and the flow of the story interrupted.

The third year I told "The Wizard's Tale," I ad-libbed a great deal. As a result the story did not always flow as smoothly as it would have had I read the manuscript. Fortunately the children were alert enough to pick up the thread of the story and fill in any gaps without interrupting the tale with "I don't understand." These children were also more inhibited than the previous group. If I had my nose in the manuscript instead of watching what they were or were not doing, I might have missed the breakdown in some groups' interactions because the children did not speak up if they did not understand something. The story would have become disjointed as some groups went ahead while others lagged behind. My ad-libbing enhanced the story. For example, if I saw a group feeling shy about making bulldozer noises, I would get the group's attention by saying something like, "As the bulldozer carried the little ones cubes, the bulldozer, especially the one in Group Two, made a loud 'vroom-vroom' sound." This usually worked to get shy children back into the flow of the story. This illustrates the advantage of telling a story compared to reading it.

HOW ORAL STORYTELLING AFFECTED CHILDREN

One of my main goals is for my fourth graders to like math when they leave me. At the end of the year, I have them write about what they liked best about math during the year. They all wrote about how much they liked "The Wizard's Tale." To me that is the most important indicator of how oral storytelling helps children improve their attitude about math.

"The Wizard's Tale" helped my children better understand mathematics. Unlike prior years when I reviewed addition, children did not disengage from my lessons but embraced them. Later in the year when I taught multiplication and division, the children more easily identified with the mathematical algorithms related to the base ten blocks than had children in prior years.

There are also other indicators. For example, during the second year after the children had experienced the story in September, I heard all year long, "Don't do that; you'll turn to stone!" The speaker was not just referring to the addition algorithm. This was a phrase that the children used to remind each other of potential procedural mistakes. This is an example of how imagery that developed during the story affected the mathematical culture of the classroom for the entire year.

HOW ORAL STORYTELLING AFFECTED MY GROWTH AS A TEACHER

"The Wizard's Tale" helped me become a better teller of mathematical stories. I have always told my fourth graders stories, although it would be more accurate to say that I told the children interesting bits of historical trivia. For example, at holiday time I might explain the origin of the Christmas tree. The closest I ever came to telling stories was during religion time when I would tell Bible stories.

During the first year I did not recognize the intrinsic power of an oral story. I wanted to be able to tell the story from memory because I felt it would free my hands and eyes so I could help the children "correctly" manipulate the materials.

The second year, Michael had a new draft of the story, which was very similar to the original. I had enough of the story memorized that I could tell parts of it without having to read the manuscript. The result of the new draft was that I realized the story was not carved in stone—it could be changed! Therefore, if I told a part of it and couldn't remember what came next, I improvised. However, that made me very uncomfortable. The story, after all, was written to help children understand the addition algorithm. What if I jumped ahead, or skipped over an essential ingredient in the process? Thoughts like these prevented me from straying too far from the story manuscript.

The third year I decided to *read* some of the narrative parts and *tell* all of the parts involving the children actually acting on the manipulatives. I decided to read some of the narrative parts of the story to take advantage of some of Michael's wonderful language. I realized the year before I hadn't given myself enough credit for knowing the process the children go through to understand the addition algorithm. So when it came time for the children to pretend they were Tinkerbell, Gandalf, or Habble and turn themselves into the bulldozer, parrot, or gorilla, I could circulate around the classroom, helping the children and telling the story as I moved about.

During the third year I became more comfortable changing the story as I felt necessary. As stated, the intellectual range of this class was broader than the previous two. As a result they didn't quite need all the repetition of actually doing the addition problems. I still, however, read Michael's imaginative descriptions of, for example, "cavern walls starting to glow violet and appearing to have hundreds of bumble bees eating away at them making loud crunching sounds." Those descriptive parts fascinate the children. I was not about to tamper with that. But I tried to stay as independent of Michael's script as possible, for I discovered that telling oral math stories without a script adds to the richness of personalization during instruction in a way that is not possible when there is—in a manner of speaking—the barrier of the manuscript between myself as storyteller and my students.

My growth as a storyteller who could take charge of a story was very important for me during the third year. It is significant that it took me 3 years to obtain confidence in myself as an autonomous teller of stories, someone who is in control of the story I was telling rather than as a mouthpiece of someone else's story.

August, 1996

Part II

"THE EGYPT STORY":
ORAL STORYTELLING, PROBLEM
SOLVING, AND MULTICULTURAL
MATHEMATICS

Chapter 7

"THE EGYPT STORY"

Doris Lawson Tells
Sixth Graders an Oral Story

Doris Lawson taught fourth grade for many years. In 1997 she moved from teaching all subjects to fourth graders to teaching mathematics and social studies in Grades 6, 7, and 8. When she changed grades, she asked me to write her a story that integrated content she had to teach her sixth graders. She suggested problem solving from the mathematics curriculum and ancient Egypt from the social studies curriculum. I wrote a story; and over the next four years Doris taught it and I revised it based on her feedback. She calls it "The Egypt Story."

"The Egypt Story" has eleven sessions, most of which last one class period. The first time Doris told the story in 1998, she did so in 11 consecutive days. The next year she told it every Friday for 11 weeks. The following year she told it on occasional Fridays, and it lasted almost the entire year. In 2001 her school had a project week, and she completed the story in 1 week—spending half a day on the story for 5 consecutive days. Usually Doris tells the story during mathematics period, although her students work on some activities during social studies. When Doris cannot complete a session in one class period, she finishes it the next day.

Let us now listen to Doris as she tells "The Egypt Story." In what follows, Doris's actual words are presented, as well as commentaries on what is occurring in her classroom. This is an abridged version of the story. The accompanying CD provides a full description of what occurs in Doris's classroom and has full-size reproducible copies of all class materials.

DAY 1

Doris announces "The Egypt Story" by saying, "Settle down. I want to tell you a story." When her class is quiet, she begins. As she speaks, she moves about the classroom gesturing with her arms and changing her tone of voice to accentuate what she is saying. She is wearing earrings that are replicas of statues of ancient Egyptian gods and a skirt with a design from an ancient Egyptian tomb painting.

> I want to tell you a story about what happened to two of my students several years ago. Their names are Maria and Regi.
>
> Maria had shoulder-length black hair and was high spirited. She always had a little bounce in her walk, and she frequently skipped with a big grin. In this story she wears a red and white checked shirt, blue jeans, and sneakers.
>
> Regi was a little plump, read a lot, remembered all sorts of facts, asked lots of questions, and got bored easily. He wore a gray tee shirt, jeans, and sneakers.
>
> I am telling you this story because last night a computer named π^3 visited me from the future. π^3 asked if we could help Maria and Regi return home from a place he sent them. Actually, they had already returned home several years ago, but because of the way time travel works, π^3 wants us to do some things that will help events in the past occur as they are supposed to.
>
> Maria and Regi told me about what happened to them several years ago and I am now going to tell you. I just never knew that what we are going to do in our class is what saved their lives.
>
> Everything started on a class trip to the museum to see an ancient Egypt exhibit. Maria and Regi were in a tomb with a mummy. Regi was poking the mummy—right next to the "Do Not Touch" sign—when the tomb's door suddenly closed with a great BOOM! . . . and locked them in the tomb. This activated π^3, which had been hidden in the tomb 3,500 years ago.
>
> π^3 told Maria and Regi that they were now in a time machine traveling back 3,500 years to ancient Egypt. π^3 told Maria that she was going to visit one of her ancestors, An-Nab. He had done π^3's creators a favor 3,500 years ago and as a reward was given the ability to have his ancestors from the future visit him.
>
> π^3 then hung a round amulet around Maria's neck and told her that jewels in it would light up when she solved problems. To return home she and Regi would have to solve eleven problems. π^3 also told Maria and Regi that it was giving them the ability to understand, speak, and read ancient Egyptian.

Doris now gives her students amulets to hang around their necks while she tells the story. She tells them that they will color in its eleven empty circles as the story progresses. The twelfth hole at the top is for the string that goes around their necks. Doris reproduced the amulets on her school's copying machine, cut them out, and put a string through their top holes. Doris has a large copy of the amulet hanging on her bulletin board. When all students finish hanging the amulets around their necks, Doris continues the story.

> Soon afterward Maria and Regi found themselves seated on the ground next to a mud building watching the sunrise.
>
> Maria said, "Wow! Look at that sunrise! Isn't it awesome that we are going to visit my ancestors? I never knew I had Egyptian in me. I knew I was

Exhibit 7.1   Student Amulet

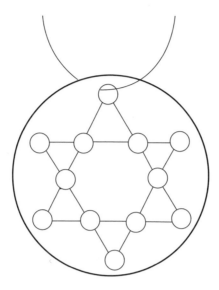

some Indian, and some Spanish, and some of a lot of other things. But just think! I am also Egyptian!"

In the distance the children could see an immense river. "That must be the Nile," Regi said. "I knew it was big. But look at it! It's gigantic! It must be a mile across."

Just then some young children came running around the side of the building and saw Maria and Regi. They stopped, stared at Maria and Regi, and then took off yelling for help. Suddenly adults with swords appeared asking a lot of questions. Thanks to π^3, Regi and Maria could understand everything being said. Maria told the adults, in Egyptian, that they were looking for An-Nab. An-Nab was sent for immediately.

Soon an old man dressed only in a white loincloth arrived, clapped his hands in delight, gave them both a hug, and welcomed them. He seemed to know who they were and why they had come. He told the other Egyptians that he had been expecting Maria and Regi, and that they would be visiting him. [*As she says this, Doris points to a copy of an ancient tomb painting of a man wearing a loincloth, which she has posted on her bulletin board.*]

An-Nab told Maria and Regi—quietly so that no one else could hear— how some other people from the future had arrived many years before and that he had saved their lives. He said that as a reward they gave his descendants the ability to come back through time to visit him. Maria told him that they had come from 3,500 years in the future.

An-Nab was surprised that Maria had come back 3,500 years. He wondered how many generations had passed and how many babies had been born to get from him to Maria. Maria was also curious about this and suggested that they figure it out. She said it was an easy problem. All they had to know were two things: how many years had passed from An-Nab's time to hers and the length of a generation (or how old women were when they had their middle child).

An-Nab said that a generation was usually about 15 to 20 years, for women in Egypt usually got married between the ages of 12 and 14 and then started having children about a year later. They usually had four to six children. He said that men usually got married between the ages of 14 and 20, right after they got their first job.

Maria told An-Nab that most women from her time did not get married until they were about 25 years old and that they only had one or two children. An-Nab had a hard time believing this. He said that most Egyptian women died between the ages of 30 and 40. He was surprised when Maria told him that in the future women live to be about 80 years old.

Regi got bored with all of this talk and just wanted to solve the problem of how many generations there were between An-Nab and Maria. He suggested that they decide on the length of a generation and divide. He said they had all the necessary information: the age at which women get married and the number of children they had. All they had to do was decide when the middle child was born and they were ready to solve the problem. Regi picked up a twig and started scribbling in the sand to solve the problem.

But something strange happened when π^3 sent Maria and Regi back to ancient Egypt. Neither of them could say or write anything having to do with mathematics in Egyptian. It was as if the translator into Egyptian that π^3 gave them did not allow them to speak or write Egyptian mathematics.

And this is where we come into the story. π^3 asked us to provide Maria and Regi with answers to problems that they have to solve in ancient Egypt. I know it sounds strange, but we have to help Maria and Regi answer mathematical questions, so that they can return home from ancient Egypt. We are now going to have to help things occur that actually happened to Maria and Regi years ago. Things like this sometimes occur when time travel exists. π^3 has given us a special magical ability to transmit our answers to mathematical problems back in time so that our answers come out of Maria and Regi's mouths as though they were their own words. So you have a very important role to play in this story. You must save Maria and Regi.

This is the first problem you must solve: How many generations are there between An-Nab and Maria over the 3,500 years? You have all of the necessary information.

Get into two-person groups. Decide which member of your group will be a writer and which will be a speaker—you need one of each. The writer must record on a sheet of paper how you determined the length of a generation and your answer. The speaker must be able to read the answer aloud and explain it. Make decisions about the length of a generation and do your calculations. When everyone finishes, we will discuss your answers, make a decision about what to send back to Maria and Regi, and transmit it to them so they can say it in ancient Egyptian.

Doris puts students into groups and then circulates among them as they work, answering questions as necessary. As small groups complete the problem, Doris encourages students to discuss comparisons between ancient Egyptian and current-day birth, marriage, and death rates.

When everyone completes the problem, Doris asks speakers of the groups to explain their calculations. Then she has students decide on a single answer to send back to Maria and Regi. Over the years students have decided this in a number of ways including voting, finding an average, and reaching a consensus based on the presentations of speakers. This year her students decide that a generation is 18 years (age 13 at marriage + 1 year for the first child and 2 years between each of the next two children) and that there were 195 generations (3500 ÷ 18 = 194.44 and round up). Once an answer is agreed on, Doris continues the story.

Now that we have made our decision, we must send our answer back to Maria and Regi so that they can tell it to An-Nab. First, in your small groups, write how we determined the length of a generation and the number of generations on a sheet of paper. Raise your hand when you are done. [*Doris waits until students compete this.*]

Now, according to π^3 we must do the following in unison to send our conclusions to Maria and Regi. On the count of three, everyone clap your hands three times, then rap your knuckles on the answer sheet three times, then clap your hands three more times.

OK, get ready. 1, 2, 3! . . . [*Doris orchestrates the event so that her class claps and raps in unison.*]

Maria and Regi tell An-Nab our information as soon as we finish clapping. He is surprised at how quickly they calculated and delighted that there were so many generations of his descendents. He wonders how many children might have been born to all of his descendents, that is, how many children he had caused to be born.

Just then a child came running up to An-Nab and asked him to open the school. As head scribe of the village, he had to open the school each day. So calculations were put aside as An-Nab hurried to school with Maria and Regi following him.

On the way to school, Regi looked at Maria's amulet. It now had a bright emerald green light glowing on it. They must have just completed one of the problems they needed to solve to return home.

This is where our story ends for today. But before we end class, I want you to take your amulet off, get an emerald green crayon out of your crayon box, color one of its circles green the way I am, and then put your amulet in your desk until I tell more of the story. [*As she says this, Doris colors one of the circles green on the large amulet posted on her bulletin board.*]

DAY 2

As her sixth graders enter her classroom, Doris tells them to get out their Egyptian amulets and put them around their necks. Then she continues the story.

As Maria and Regi follow An-Nab through his village, they see many one- and two-story mud brick houses. Many houses have brightly painted front doors and a couple of palm trees near them. There are only a few narrow streets in the village, and they twist around the houses.

When they get to the school, An-Nab opens its brightly colored front door and people rush inside. Inside are several connected buildings surrounded by a high wall. The buildings all face into a central courtyard that contains a small garden with a pond, flowers, and palm trees.

An-Nab tells Maria and Regi that his school has two parts. In one part scribes do their work, and in another part children study to be scribes. Scribes are people whose work is reading, writing, and doing mathematics for others. The scribes are also the teachers in the school, and when students know enough to help the scribes, they apprentice themselves to scribes and help them with their work.

An-Nab says he has some business to do and points to where his office is. He then stops a boy named Na-Ban, who looks about 6 years old, and tells him to take Maria and Regi to class with him.

Na-Ban takes Maria and Regi to a small mud building with a large door and several large windows. This is his classroom. Na-Ban says that his class is reviewing how to count and write numbers.

Na-Ban introduces Maria and Regi to his teacher. The teacher welcomes them and tells them to sit on the floor with the rest of the children. When she sits down Maria feels something vibrating on her chest. It is her amulet. It has a small red light blinking on it. She says to herself, "I bet this means we are facing another problem." As the two children sit quietly, all they hear is the slapping of the palm tree leaves on each other, and the teacher asking, "What number comes next?" and "How do you write that number?"

Eventually the teacher asks Regi what number comes next. Regi says he does not know because he was not paying attention. He is given a scolding and told to pay attention, for he is in the House of Life. He is told that being in school is a privilege that only a few people are given, and that learning to read, write, and calculate makes their lives much easier than the lives of others. "After all," the teacher asks Regi, "would you rather labor in the fields or write and calculate?"

When the teacher goes on to the next child, Regi whispers to Maria, "We better figure out how ancient Egyptian numbers work." Maria agrees, and the two children begin paying attention. Before long, Regi takes a piece of paper out of his backpack—which he is still wearing—and starts taking notes.

Before long Regi gives his notes to Maria and whispers, "Here, I figured it out." Maria studies the notes. Here is a copy of Regi's notes.[1] [*Doris passes out copies to her students; see Exhibit 7.2.*]

Exhibit 7.2   Regi's Notes

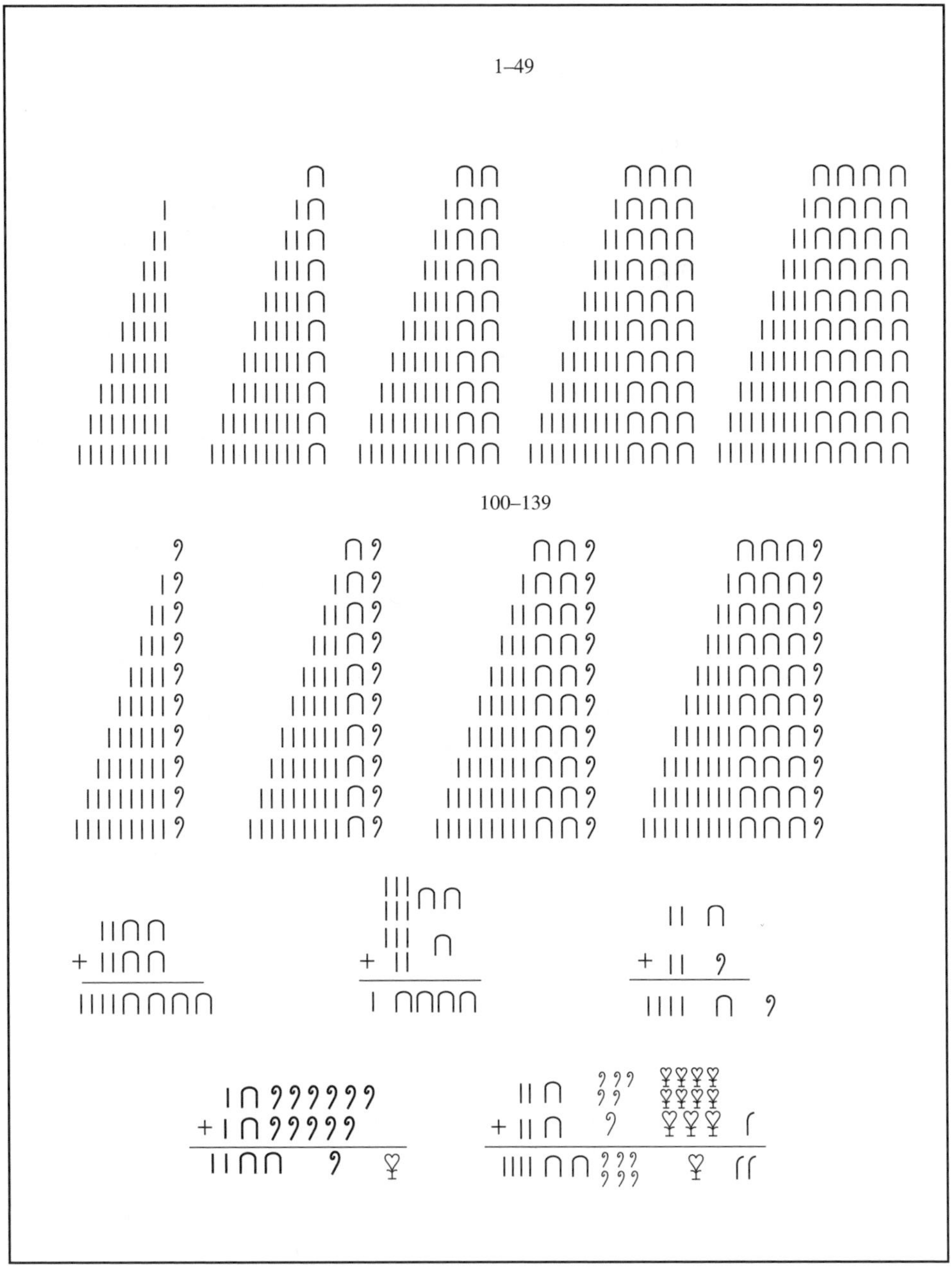

1–49

	∩	∩∩	∩∩∩	∩∩∩∩
׀	׀∩	׀∩∩	׀∩∩∩	׀∩∩∩∩
׀׀	׀׀∩	׀׀∩∩	׀׀∩∩∩	׀׀∩∩∩∩
׀׀׀	׀׀׀∩	׀׀׀∩∩	׀׀׀∩∩∩	׀׀׀∩∩∩∩
׀׀׀׀	׀׀׀׀∩	׀׀׀׀∩∩	׀׀׀׀∩∩∩	׀׀׀׀∩∩∩∩
׀׀׀׀׀	׀׀׀׀׀∩	׀׀׀׀׀∩∩	׀׀׀׀׀∩∩∩	׀׀׀׀׀∩∩∩∩
׀׀׀׀׀׀	׀׀׀׀׀׀∩	׀׀׀׀׀׀∩∩	׀׀׀׀׀׀∩∩∩	׀׀׀׀׀׀∩∩∩∩
׀׀׀׀׀׀׀	׀׀׀׀׀׀׀∩	׀׀׀׀׀׀׀∩∩	׀׀׀׀׀׀׀∩∩∩	׀׀׀׀׀׀׀∩∩∩∩
׀׀׀׀׀׀׀׀	׀׀׀׀׀׀׀׀∩	׀׀׀׀׀׀׀׀∩∩	׀׀׀׀׀׀׀׀∩∩∩	׀׀׀׀׀׀׀׀∩∩∩∩
׀׀׀׀׀׀׀׀׀	׀׀׀׀׀׀׀׀׀∩	׀׀׀׀׀׀׀׀׀∩∩	׀׀׀׀׀׀׀׀׀∩∩∩	׀׀׀׀׀׀׀׀׀∩∩∩∩

100–139

(Egyptian numeral chart continuing with the coil/loop symbol "9" representing 100, combined with the units and tens from the table above.)

Addition examples:

```
  ׀׀∩∩                ׀׀׀∩∩               ׀׀ ∩
+ ׀׀∩∩              + ׀׀׀ ∩            + ׀׀ 9
----------          ----------          ----------
 ׀׀׀׀∩∩∩∩            ׀ ∩∩∩∩              ׀׀׀׀ ∩  9
```

```
  ׀∩99999 9              ׀׀∩ 999 ♀♀♀♀
+ ׀∩99999              + ׀׀∩ 9   ♀♀♀♀ ⌐
----------------        --------------------------
 ׀׀∩∩ 9  ♀              ׀׀׀∩∩999 ♀ ⌐⌐
```

Just as she finishes studying Regi's notes, the teacher asks Maria, "Can you show us the proper way to write the number 234 in the tomb of a great Pharaoh?"

Now children, you must again help Maria and Regi, for they can neither write nor speak mathematics in Egyptian. You must figure out answers to the teacher's questions, and we will send them back 3,500 years to Maria.

Get into your groups of two. Decide who will be your writer and speaker. Figure out how ancient Egyptian numbers work: how to read, write, and add in ancient Egyptian. All of the information you need is in Regi's notes. Then record 234 as ancient Egyptians would on a piece of paper and hold the answer up facing me.

Doris circulates among students providing help as needed. When all groups have the answer, Doris holds a short whole-class discussion in which a speaker from one group describes how she arrived at their answer while her partner displays it. Doris then has her class send their answers back to Maria using the clap-rap-clap procedure.

As if by magic Maria's hands move and write the Egyptian numeral 234. The teacher says, "Very good. Now try these problems."

Doris now has her class solve each of the following problems in their small groups, discuss them, and transmit answers to Maria using the clap-rap-clap process before solving the next problem. Addition problems must be worked using ancient Egyptian numerals. Doris uses the problem about 1,000 and 999 to highlight the difference between "numbers" and "numerals." (Is the numeral with the smallest number of characters [1,000] smaller than the numeral with the largest number of characters [999]?)

Write 4321.

Write 405.

Write 1,000 and then 999. Which is larger?

Write and solve 32 + 33.

Write and solve 63 + 57.

Write and solve 102 + 130.

When Maria finishes the last problem, the teacher exclaims, "Excellent! You may now all take a break and cool off in the courtyard, for it is getting hot as our desert sun beats down on us."

Maria and Regi follow the other children to the courtyard. The Egyptian children go over to the pond, plunge their hands into its water, splash it on their faces, and drink it. Maria is horrified. "Getting splashed with water looks cool," she says to Regi, "but who would ever want to drink such dirty water? Those kids are going to get sick, sick, sick."

Na-Ban and a friend of his come over to Maria and Regi and ask if they want to play The Game of Snake. Maria says that she does not know the

Exhibit 7.3   The Game of Snake Playing Board and Sample Problems

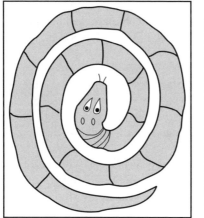 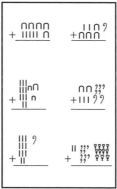

rules but would love to play. [*Doris holds up The Game of Snake playing board as she describes how to play it.*]

Na-Ban gets his snake board and a small linen bag full of scraps of papyrus with addition problems on them, and the four children squat down in a quiet part of the courtyard. Na-Ban gives Maria and Regi each a different colored stone and shows them how to place their stones on the last joint of the snake's tail. He tells them that during each round of the game, they each pick a problem from the linen bag, do their own problem, share their answer with the others, and check each other's answers. The player with the largest answer moves his marker four spaces clockwise around the snake's body, the player with the second from largest answer moves three spaces, the player with the third from largest answer moves two spaces, and the player with the smallest answer moves one space. If a player calculates incorrectly, the player does not move. When everyone takes their turn moving, another round then begins. The first player to move his or her marker onto the snake's head wins. Then Na-Ban said, "Let's begin."

Last night π^3 sent me copies of the game so that you can play it while Regi and Maria are playing. π^3 said that your activity while playing the game will make it possible for Regi and Maria to give answers to problems while playing the game in ancient Egypt. All you have to do at the end of each round of the game is to clap your hands three times, rap your knuckles on your desk three times, and then again clap your hands three times. Combine your groups of two into groups of four, and play the game for about 10 minutes. And remember to do your calculations using ancient Egyptian numerals.

Before class Doris photocopied game boards and sets of problems, cut up the problems and put them in small paper bags, and collected different colored polished stones from a nearby stream for her students to use as game markers.

Doris helps students get into groups and distributes materials to each group. She tells them to shake the bag to mix up its problems before drawing a problem from it. Problems are not to be placed back into the bag until the bag is completely empty. As soon as someone wins the game, they are to begin another game. Doris emphasizes that their playing boards for The Game of Snake are modeled after real game boards found in ancient Egyptian tombs. After about 10 minutes Doris continues the story.

> Class, you did an excellent job playing The Game of Snake. By playing the game you provided Regi and Maria with all of the answers they needed to play the game in ancient Egypt. When they played the game, answers to problems just slipped out of their mouths without them having to do anything.
>
> After playing the game several times, Maria and Regi went to An-Nab's office to ask him some questions. On the way Regi noticed that the blinking light on Maria's amulet had turned into a constantly shining red light. Now there were two lights on her amulet.
>
> This is where our story ends for today. Before we end class, I want you to take your amulet off, get a red crayon out of your desk, color one of the circles red, and then put your amulet in your desk until I tell more of the story.

DAYS 3 AND 4

This installment of "The Egypt Story" lasts for two class periods and launches a class project in which students build scale models of An-Nab's tomb during social studies.

Doris has students help tell this installment of "The Egypt Story" by having them read a play that describes what happened in An-Nab's office. The play is modeled after a type of play performed in Egypt thousands of years ago (similar to Greek tragedies with choruses). It provides background knowledge of ancient Egyptian beliefs about life after death and sets up a problem that Doris's class must solve concerning how to furnish An-Nab's tomb on a budget of 2,000 deben.

Doris continues the story from where she left off.

> When Maria and Regi enter An-Nab's office, they find him writing on papyrus.
>
> Rather than tell you what occurred in An-Nab's office, I would like to have us read a play that describes what occurred. π^3 wrote the play, and it matches what Maria and Regi described.

Doris distributes photocopies of "The Play of the Tomb" to students and tells them to silently read it to themselves. When they finish, they form a circle and take turns, in clockwise rotation, reading the parts of An-Nab, Maria, and Regi. Doris reads the opening scene to set the stage. The whole class in unison loudly chants the chorus. One year Doris had students perform the play for parents during a parent-teachers organization meeting.

The Play of the Tomb

Opening Scene: Maria and Regi enter An-Nab's office. It is a small room with mud walls, a dirt floor, and two windows. It contains many papyrus scrolls stacked in baskets. An-Nab is sitting on a reed mat on the floor writing hieroglyphics. Next to him is a basket that contains small pieces of papyrus with illustrations and writing on them.

Maria: Hello, An-Nab. What are you writing?

An-Nab: Hello, Maria. I am finishing my copy of *The Book of the Dead* for my tomb.

Maria: Why would you write about dead people?

Regi: It is not about dead people, Maria. *The Book of the Dead* is a list of spells and stories about the Egyptian underworld.

An-Nab: That's correct, Regi. Once you enter the underworld, the ba must pass many tests before the final judgment, and *The Book of the Dead* tells it how to do so.

Chorus: *The Book of the Dead*
           The Book of the Dead
           Guide Book to the Underworld
           Guide Book to Eternal Life
           Eternal Life for the Ka and the Ba

Maria: Are you going to be buried in a tomb? I thought Egyptians were buried in pyramids.

Regi: Don't you read anything, Maria? Ancient Egyptians were buried in different ways. The poorest people were just tossed into the Nile or covered with sand without even being embalmed.

An-Nab: Yes, Regi. The poor are not even embalmed while the rich embalm their pet cats before burying them in cat graveyards. People with even a small amount of money are embalmed and put in a House of Eternity with others.

Regi: I read that some mass graves have hundreds of mummies in them.

An-Nab: Yes. And people with more money are embalmed and buried in their own tomb. If they are wealthy and related to Pharaoh, they are buried either in a cave carved out of a mountain or in a stone mausoleum. Stone mausoleums are very beautiful. Some pharaohs are buried in a pyramid in as many as four caskets, one inside the other. Most pharaohs are buried in mountain tombs.

Regi: I read that lots of tombs are carved out of stone in the mountains and have tunnels cut through the stone that lead to secret burial chambers.

Chorus: Embalm the Dead
Embalm the Dead
Bury them in a Tomb
Bury them in a Cave
Bury them in a Pyramid
Eternal Life for the Ka and the Ba

An-Nab: Yes, and the chambers hold objects we need in the underworld. I am rich enough to have my tomb cut into a mountain. It is already complete. It has an entry hall and a small room for my ka and my ba. The entry hall is 10 cubits long, 3 cubits wide, and 5 cubits high. The room is 12 cubits long, 10 cubits wide, and 6 cubits high.

Maria: Your tomb sounds beautiful, An-Nab. But what are a ba and a ka?

An-Nab: You are made up of two parts, ba and ka. The ba is your soul, and it can leave and return to your body as it pleases once you are dead. It is also the part of you that must make it through the final judgment. The ka is your physical body, which must be protected and fed after you die.

Regi: Maria, don't you remember seeing tomb paintings of people bringing food to tombs of the dead? An-Nab, isn't it expensive to keep bringing food to your ancestors' graves year after year?

An-Nab: Real food is not delivered year after year. Food is delivered to the ka through wall paintings or through the ushabti. Wall paintings show food being delivered to our ka. Ushabti statues represent servants who prepare and deliver food to us. We always leave food for ushabti to prepare for us. I will have wall paintings and ushabti.

Maria: But why does the ka need food if it is dead?

An-Nab: The ka must be fed because the ba returns to the ka every night after visiting the underworld in search for eternal life. The ka must be fed so that it can give new strength to the ba, so that the ba can keep searching for eternal life. The ba has to keep searching for eternal life until it finds it and faces the final judgment. The ba uses *The Book of the Dead* to navigate through the underworld. A person must have a House of Eternity because that is where the ba finds the ka. You must have your name in your House of Eternity so your ba can easily find its ka.

Chorus: The Ka and the Ba
The Body and the Soul
In Search of the Final Judgment
In Search of Eternal Life
Eternal Life for the Ka and the Ba

Maria: So your tomb is your House of Eternity. What else goes in it besides wall paintings, ushabti statues, food, and the mummy?

An-Nab: Each tomb has a statue of your ka, coffins that contain your mummy, and your life mask, which is painted to look like you. It has wall paintings of important things like your work and your family. It also has statues of the gods you will need to appease in the underworld and amulets to protect you from danger.

Chorus: Into the Tomb
Into the Tomb
Paintings and Statues
Amulets and Coffins
The Book and The Mummy
Eternal Life for the Ka and the Ba

An-Nab: My tomb cost me most of my wealth. I have already paid for my embalming. Now I must decide what to place in my tomb, have it decorated, and have my coffins built. I have 2,000 deben left to spend.

Maria: What is a deben? And what is a cubit?

Regi: Maria, don't you read? A cubit is the length of your forearm, from elbow to outstretched fingers. A deben is like money, except that it is a piece of metal—like copper or silver or gold—that has a certain value because of its weight. In a regular trade if you make linen and you want bread, you trade some linen for bread. When you trade with deben, you might trade a piece of copper worth a deben for three fish. Isn't that right, An-Nab?

An-Nab: Yes, Regi. In fact, if you look at people you will see them wearing thin anklets and bracelets of different materials. Look, I am wearing copper anklets. Most anklets and bracelets are made so they weigh a deben. Copper ones are worth the least, and gold ones are worth the most. We trade them for things we want when we don't have goods to trade. This morning I traded one copper anklet for three loaves of bread. And this morning one of my students paid me for this week's instruction with a copper anklet that weighed a deben. I have a budget of 2,000 copper deben to spend in furnishing and decorating my House of Eternity. It is quite a puzzle to figure what to take with me to the next life, given my budget.

Chorus: 2,000 copper deben to furnish his Tomb
          2,000 copper deben to furnish his Tomb
          Paintings and Statues
          Amulets and Coffins
          The Book and the Mummy
          Eternal Life for the Ka and the Ba

Maria: Maybe we can help you.

An-Nab: I would like to know your thoughts. Let me show you my notes about what I need. I have narrowed down the list of items that can go in my tomb and made notes on small pieces of papyrus that I keep in this basket. [Doris holds up a basket with tomb cards.] Each note has one object drawn on it that can go into my tomb, different materials it can be made out of, and its price. Each thing I put in my tomb must help me obtain everlasting life. Given my budget I can't take everything, for I want some nice things and not just one of everything. Having a gold statue of a powerful god is more help to me in the underworld than just having one of everything. One powerful god will provide more underworld protection and guidance than three not so powerful gods.

Chorus: 2,000 copper deben to furnish his Tomb
2,000 copper deben to furnish his Tomb
Paintings and Statues
Amulets and Coffins
The Book and the Mummy
Eternal Life for the Ka and the Ba

Regi: How do we make decisions about what you take with you?

Maria: We have to consider all options in terms of the help they will give An-Nab in obtaining everlasting life. For example, we have to consider that a wood coffin costs less than a stone one, but that it will not last as long. And we do not want An-Nab's coffin rotting and him falling out of it!

Regi: Are there other things that we need to consider?

An-Nab: You can use my father's tomb as a comparison for mine. His tomb contained two coffins (one inside the other), two amulets, two god statues, a few small wall paintings, and two ushabti statues. I want at least one more of each of these items in my tomb. That way when I see my father in the underworld, he will be proud of me because of my tomb's wealth. And remember that statues and amulets hold more power for my ba if they have my name written on them because my name will make them always stay with me instead of going to someone else's aid in the underworld.

Regi: And we must spend no more than 2,000 deben and can only consider items on the papyrus notes.

An-Nab: Yes, Regi. I have an errand to run now but will be back soon to hear your recommendations.

Chorus: 2,000 copper deben to furnish his Tomb
          2,000 copper deben to furnish his Tomb
          Paintings and Statues
          Amulets and Coffins
          The Book and the Mummy
          Eternal Life for the Ka and the Ba

Ending Scene: An-Nab leaves his office. Maria and Regi are left holding a basket of small pieces of papyrus, with notes on them.

The End

When the performance of "The Play of the Tomb" is complete, Doris continues the story.

Since Maria and Regi cannot do any Egyptian mathematics, you, class, have to solve their problem for them. I am going to put you into four-person groups to help Maria and Regi decide what to put into An-Nab's House of Eternity. In your groups choose two writers and two speakers. Writers record the items that you decide to put into An-Nab's tomb and their prices. Speakers must be able to explain why you chose each item. Later, during social studies class, you will build scale models of An Nab's tomb that contain the things you decide to put into his House of Eternity.

I have two things to help you: tomb cards and tomb contents. Tomb cards contain the information on An-Nab's papyrus notes. Tomb contents contains An-Nab's specifications about what needs to go into his tomb. Use them to help you make your decisions. Spend no more than 2,000 deben.

When you decide what to include in An-Nab's House of Eternity, make a list of the items and the price of each using ancient Egyptian numerals, and do your addition in ancient Egyptian. Then check your addition using a calculator and our number system. Make sure you know each item's significance so you can defend its inclusion in the tomb to the rest of the class.

Doris distributes tomb contents and tomb cards as she helps students get into four-person groups, choose writers and speakers, and get started on the problem. Mathematics class ends before students complete the problem. Doris tells students to work on the problem for homework.

During social studies class later in the day, Doris introduces the activity of building scale models of An-Nab's tomb, an activity that takes several weeks of intermittent work to complete. This is one of the highlights of the year for her sixth graders. Students use graph paper to design tombs according to An-Nab's specifications in the play, then construct tombs

Exhibit 7.4

Tomb Contents

At least one thing from each category is needed.
At least three items from each starred category are needed.

Book of the Dead

Ka Statue (Scribe)
* Ushabtis
Furniture: headrest, bed, stool, table, etc.
Clothing: loincloths for men, dresses for women, sandals
Tools: for your food preparation, hobbies, body, job (a scribe needs: palette, paints, papyrus, and pens)

* Wall Paintings
    of the activities of your work   of the final judgment   of your family
    of your domestic and everyday life   of provisions for the Ka   decorations
    prayers and spells for protection   games, work, mealtime   name

* Coffins
Name Plate
Name Inscribed on Objects in Tomb (amulets, god statues, etc.)
Hieroglyphic Letters
Cartonnage Mask
Containers: pottery and baskets (used for serving food, carrying water, holding materials)

* Statues of the Gods
    Amen-ra   Amsu   Bes   Shu   Amenait   Osiris
    Anubis   Hapi   Ma'at   Thoth   Isis

* Protective Amulets
    ankh   djed pillar   heart
    udjat eye   isis amulet   scarab

      ***Tomb size: entry hall = 10 cubits long, 3 cubits wide, 5 cubits high
      main room = 12 cubits long, 10 cubits wide, 6 cubits high

---

Exhibit 7.5   Fronts and Backs of Three Tomb Cards

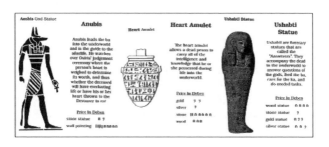

out of cardboard, determine by what percentage to shrink or enlarge tomb cards so they are sized correctly to decorate and furnish An-Nab's tomb (Doris does this on the school photocopy machine), write An-Nab's name on the tomb using hieroglyphic ink stamps, and build scale models of coffins for their tombs. In this integrated unit students learn about mortuary practices and budgeting in mathematics and use fractions, decimals, percents, and ratios during social studies.

When students arrive in class the next day, Doris has them complete the problem and check their calculations. She then holds a brief whole-class discussion during which speakers describe and justify their groups' decisions. Students then transmit to Maria and Regi their lists using the clap-rap-clap procedure. Doris then continues the story.

> Maria and Regi receive your lists written in ancient Egyptian. They read all the lists and choose one to give to An-Nab.
>
> When An-Nab returns to his office, they give him their chosen list, as well as all of the other lists. An-Nab is amazed at all their work. He immediately begins examining it.
>
> While An-Nab studies your lists, Regi says, "Maria, I am surprised at how different the Egyptian number system is from ours."
>
> "How so?" asks Maria.
>
> "Think about how our numbers work if we put them on a place value chart," says Regi. "For example, if we put 321 on a place value chart, we put a 3 in the hundreds column, a 2 in the tens column, and a 1 in the ones column." As he speaks, Regi scribbles this on the sand floor of An-Nab's office. [*Doris replicates Regi's sand scribbles on her chalkboard; see Exhibit 7.6.*] "The Egyptian number system also seems to work this way. For example, they write 321 with 3 hundred symbols in the hundreds column, 2 tens symbols in the tens column, and 1 one symbol in the ones column. But things are not the same. For example, consider the number 102. In our number system, we write a 1 in the hundreds column, a 0 in the tens column, and a 2 in the ones column. But the Egyptian number system does not have a 0 in it,[2] so they write a hundred symbol next to 2 one symbols. That is, they put a hundred where the tens column should be and 2 ones in the ones column. Even though their ones, tens, and hundreds are written down in groups of increasing size next to each other from smallest to largest, their number system is not a place value system like ours because the values of digits are not based on their position in the number but by their shape."
>
> An-Nab exclaims, "Impossible! The number system of the future cannot possibly be different from our number system. Numbers are numbers. What could be different?"
>
> Regi answers, "Oh, there are so many things that are different! For example, it takes you more writing to record your numbers than it takes us. For us to write 345 we only need to make three marks: one digit for the 3 hundreds, one digit for the 4 tens, and one digit for the 5 ones. In your number system you have to make 12 marks: 3 hundred marks, 4 ten marks, and 5 one marks."

Exhibit 7.6   Regi's Sand Scribbles

hundreds	tens	ones
3	2	1

Our number 321

hundreds	tens	ones
1	0	2

Our number 102

ones	tens	hundreds
I	∩ ∩	999

Egyptian number 321

ones		
I I	9	

Egyptian number 102

An-Nab laughs and replies, "But we have two number systems. One is for important official things like tomb writing and Pharaoh's decrees. The other is for less important matters such as keeping track of how many loaves of bread someone has or how much a person owes in taxes. You saw our students practicing our official number system. It is called 'hieroglyphic.' Our everyday number system works the same way except we have a short-hand way of writing 4 tens with a single symbol or 3 hundreds with a single symbol. It is called 'hieratic.'"

Maria asks, "Why do you have two number systems? Why would you want one number system for official use and another for everyday use?"

"That is the way everything works," An-Nab answers. "There are pharaohs and nobles who are related to the gods, and then there are the rest of us common people. Our society contains two types of people, so why shouldn't we have two number systems, one for the royalty and one for the rest of us? Doesn't society in the future have two social classes, with different burial grounds, different laws, and different number systems for each of them? After all, our number systems are simply a reflection of our world. Our official number system is like a beautiful painting in which everything is perfect and decorative. It is something made for the gods. Our everyday number system is similar to the official one except it is not so beautiful. It shortens things by letting one pictogram stand for 5 tens rather than using 5 ten symbols. Common people do not need the beauty required by Pharaoh and the royal family."

"But honorable ancestor," Maria replies, "in the future we believe that all people should be treated equally. We don't have royalty. There is only one social class, even though some people are richer than others. Everyone is buried in the same burial grounds and everyone has to obey the same laws. And we only have one number system."

"Well 3,500 years is a long time, and I guess things change over time," says An-Nab. "But I never would have believed that society would change so much and that our number system would no longer be used. But I guess a number system is a reflection of the society that uses it, and if society changes, then its number system will also change."

"That is only one way our number systems are different. There are also lots of other ways," adds Regi.

"Well, tell me other ways in which our number systems are similar or different," says An-Nab. "That will let me know how Egyptian culture has changed, for it is said among scribes that the essence of a culture is reflected in its number and writing systems."

Class, you have to help Maria and Regi again, for they cannot talk Egyptian mathematics. Get into four-person groups and discuss ways in which our number system is different from or similar to the ancient Egyptian official number system. Writers should record phrases that summarize your answers in a table that indicates something about our number system in one column and the corresponding thing about the ancient Egyptian official number system in another column. Whenever possible, speculate on why the Egyptian official number system might be different from ours. Later, speakers will report your ideas to the class. Then we will transmit answers back to Maria and Regi.

Doris's students begin work in their small groups. Doris circulates among them listening to, interacting with, and helping them as needed. After small groups discuss similarities and differences, Doris leads a whole-class discussion (based on reports from group speakers) during which she records students' ideas in a table (see Exhibit 7.7).

Whenever students note a similarity or difference, Doris asks them to speculate on how the number system comparison relates to a comparison between our current-day society and ancient Egyptian society. Student speculations about cultural comparisons include the following: ancient Egyptians had god kings and common people (a dualistic society) while we just have common people (a more monolithic society); Egyptians viewed written numbers as art while we view them as a (technological) tool; (celebratory) hieroglyphics were for the gods and posterity (they live forever in tombs) and thus deserved careful drawing to celebrate the eternal, while our numerals simply function in the present without anything sacred about them.

Doris concludes the discussion by having students send their thoughts back to Maria and Regi using the clap-rap-clap transmission method. Doris then continues "The Egypt Story."

As soon as our information reaches Maria and Regi, they convey it—in ancient Egyptian—to An-Nab. He is amazed by all the differences, but before he can comment, a student named Nila enters the office and says that An-Nab is needed at the front door.

An-Nab tells Maria and Regi to go to class with Nila. Nila tells them to hurry or they will be late.

Exhibit 7.7   Number System Comparisons

Our Number System	Ancient Egyptian Number System
Our digits are symbolic and disconnected from the quantities they represent.	Number symbols are pictorial and concrete. Ones are like fingers and tens are like two arched hands.
Our number system has one set of numerals.	Ancient Egyptians had two sets of numerals, one for royalty and one for the common people.
The positional location of a digit in a number conveys its value. In 45, the 4 is in the tens column, and the 5 is in the ones column.	The shape of the number symbols tell their value. Numbers are pictorially defined rather than positionally defined.
Our numbers require only one digit in each column to designate the number of ones, tens, hundreds, etc. 56 means 5 tens and 6 ones.	(Official) numbers required multiple symbols to tell the number of ones, tens, etc. in a number. 56 requires 5 ten symbols and 6 one symbols.
We read our numbers from left to right with the largest quantities recorded to the left.	Egyptians read their numbers from right to left with the largest quantities recorded to the right.
We have a base ten system, with the trade between basic units (ones, tens, hundreds, etc.) being ten.	Egyptians had a base ten system, with a ten for one trading rule.
We have a digit that stands for nothing (0).	Ancient Egyptians did not have a zero (0)

On the way to Nila's class, Regi points to Maria's amulet. It has two new lights on it that are bright turquoise blue.

This is where our story ends for today. Take off your amulets, get a blue crayon from your desk, color two of the circles blue, and then put your amulet in your desk until I tell more of the story.

DAYS 5 AND 6

This session of "The Egypt Story" lasts for two class periods. Doris tells as much as she can in one day and then tells the rest the next day.

When we last left Maria and Regi they were following Nila to his classroom. When they reach his classroom they discover a frog race in progress. Children are poking and yelling at three large frogs in an attempt to urge them to jump from the center of a circle across its circumference. The teacher enters the class before the race is over but just watches until one frog wins the race. Then he slams his scepter on the mud floor and yells, "To your places! And get rid of those frogs!" Maria is amazed to see three children pick up the frogs and stuff them in their loincloths. She certainly would not like to have a frog wiggling around in her underpants.

The teacher continues, "Today we calculate the area of rectangles by doing multiplication. Scribes must be able to find the area of farmers' fields because taxes are based on the size of farms. If you calculate incorrectly and say a farmer's fields are larger than they actually are, at the end of the growing season the farmer will have to give Pharaoh more of his harvest for taxes than he should. If you calculate incorrectly and say a farmer's fields are smaller than they really are, then you will cheat Pharaoh out of his fair share of the farmer's crop when taxes are paid. You must accurately calculate area to be fair to both Pharaoh and farmers. And you will be doing lots of area calculations because each year you must recalculate the area of all fields. In the winter when the Nile River rises, all field markers are washed away. In the spring, when the Nile recedes, fields must be resurveyed and remeasured, and you will have to recalculate their area to determine how much of a farmer's crop must be given to Pharaoh in taxes."

"We start today's lesson by finding the area of a rectangular plot of land that is 6 cubits long and 9 cubits wide. Remember that a cubit is the length of the forearm from the elbow to the outstretched tip of the middle finger. Our standard cubit is the distance from Pharaoh's elbow to the tip of his middle finger."

The teacher then goes over to a box of sand on the classroom floor and scrapes its surface flat. He says that you find the area of a rectangular plot of land that is 6 cubits long and 9 cubits wide by multiplying "six times nine." Then he asks a child to come to the sandbox and do the problem. This, using our numerals, is what Regi and Maria see the child write and hear the child say:

Exhibit 7.8

This Is What Was Written		This Is What Was Said
1	9	1, 2, 4; I will use 2 + 4 to make 6.
\ 2	\ 18	6 times 9....so....9, 18, 36.
\ 4	\ 36	I used 2 + 4 to get 6, so I use 18 + 36
Totals 6	54	and get 18 + 36 = 54

Doris writes these calculations on her chalkboard as she says aloud the adjacent statements. She does this in such a way that students can clearly see and hear what she is doing but without telling them what she is doing or why she is doing it.

First she writes the numbers in the left column, saying each as she writes it. Each is double the number above it, until the line is reached. As Doris doubles the numbers, she adds aloud until she gets a sum of doubles that equals the first number of the multiplication problem (the *multiplier*)—in this case 6. When she finds a set of numbers that equals the multiplier, she puts a mark to the left of each number and then writes their sum (the multiplier) below the line.

Next Doris writes 9 in the right column adjacent to the 1. This is the *multiplicand,* or the second number in the problem. She then doubles that number and writes the result next to the 2, and doubles that number and writes the result next to the 4. She now points to the mark next to the 2 and makes a corresponding mark next to the 18. She then points to the mark next to the 4 and makes a corresponding mark next to the 36.

She now points to 2, 4, and 6 and says, "2 + 4 = 6." Next she points to 18 and 36 and says, "18 + 36 = 54" and writes 54 below the line under 36.

> When finished, the student proudly announces, "To find the area of a rec-
> tangular plot of land that is 6 cubits long and 9 cubits wide, I multiply the
> length of one side by the length of the other side. 6 times 9 is 54! The area
> is 54 square cubits!"
>
> The teacher exclaims, "Excellent! Your answer honors your parents."
>
> Regi whispers to Maria, "They don't seem to be multiplying, just doubling
> and adding!"

Doris tells her students to get into groups of two and spend 2 minutes discussing how they think ancient Egyptian multiplication works—or what is occurring when ancient Egyptians multiply. After 2 minutes Doris continues the story.

> The teacher scrapes the sandbox flat again and gives Nila this problem:
> "Find the area of a rectangular royal raft that would carry Pharaoh on the
> Nile River. The raft is 9 cubits long by 8 cubits wide."
>
> This, using our numerals, is what Regi and Maria see Nila write in the
> sandbox and hear him say. [*Doris does the problem as before.*]

Exhibit 7.9

This Is What Was Written		*This Is What Was Said*
\ 1	\ 8	1, 2, 4, 8; I will use 1 + 8 to make 9.
2	16	9 times 8....so....8, 16, 32, 64.
4	32	I used 1 + 8 to get 9, so I use 8 + 64
\ 8	\ 64	and get 8 + 64 = 72
Totals 9	72	

> When he finishes, Nila proudly says, "To find the area of a rectangular
> raft that is 9 cubits long and 8 cubits wide, I multiply its length by its width.
> 9 times 8 is 72! The area is 72 square cubits!"
>
> The teacher responds, "Excellent Nila! You honor your grandfather with
> your answer."
>
> Regi whispers to Maria, "I think I get it! Do you see what is going on?"

Doris tells her students to spend 2 more minutes in their groups discussing how they think ancient Egyptian multiplication works. She then continues the story.

"Quiet!" yells the teacher [and Doris].

A second later a student is lying on the ground with another student on top of him. The bottom student yells, "Tuauf, wait until I get you after school. Stop leaning on me when you fall asleep! You weigh a ton, you lazy hulk!"

The teacher slams his scepter against the wall with a loud bang and then snarls the following scolding. [Doris projects "Tuauf's Scolding" on a large screen using an overhead projector as she reads it.]

Tuauf's Scolding

Tuauf, Tuauf, pay attention.
You are in the House of Life.
You are in a school for scribes.

No fooling around in class. No falling asleep. No doodling. No hunching. Stay awake and pay attention to your teacher.

You have been chosen to be a scribe. Even as a beginner you will be honored and consulted by others for your knowledge. The profession of scribe has no equal on Earth. Because of his knowledge a scribe will never be short of food, a scribe will never lack riches, a scribe will always be honored and have the respect of others.

Would you rather be a coppersmith who has to work in front of his blazing furnace? His fingers are like crocodile legs, and he stinks more than rotten fish.

Would you rather be a water carrier who slowly shrinks under the weight of his water buckets as he delivers water at other's commands? He is stung to death by gnats and mosquitoes and chokes from the stench of the canals.

Would you rather be a potter? He works under the soil as if he already belongs among the dead. He grubs in the mud more than a pig to fire his pots.

Would you rather be a weaver, who must give his overseer his dinner in order to leave his looms that have only white cotton on them so that he can see daylight and the many beautiful colors of the world? His thighs are drawn up to his body so he can hardly breathe. The day he fails to do his work he is dragged from the weaving hut like a lotus from a pool and cast aside.

Or would you rather be a reed cutter who works naked among the reeds all day? His fingers stink like the fishmongers, his eyes are dull and lifeless, and his skin bakes like bread in an oven as he works from morning to night.

You are in the House of Life.
You are in a school for scribes.

Love learning and books as you love your mother and life, and behold their beauties.[3]

"Wow!" whispered Maria. "Sounds sort of like my teacher when she gets upset. I wonder if all teachers think that sort of thing when they get upset with kids."

After catching his breath, the teacher scrapes the sandbox flat again and gives Tuauf this problem: "Find the area of a small rectangular plot of land in which melons are grown. The plot is 13 palms long and 14 palms wide. Remember, a palm is the width of a hand. Our standard palm is the width of Pharaoh's palm. There are 7 palms in a cubit."

This, using our numerals, is what Regi and Maria see Tuauf write and say. [*Doris does the problem as before.*]

Exhibit 7.10

This Is What Was Written		*This Is What Was Said*
\ 1	\ 14	1, 2, 4, 8; I will use $1 + 4 + 8$ to make 13.
2	28	13 times 14....so....14, 28, 56, 112.
\ 4	\ 56	I use $1 + 4 + 8$ to get 13, so I use $14 + 56 + 112$
\ 8	\ 112	and get $14 + 56 + 112 = 182$
Totals 13	182	

"One hundred eighty-two!" announces Tuauf.

"Don't just say a number!" says the teacher. "Put the answer in the context of the problem."

"The area of a rectangular melon plot that is 13 palms long and 14 palms wide is 13 times 14! 13 times 14 equals 182. So, the area is 182 square palms."

"Excellent," smiled the teacher. "Your great grandfather in the underworld would be proud of you."

Regi whispers to Maria, "I've figured it out. Just wait till he calls on me. Since I know my multiplication tables, I don't have to use the sandbox."

Doris again tells her students to spend 2 minutes in their groups discussing how they think ancient Egyptian multiplication works. After about 2 minutes Doris continues the story, giving another child this problem: "Find the area of a small rectangular plot of marshland in which frogs are raised. The plot is 21 palms long and 12 palms wide." Following the problem, Doris again has her students spend 2 minutes discussing Egyptian multiplication before continuing the story.

The teacher scrapes the sandbox flat again, walks over to Regi, and says, "You sure like to talk a lot. Let's see you do this problem in the sandbox: Find the area of a square flower pot that is 6 fingers long and 7 fingers wide.

As anyone in Egypt will tell you, a finger is the width of a finger. Our standard finger is the width of Pharaoh's finger. There are four fingers in a palm."

Regi immediately says, "I have no need of a sandbox. The answer is . . ."

Regi forgot that he could neither speak nor write ancient Egyptian mathematics. So you, class, have to help him. Decide who will be the writer and speaker in your group. Figure out how the ancient Egyptians did multiplication. Then do the problem 6 times 7 as an ancient Egyptian would, but using our number system. Record your calculations and be prepared to discuss them. Raise your hands when your group finishes. When everyone finishes, we will discuss your answers and send them to Regi.

Doris circulates among her students as they work, providing help as needed. She examines answers as students hold their hands up. If answers are correct, she suggests that the group try to figure out *why* ancient Egyptian multiplication works. When everyone finishes the problem, Doris holds a class discussion in which speakers describe their answers and *try to explain how and why* ancient Egyptian multiplication works, while writers display their calculations. Some groups work the problem as 6 times 7 and others work it as 7 times 6. Both are accepted and examined to see differences. This is what the written work looks like:

Exhibit 7.11

	1	7			\ 1	\ 6
	\ 2	\ 14	or		\ 2	\ 12
	\ 4	\ 28			\ 4	\ 24
Totals	6	42		Totals	7	42

When the discussion is complete, Doris has the class send their work to Regi using the clap-rap-clap transmission method and then continues the story.

As soon as we transmit, Regi yells out in Egyptian, "The area of a square flower pot that is 6 fingers long and 7 fingers wide is 42 square fingers!" He then walks over to the sandbox and quickly records how to do the problem.

The teacher exclaims, "That's amazing! How did you get the correct answer so quickly and even before you did the written work? Excellent! But you must talk out loud while you write in the sandbox!"

"Why must I talk aloud while writing?" asks Regi.

"So that I can hear that you are thinking correctly," says the teacher. "If you don't talk aloud, I will not be sure that you are thinking in the correct way. And there is only one correct way to do multiplication."

The teacher scrapes the sandbox flat and continues, "Regi, here is another problem: Find the area of a rectangular piece of papyrus that is 14 fingers long and 15 fingers wide. Remember there are 4 fingers in 1 palm. Start your work."

As before, Doris has her class help Regi do the problem by working in small groups. When everyone finishes the problem, Doris holds a class discussion in which speakers describe their answers and *try to explain why* ancient Egyptian multiplication works. During the class discussion, Doris's students begin to be able to verbalize their understanding of the ancient Egyptian multiplication algorithm. They explain that numbers in the left column are multiples of two, that the sum of these checked off multiples is the total at the bottom left, and that this is the multiplier. They explain that the number at the top of the right column is the multiplicand, that each number in the right column is equal to the corresponding number in the same row to the left times the multiplicand, that by summing the checked off numbers in the right column you obtain as a total in the right column the sum of the result of multiplying each of the corresponding numbers in the left column by the multiplicand, and that the number in the bottom row of the right column is the product that results from multiplying the multiplier by the multiplicand. When the discussion is complete, Doris helps her students transmit their answers back through time to Regi using the clap-rap-clap method, and then Doris continues the story.

> As soon as we transmit, Regi yells out in Egyptian, "The area of a rectangular piece of papyrus that is 14 fingers long and 15 fingers wide is 210 square fingers!" He then walks over to the sandbox and quickly records how to do the problem while saying the calculations out loud.
>
> "Amazing! You again are first to answer the problem and then show how to solve it," says the teacher. "I wonder if Maria can do the same." He scrapes the sandbox flat and says, "Maria, what is the area of the rectangular floor of a house that is 25 cubits long and 12 cubits wide?"

Doris repeats the process described above. After the discussion and the transmission of student work to Maria, Doris continues the story.

> As soon as we transmit, Maria yells out in Egyptian, "The area of the rectangular floor that is 25 cubits long and 12 cubits wide is 300 square cubits." She then skips over to the sandbox and quickly records how to do the problem while saying the calculations out loud.
>
> "Amazing! How did you work so fast?" exclaims the teacher as he scrapes the sandbox flat. "I wonder what you would do with a really tough problem like finding the area of a rectangular field of barley that is 51 cubits wide by 15 cubits long."
>
> "Oh come on!" responds Maria. "If you want to give me something difficult, try something like a barley field that is 125 cubits long by 15 cubits wide."
>
> The Egyptian children in that class 3,500 years ago gasp. Problems like that are reserved for the most advanced class in scribe school.
>
> The scribe says, "If you are willing to try a problem like that, let's see what you can do. If you get it correct, I will let class out early."
>
> All of the children in the class yell, "Go, go, go, Maria!"

Doris again repeats the process described above. The discussion is similar to the previous one except that students' descriptions of how and why the algorithm works are increasingly sophisticated. After the discussion, Doris's students transmit their work to Maria, and Doris continues the story.

> As soon as we transmit, Maria yells out in Egyptian, "The area of a rectangular barley field that is 125 cubits long by 15 cubits wide is 1875 square cubits." She then does a cartwheel over to the sandbox and quickly records how to do the problem.
>
> "Unbelievable!" exclaims the teacher. "Class is dismissed early. Go play with our visitors and see what you can learn from them."
>
> The Egyptian children cheer and lead Maria and Regi out of the classroom. Regi notices that Maria's amulet has a new light that is jade green.
>
> When they reach the courtyard the class heads for the pond, splashes water on their faces to cool off, and drinks from cupped hands. It is getting really hot. Maria and Regi, of course, do not drink the water, but they do enjoy splashing water on themselves.

Doris now has Nila and one of his friends teach Maria and Regi how to play The Palm Tree Game, the game board of which is similar to ones found in ancient Egyptian tombs. The game gives Doris's students practice using ancient Egyptian multiplication. The CD accompanying this book has instructions and a reproducible copy of the game board. After students play The Palm Tree Game for about 15 minutes, Doris ends the story for the day by saying the following.

> Before we end class, I want you to take your amulet off, get a jade green crayon out of your crayon box, color one of its circles green, and then put your amulet in your desk until I tell more of the story.

DAY 7

As her sixth graders enter her classroom, Doris has her students put their amulets on.

> After playing The Palm Tree Game, Nila's classmates led Maria and Regi to a large playing field behind the school and asked them what game they would like to play next. Maria asked what their choices were.
>
> Nila answered, "We have archery, where we use a bow and arrows to shoot at a target. We have throwing sticks, which we try to hit a target with. We have footraces that are great fun. We have stick fighting with sticks about the length of our arms, but most of our moms will not let us play that since Tuauf got three teeth knocked out stick fighting. We sometimes have great fun playing leapfrog where we jump over each other's backs. We love to play bowling with a ball and pins, but I don't think we have any pins here at school. We play tug of war, where two captains hold hands and draw a line between them. Then the rest of us form teams that pull on the captains and try to get one of them to move across the line. We also love to wrestle. Do you like any of these games?"[4]

Doris now tells how Maria and Regi play a wrestling game with the Egyptian children. (See the accompanying CD.) After the game Maria and Regi go to An-Nab's office. On the way a new light starts blinking on Maria's amulet.

When they reached his office, An-Nab asked, "You seem to be marvelous multipliers. How do you find answers so quickly?"

Regi answered, "Our teachers make us memorize lots of multiplication facts. Then we don't have to do very many calculations."

An-Nab responded, "You memorize everything? That must take years. And what a waste of heart power!"

"What do you mean 'heart power'?" Maria questioned. "What does the heart have to do with memorizing things?"

"Maria," Regi said, "I remember reading that ancient Egyptians thought that the heart is where people did all of their thinking and reasoning and memorizing. They thought it was the brain."

An-Nab queried, "I wonder what is best—your system of doing multiplication that requires lots of memorizing or our system that requires calculation?"

Regi replied, "I read about Egyptian multiplication. People all over the world used it for thousands of years. It was only about a thousand years before I was born that other ways of doing multiplication were invented. You know, I read that in England they did not even teach children multiplication until after 1650. Until then only college graduates learned multiplication. An-Nab, that was 350 years ago in our time.[5] From what I have read, our way of doing multiplication is pretty new, and after seeing your method, I am not sure that our method is worth the effort it takes to learn it."

Maria interrupted Regi and asked, "How do you know all about this?"

"I read a lot, Maria, compared to others who spend their time wrestling."

Just then, a scribe ran into An-Nab's office and said that a messenger from Pharaoh had arrived outside of the school and that he should come quickly. Before he left, An-Nab told Maria and Regi, "While I am gone I want you to think about whether your way or my way of doing multiplication is best. When I return, I want you to tell me the advantages and disadvantages of each way. I also want you to decide if I should or shouldn't learn your way of doing multiplication, and why you think so." And with that he was gone.

"Drat!" said Maria. "I hate not being able to speak Egyptian mathematics. How are we going to give An-Nab an answer?"

Regi responded, "Well, someone is helping us, so I guess we just have to wait for them to put the words in our mouths. They have been doing a good job so far. I hope they consider whether or not they think our way of doing multiplication is good enough to change history by telling An-Nab about it. And whether they want generations of kids to have to memorize multiplication tables like we had to."

Class, this is where you again enter the story. To help Maria and Regi, you are going to have to compare the ancient Egyptian multiplication method with our method. You are going to have to decide what the relative strengths and weaknesses of each are. In addition, you are going to have to make a recommendation about whether or not we should change history and teach An-Nab our way of doing multiplication.

Doris puts her students into groups of four, has them choose writers and speakers, and has them begin discussing. After the small-group discussions have lasted long enough, Doris holds a whole-class discussion during which speakers report group findings. Doris puts their comparisons in a chart.

As each comparison is recorded and discussed, Doris asks her students to relate it to the question, "Should Maria and Regi teach An-Nab our way of doing multiplication?" The purpose of this question is to have children determine if our way of doing multiplication in our highly technological society (in which abstract thought and concern with efficiency is the norm) would really be better for the ancient Egyptians than their way of doing multiplication (that is more consistent with their holistic agricultural society in which most problems worked are of a very practical nature). These are some of the comparisons that Doris's classes have suggested over the last 4 years.

Exhibit 7.12   Comparisons of Modern-Day and Ancient Egyptian Multiplication Methods

Attributes of Our Multiplication	Attributes of Egyptian Multiplication
A lot of energy and time is spent memorizing many multiplication facts.	You don't have to memorize hardly anything.
It requires a place value number system with a zero. Our number system contains these. The Egyptian number system does not.	It does not require a place value number system or the use of a zero. Can be used with almost any number system.
You are less likely to understand multiplication because of the complexity of what is occurring. You can lose sight of the multiplier and multiplicand as whole numbers when you multiply each of their digits by the other number's digits as separate items.	You are more likely to understand multiplication because of the simple way it is treated as repeated addition.
We do not have to talk out loud while multiplying.	They have to speak aloud while multiplying.
It is harder to learn because the operation is more complex and because of all the memorizing of facts.	It is easier to learn because it is less complex and very little has to be memorized.
It is more efficient in terms of the number of different multiplications, additions, and recordings required.	It is less efficient in terms of the number of things you have to do—add, double, and record to get an answer.
It takes less space and pencil lead to do a problem.	It takes more space and sand scribbles to do a problem.

After the whole class discussion, Doris has her students discuss and then vote on whether or not Maria and Regi should teach An-Nab our way of doing multiplication. They vote not to teach him our way of doing multiplication.

When the discussion and voting are complete, Doris has her students send their thoughts back to Maria and Regi using the clap-rap-clap method of transmission.

> Just as we send our answers back through time, An-Nab returns to his office and tells Maria and Regi that the magician Bu Bop will visit the school later in the day to announce Pharaoh's latest military victory. Then he asks Maria and Regi for answers to his questions.
>
> As if by magic, Maria and Regi communicate our ideas to An-Nab.
>
> An-Nab thinks about what they said for several minutes until suddenly a young girl about 13 years old bursts into An-Nab's office and says, "Dad, it's time to go home for lunch and a short nap." An-Nab introduces Maria and Regi to Isi, his daughter. He tells them that she is one of the few women in the school and that she will soon graduate and get married. He tells Isi to take Maria and Regi home with her for lunch and that he will join them soon. Isi immediately leads Maria and Regi out of the school and toward home.
>
> On the way out of school, Maria tells Regi to look at her amulet. It has a new amethyst purple light shining on it.
>
> This is where we end the story for today. Before we end, class, take your amulet off, get a purple crayon out of your crayon box, color one of the circles purple, and then put your amulet in your desk until I tell more of the story.

DAY 8

Three things occur during Day 8. First, Maria and Regi accompany Isi to An-Nab's house for lunch. During this segment of the story, Doris's class learns about the architectural structure of An-Nab's house, how and why ancient Egyptians washed their hands before eating, how they ate, and the types of foods they ate. Second, a mathematics problem is presented. Third, Maria and Regi accompany Isi back to school. On the way they visit a public bathhouse, have their skin oiled, and discuss hair and hair lice. Only the second part of the story is presented here. The rest is on the accompanying CD.

> After lunch, Isi told Maria and Regi that it was nap time. Maria asked, "Do you really take a nap after lunch?"
>
> Isi replied, "You don't have to nap. I have some math homework to do before returning to class, and you can help me. We frequently take naps in the afternoon because we get up early at sunrise and don't go to bed until late at sunset and because it is usually too hot in the afternoon to do much work."
>
> Isi led Maria and Regi to a quiet part of the courtyard, and the children sat on the ground in the shade of a date tree. She told them they were going to be learning how to find the area of a circle that afternoon and that her teacher had given her this problem to solve before class: A sheep farmer keeps his sheep in a circular corral. If the diameter of the corral is 9 rods, what is its area?

Isi said her class has not yet learned how to find the area of circles. But her teacher wants them to see how close they can come to finding the area of the circular corral with a diameter of 9 rods before he shows them how to calculate the area of circles.

Maria asked, "I know what a finger, palm, and cubit are. What is a rod?"

Isi answered, "A rod is a hundred cubits long. It is the unit of measure we use most often when finding the area of large fields." Isi then picked up a twig and drew a circle on the ground and said, "Since you are going to be joining me in class this afternoon, you should try to solve the problem also, for you can be sure my teacher will ask you for your estimate." And with that Isi started drawing all sorts of lines and numbers around her circle.

Class, we must prepare Maria and Regi for the afternoon class they will visit. Get into your groups of two students and decide who will be writer and speaker. Then discuss what you know about circles and how you might find the area of a circle with a diameter of 9 rods. I am giving you each a piece of graph paper with a circle drawn on it. Assume that the distance between the lines is one rod, and that the circle has a diameter of 9 rods. After discussing one or more methods for finding the area of a circle, decide on a method, and use it to estimate the area of the circle. Pretend that you are in the same predicament as Isi and that you have never been taught how to find the area of a circle. Pretend that you have no tools to use in calculating area other than paper and pencil—or sand to draw in and a stick to draw with. Do not use a calculator or the formula $A = \pi r^2$. Now get to work.

Doris helps students to get into groups of two, decide on writer and speaker, and gives them about 10 minutes to solve the problem. She then begins a whole-class discussion of the different ways they invented to solve the problem. The focus is on different methods for finding the area of a circle and being able to describe the method to others, not just getting an answer. Before the discussion is complete, Doris stops the discussion by putting her hands over her ears and yelling, "Stop! Stop! Stop!" She then continues the story.

Stop! Stop! Everyone quiet! I am getting an emergency transmission from π^3. It says that it cannot transmit information to ancient Egypt for the next 11 hours because of irregular sun spot activity that might change information. It says it wants you to go home and rethink your methods of finding the area of the circle and recalculate your answers. It says we are to transmit our answers tomorrow.

We will continue our discussion tomorrow. Here is another piece of graph paper with the circle drawn on it. For homework try to invent the best method of finding the area of the circle you can, and try to do your best to determine the area of a circle that has a diameter of 9 rods. Record both your method and the area on the back of the graph paper. And remember, imagine you have the same tools and knowledge as the ancient Egyptians. Do not use formulas or calculators.

Meanwhile, back in ancient Egypt, a giggling Isi awakens Maria and Regi from naps. She says, "So you wanted to know why we take naps. Well, the

Exhibit 7.13   First Circle Area Calculation Worksheet

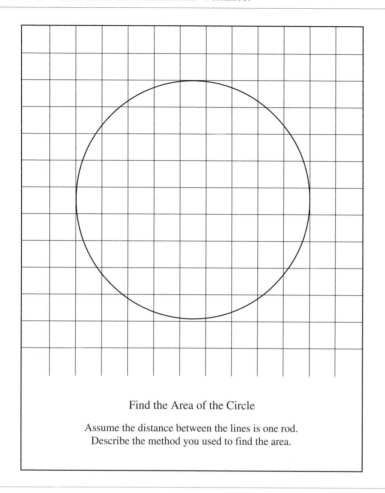

Find the Area of the Circle

Assume the distance between the lines is one rod.
Describe the method you used to find the area.

two of you have been sleeping soundly for quite a while. It is now time to have a bath and hurry back to school, or else we will be late." And with that Maria and Regi get up and follow Isi to the communal bathhouse.

Doris concludes this session of the story by telling about Maria, Regi, and Isi's visit to the public bathhouse.

DAY 9

Doris begins Day 9 with a whole-class discussion about homework—finding the area of a circle 9 rods in diameter. Students describe their solution strategies, and Doris writes their answers on her blackboard in an ordered list. Answers range from 42 to 83 square rods. Doris has her class decide which answer to send to Maria and Regi, and they decide on 65 square rods (the mean of the numbers on the blackboard). Doris has her students write 65 square rods on a sheet of paper and prepares them to transmit it to Maria and Regi. Then she continues the story.

When they reach school, Maria and Regi follow Isi to her classroom. Each student in the room has a small sandbox and a writing stick.

When Isi's teacher enters the room, he welcomes Maria and Regi and says, "Now, future scribes of Egypt, what is the area of a circular corral with a diameter of 9 rods?"

Answers range from 37 square rods to 85 square rods. The teacher is interested in Maria and Regi's answers.

Maria says, "Honored teacher, the area of a circle 9 rods in diameter is . . ."

Doris now has her class transmit their answer to Maria using the clap-rap-clap method.

As soon as Maria receives our message, she says it in ancient Egyptian. Regi says he agrees with Maria's answer.

"Now listen carefully, future scribes of Egypt, for I am now going to show you how to calculate the area of a circle," continues the teacher. "I am going to show you how to find the area of a circular piece of land designed for the wrestling game that some children were playing earlier today. The diameter of most wrestling circles is 36 palms. Do the following to find the area of a circle with a diameter of 36 palms:" And this is what the teacher writes as he speaks:[6] [*Doris writes these calculations on her chalkboard as she speaks.*]

"First, state the diameter of the circle."
He writes the number 36 in a sandbox.   36
"Then find one ninth (1/9) of the diameter. It is 4."
He writes the number 4 in the sandbox.   4
"Now, take away from the diameter one ninth (1/9) of the diameter. The remainder of 36 - 4 is 32."
He writes the number 32 in the sandbox.   32
"Finally, multiply the result by itself. That is, find 32 × 32."
He writes the equation 32 × 32 in the sandbox.   32 × 32
"Then do the multiplication like this:"

Exhibit 7.14

	1		32
	2		64
	4		128
	8		256
	16		512
	\ 32		\ 1024
Totals	32		1024

"This equals 1024, and therefore the circle contains 1024 square palms of land."

"That is how you do it. To find the area of a circle, find the diameter, find one ninth of the diameter, subtract from the diameter one ninth of it, and then multiply the result by itself."

"Now do as I have done. Here is your first problem. Find the area of a circular pond 18 cubits in diameter."

His students take up their sandboxes and writing sticks, smooth out the sand, and go to work. Maria and Regi watch Isi. This is what she writes and says [and what Doris says and writes on her blackboard]:

18	that's the diameter
2	that's one ninth (1/9) of the diameter
16	that's the diameter less one ninth of the diameter
256	that's the difference times itself
256 square cubits	that's the area of the circle.

Exhibit 7.15

	1	16
	2	32
	4	64
	8	128
	\ 16	\ 256
Totals	16	1024

The teacher comes and examines Isi's work and says, "Excellent. But why aren't Maria and Regi also doing the problem?" He goes and gets two sandboxes and writing sticks for them and tells them to try the next problem. He then examines everyone else's answers and continues his lesson.

"Now, class, find the area of a circular tabletop that is 27 fingers in diameter."

To help Maria and Regi, Doris has her students get into groups of two, select a writer and speaker, and solve the problem. When they are done and Doris has examined everyone's work, she has one group's writer hold up his answer while its speaker explains what was done. Doris then has her class transmit their answer to Maria and Regi using the clap-rap-clap method and continues the story.

As soon as Maria and Regi receive our message, they say the answer and write it in their sandboxes in ancient Egyptian. The teacher examines Maria's, Regi's, and everyone else's work as they finish.

The teacher then announces, "Here is a harder problem: Find the area of a flat circular plate that is 4½ fingers in diameter."

Doris again has her students solve this problem and transmit the answer to Maria and Regi.

As soon as Maria and Regi receive our message, they say the answer and write it in their sandboxes. The teacher examines their work while everyone else in his class keeps working. He says, "I do not understand how you got the answer so quickly."

Regi replies that the problem is so easy that he can do it in his head.

The teacher stares at Regi. He then examines everyone else's work as they finish.

The teacher then says, "Class, Regi thinks that the area problems we are doing are easy. So I am going to give him a hard problem, and we are going to see just how good a mathematician he is."

Regi asks, "Honored teacher, where I come from we use a different method than you use to find area. Can I use my method?" Maria's mouth falls open when Regi says this.

The teacher responds, "Use any method you desire."

Regi takes off his backpack, finds his calculator, and says, "I'm ready."

The teacher says, "Find the area of a circular grain silo that is 45 hands in diameter."

Regi pushes these buttons on his calculator: $\pi \times 22.5 \times 22.5$. Amazingly the number 1590 shows up on the calculator display screen in ancient Egyptian numerals. Regi is surprised. He just shows the calculator display to the teacher since he cannot talk Egyptian mathematics.

The teacher is jubilant and declares, "Your answer is incorrect!"

"That is because I use a different area method than you," answers Regi.

The teacher replies, "Now figure out the area of a circular grain silo that is 45 hands in diameter using my method."

As before, Doris has her class calculate the area of a circular grain silo that is 45 hands in diameter using the ancient Egyptian method and transmit the answer to Regi using the clap-rap-clap method.

As soon as Regi receives our message, he says the answer and writes it in his sandbox.

The teacher responds, "Well, you have now correctly—and very quickly—found the area of the circle. The black box says the area is 1590 square hands, while your sandbox says the area is 1600 square hands. How do you explain the difference?"

Regi looks at his calculator and knows that he is in trouble. Maria tries to hide behind Isi, for she knows Regi should never have taken out his calculator.

Regi replies, "Where I come from, we use a different method for finding the area of a circle. I guess our methods give different answers."

The teacher says, "Well I have heard that the Babylonians, Indians, and Chinese have different methods of calculating area than we do. Can you describe how and why your method works?"

Regi asks, "Can you describe why your method works?"

The teacher responds, "I certainly can. In fact, that is the next part of our lesson. Why don't I prove why our method works, and then you can explain why your method works."

Regi groans.

Just as the teacher is about to begin his proof, a child bursts into the classroom and yells, "Bu-Bop is here! He is going to do magic! Come quickly!" Everyone rushes from the classroom into the courtyard where all the other children in the school are gathering.

Bu-Bop is a slender man about 5 feet tall. He wears a white loincloth and has jewelry around his neck and arms. His hair has little tight braids all around the bottom and curls all over the top.

Children sit all around Bu-Bop. Bu-Bop has come to announce Pharaoh's military victory and help people celebrate by doing mathematical magic. Maria elbows Regi and says that she wishes that Bu-Bop would do something like float on air rather than mathematical magic. Regi elbows Maria back and points at her amulet. It contains a new pink gem.

Bu-Bop tells everyone to clear a small flat area of sand in front of them so that they can write some numbers. He also tells them to do their magic individually.

Regi gets a sheet of paper and a pencil out of his backpack because he wants to keep a record of the magic.

Doris tells her students to get out paper and pencil and follow along with what is happening. They are to do the magic also. They are to use our modern numerals rather than ancient Egyptian numbers.

Bu-Bop says, "Everyone write down a number of your own choosing with hundreds, tens, and ones—in which the number of hundreds is one more than the number of tens and in which the number of tens is one more than the number of ones. An example of this type of number is 5 hundreds, 4 tens, 3 ones—or 543. Make sure that I cannot see what you are writing." Everyone hurriedly writes down a number. Maria chooses 543. Regi chooses 432. No one chooses 210, for the Egyptian children do not use zero.

Bu-Bop continues, "Now reverse the number of hundreds, tens, and ones and write the new number below the first. For example, if your number is 5 hundreds, 4 tens, 3 ones—or 543—you will now write 3 hundreds, 4 tens, 5 ones—or 345." Everyone does this. Maria writes 345 in the sand. Regi writes 234 on his paper. [Doris's students do the same with their numbers.]

Bu-Bop now says, "Now subtract the bottom number from the top number. Then cover up your work, concentrate on your answer, and raise your hand. I will come around and tell you your answer. As soon as I have told you the answer, erase your work if I am correct." Everyone does this, and Bu-Bop walks from child to child, pretending to read their minds and whispering their answers in their ears.

Doris also walks around her class and whispers into her students' ears the number 198 as they raise their hands after completing their calculations.

The Egyptian children are greatly impressed and clap loudly.

Before Maria can erase her work, Regi insists upon looking at it. The answer to her problem is 198, which is the same as his answer. He says, "I bet everyone had the same answer." Isi says, "Hush up! This is really amazing! He could read everyone's mind. Listen to what he is going to do next."

Bu-Bop jumps up and down and twirls around several times. He yells, "No one can do magic like me!"

Everyone yells back, "Bu-Bop is the greatest! Bu-Bop is the greatest!"

Bu-Bop now tells everyone that he has come to announce Pharaoh's great military victory. He tells how Pharaoh's troops left Egypt on a dangerous mission to pacify some wild tribes to the south, how great battles were fought, how 1,000 of the enemy were slaughtered, how 20,000 captives were taken who will be Pharaoh's slaves, and how 66,666 cows and 237,000 goats were captured that will feed Pharaoh's people.[7]

When Bu-Bop finishes telling about Pharaoh's conquests, he twirls around several times and yells, "Let's do some more magic!"

Doris now tells her students a second mathematical magic trick of the type found in ancient Egyptian writings.[8] Both magic tricks are described on the accompanying CD.

As Bu-Bop finishes the second magic trick, a trumpet sounds outside of the school. Bu-Bop says that he must now leave and that they must now return to class. He pulls off his hair, waves it in the air, and is off, with children clapping as he leaves.

On the way back to class, Maria pokes Regi and points to her amulet—it has another gem glowing red on it like a bright red ruby.

As Isi leads Maria and Regi back to class, she says she wishes that she could do a mathematical magic trick. Regi tells Isi that he took notes on how to do Bu-Bop's magic tricks and that if she studies his notes, he is sure she can figure out how to do his tricks. He gives her his notes, and she is delighted.

Last night π^3 gave me copies of Regi's notes to give to you. Try out the tricks from Regi's notes on each other and on your friends and parents tonight for homework. See if you can figure out how they work. [As she says this, Doris distributes copies of the magic tricks to her class.]

Doris ends the story as before, by having her student remove their amulets, color in one of its circles pink and another red, and put their amulets in their desks.

DAY 10

Doris begins by asking her students to discuss Bu-Bop's magic tricks. She then continues "The Egypt Story."

> When the children in Isi's class return to their classroom after Bu Bop's departure, the teacher says that he is now going to show them a proof of his method for finding the area of a circle. This is what he says and draws in his sandbox.

Doris gives each student in her class a sheet of paper with six drawings on it. She turns on her overhead projector and projects a large copy of the first drawing above her blackboard. As she proceeds with the proof, Doris projects each of the six drawings at the appropriate time.

Exhibit 7.16   Egyptian Area Proof Diagrams

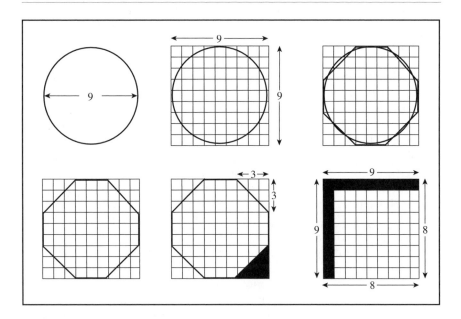

> The teacher says, "My proof is going to use a circle with a diameter of 9 fingers. First, I draw a circle in my sand box with a diameter of 9 fingers and label the diameter with the number 9. Any questions?" [*Doris points to the overhead drawing and asks her students, "Any questions?" No one has questions so she continues.*]
>
> "Second, I draw a square with a side of 9 fingers that fits exactly on top of the circle. I draw in lines at each one-finger interval, and I label the sides with the number 9. Any questions?" [*Doris points to the overhead drawing and asks, "Any questions?"*]

"Third, I draw an octagon with sides of 3 fingers that fits exactly in the square and almost exactly on top of the circle." [*Doris again points to the overhead drawing.*]

"Fourth, now notice that the area of the circle is almost exactly the same as the area of the octagon. The small pieces of area outside of the circle but inside of the octagon are almost exactly the same size as the small pieces of area outside of the octagon but inside of the circle. [*Doris points to the overhead drawing.*]

"This means that the area of the circle is the same as the area of the octagon. So if we find the area of the octagon, then we will know the area of the circle."

Maria can tell that Regi is about to say something and motions to him to keep quiet. Regi keeps quiet. Do you know what Regi saw that made him want to say something?

Doris looks inquisitively at her class. Several students raise their hands. Doris asks one what she thinks, and she says, "But how do you know the area is the same?" Doris responds, "Good thinking!" and continues the story.

The teacher continues, "To find the area of the octagon, next redraw it inside of the square without the circle and draw lines in the square at each one-finger interval." [*Doris points to the overhead drawing.*]

"Now look at the areas of the octagon and the square. The difference in their area is the area of the four small triangles in the corners of the square that are outside of the octagon. Each of these corners is 3 fingers long and 3 fingers high." [*Doris points to the overhead drawing.*]

"Now we are almost done. We next need to find the area of the four small corners. If we put 2 of the triangles together they will form a square with a side of 3 fingers. The 4 triangles make 2 of these squares. The area of each of these squares will be 3 times 3, or 9 square fingers."

"Now I will complete my proof. Next draw a square with 9 fingers on each side and draw in lines at each one-finger interval. [*Doris points to the overhead drawing.*] Now, along the left side of the large square, color in 9 little squares. This is the same as the area of two of the corner triangles that were outside of the octagon but inside of the large 9-finger square. Next color in 9 of the little squares along the top of the large square. This is the same as the area of the other two triangles. Look at my diagram and see what I have done."

Maria can tell that Regi is about to yell. She pokes him, gives him an angry look, and motions to him to keep quiet. Regi keeps quiet. Do you know what Regi saw that made him want to yell?

Doris looks inquisitively at her class. Several students raise their hands. Doris asks one what he thinks, and he says, "Isn't one square in the corner getting counted twice?" Doris responds, "Excellent thinking!" and continues the story.

The teacher continues, "Now class, the part of the large square that has sides of 9 fingers that is not shaded in has the same area as the octagon. Since the octagon had the same area as the circle, the part of the large 9-finger square that is not shaded in has the same area as a circle with a diameter of 9 fingers."

Maria reaches over and jabs Regi to keep him quiet. Do you know why Regi might want to say something?

Doris looks inquisitively at her class, waits a minute, and then continues the story without taking answers.

The teacher continues with pride, "And what is the area of the small unshaded square? It is 8 (or 9 subtract 1) times 8 (which is also 9 subtract 1). Since 1 is one ninth of 9, the area of the small unshaded square is the length of the square less 1/9 itself times itself (or 8 times 8, which equals 64). And this is also the area of the circle."

"Now let us relate this directly to what we know about finding the area of a circle with a diameter of 9 fingers:

First, find the diameter . . . that's 9 fingers.
Next, find one ninth the diameter . . . that's 1 finger.
Next, subtract one ninth the diameter from the diameter . . . that's 8 fingers.
Now multiply the difference by itself . . . that's $8 \times 8 = 64$ square fingers."

"I have shown why our method of finding the area of a circle works," says the teacher triumphantly. "Are there any questions?"

Regi's hand shoots up in the air. Maria reaches her foot out and knocks Regi over, and then gives him a karate kick that makes him yelp with pain. Maria then leans over Regi and says in a loud voice for everyone to hear, "Oh, poor boy, did you hurt yourself?" Then she whispers, "You got us in enough trouble with your calculator. Keep quiet!"

When Regi is again sitting up, the teacher asks, "Do you have a question, Regi?"

Regi casts a glance at Maria. Then he cautiously says, "Honorable teacher, your proof is brilliant. I have a question that might explain why my answer for the area of a circle is different from yours."

The teacher asks, "Well, what is your question?"

Regi says, "Honorable teacher, I am curious to know about . . ."

And this is where words fail Regi, for he cannot speak ancient Egyptian mathematics. And this is where you, class, must help Regi. Get into four-person groups. Decide on a writer and three speakers. Discuss what might bother Regi about the teacher's proof. The writer is to record several sentences, and the speakers are to prepare to describe your thoughts to our class. When you finish, hold up your paper with your comments.

When small groups finish their discussions, Doris holds a whole-class discussion. Three issues are raised:

- How do we know that the areas of the circle and octagon are the same? They might just look the same but not really be exactly the same.
- What about the little square that was counted twice in the upper left corner of the last diagram? Should not the area of the octagon be 63 square fingers and not 64 square fingers?
- Can a proof simply be a demonstration of what happens with one particular circle, or must it be generalizable to all circles? (This relates to the concrete and particularized way that ancient Egyptian mathematical thought took place, in comparison to the way that more abstract and generalizable thought takes place today. In ancient Egypt, proofs tended to reference specific situations. To demonstrate something with respect to a finite number of specific situations was sufficient for most proofs. Today, to prove something like the area of a rectangle, we use variables and formulas such as $A = h \times w$ to say that the area of *any* rectangle equals its height times its width. Key here is our current ability to use abstract generalizable algebraic symbols that represent *any* quantity, as compared to Egyptian practice of using a single fixed specific quantity such as 9 cubits.)

After her class discussion, Doris has each small group write what it wants Regi to say on a sheet of paper and transmit it to him using the clap-rap-clap method. Then she continues the story.

As soon as we send the message, Regi finishes his sentence.

The teacher stares at Regi, closes his eyes, and thinks for a long time. He then says, "You are very clever, Regi. Will you please now explain to us your method of finding a circle's area with your black box?" Regi is speechless. His mind goes blank.

Just then, a child appears at the classroom door and announces that An-Nab wants Regi and Maria to report to his office immediately.

The teacher says, "Regi, you are dismissed to go to An-Nab's office. But later I will expect an explanation of how your black box finds the area of a circle."

While on the way to An-Nab's office, Maria says to Regi, "How are you going to explain how to find a circle's area with a calculator?"

Regi answers, "I don't know. But look at the amulet around your neck. That last gem is glowing orange. Maybe that means we are done with areas of circles. I hope so."

When Maria and Regi arrive in An-Nab's office, he is waiting for them with a pile of papyrus in front of him. He asks them to sit down and says, "A little while ago I passed your classroom when you used a small black box to calculate the area of a circle. For the last 10 years I have been interested in circles and have studied how to find their areas. I stop all learned visitors to our village and ask them how they find the area of a circle. I have visited the great libraries of Pharaoh to study what his scribes know. I have discovered how the Greeks, Judeans, Babylonians, Indians, and Chinese find the area of a circle. The visitors from the future whom I saved years ago showed me a method I had never seen. I have here in front of me on papyrus descriptions of some of the different ways used. I have never seen a black box like yours, however. Will you please show me how it works?"

Regi turns scarlet. Maria says, "Oh, I am sure Regi will show you how his black box works. We call it a calculator because it does calculations for us."

Regi takes off his calculator's cover, wondering how he will explain it to An-Nab. To his surprise, all of the numbers on it are written in ancient Egyptian. He hands the calculator to An-Nab and says he can have it. He then shows An-Nab how to use it to find the area of circles.

An-Nab is amazed by the calculator and thanks Maria and Regi for their gift. He wants to use it right away. But before he does, he gives Maria and Regi a problem. He shows them five sets of papyrus that are on his table and says, "Here are my favorite ways of finding the area of circles. They come from all over the world: Babylonia, Greece, India, China, and this one is from our friends in the future. While I am studying your calculator, I want you to examine these ways of finding the area of a circle, compare them to each other and to the way you were taught, and tell me which way you think is best." An-Nab then goes out into the courtyard, sits down next to the pool, and starts working with Regi's calculator.

Regi and Maria start to study the papyrus. Maria tries to say something to Regi about one of the methods in ancient Egyptian, but only grunts come out of her mouth. She says, "I hope that whoever is helping us has copies of these. We sure need their help."

Doris explains that π^3 sent her copies of An-Nab's methods for finding the area of a circle last night. She has students get into groups of four and select writers and speakers. She gives each group instruction sheets that guide them through two methods of calculating area, along with whatever materials are needed to use those methods. She tells them to do the following:

1. Figure out how each method works.

2. Use each method to find the area of the circle in the instructions.

3. Prepare to describe to the class each method and what you discover from using it.

4. Compare the advantages and disadvantages of each method.

5. Decide which of your two methods you like the best and which you would recommend to An-Nab.

Doris gives each group sufficient materials so that each student in the group can do all of the necessary calculations. She tells them to work together but to independently do their calculations so that they can compare, check, and, if necessary, average their calculations. She tells them that when they are done, they will have a whole-class discussion.

Students begin work that class period and finish during the next class period. A few notes on each method are listed below. Worksheets that guide students in using each method are on the accompanying CD. *Squaring the Circle* (Hobson, 1913) and *A History of π* (Beckmann, 1974) both discuss ancient approaches to finding the area of a circle.

Inscribe/circumscribe method. This is an early method used by the Greeks, Babylonians, Persians, Indians, and Chinese as early as 3,500 years ago. Most ancient cultures used only inscribed polygons. The method used here lets students average the values from both inscribed and circumscribed polygons as they observe the idea of a limit being approached as the shape and area of polygons with increasing numbers of sides approach the shape and area of a circle.

Dissect and reassemble into parallelogram method. This is an early method used by Babylonians and Persians. Children use scissors and glue to cut up a circle and reassemble it into a parallelogram. They make measurements of the parallelogram using a radius ruler and use those measurements to derive a formula for the area of a circle.

Radial squares method. Finding a square with an area equal to that of a circle is a problem that ancient Greeks attempted. Children use scissors and glue to cut up a circle and reassemble it into a square when they use this method.

Circumscribed square excess method. This is a variation of the radial squares method, in which the area outside a circle but inside a circumscribed square is subtracted from the area of the circumscribed square.

Displaced objects method. Children use small objects, such as dried beans or cheerios, to cover a circle one layer high. After the circle is covered, the small objects are displaced onto a rectangle with a width equal to the radius of the circle, and its height is then found using a radius ruler. The area of the rectangle, and thus the circle, is found by using the formula for the area of a rectangle. No ancient documents describe this method, and that is why in this story An-Nab claims that it was given to him by π^3.

When small groups complete their tasks, Doris holds a whole-class discussion during which each group describes its two methods and tells the advantages and disadvantages of each. Then the class discusses and votes on which method they like best.

The last time Doris's students did this, they decided that the Dissect and Reassemble Into Parallelogram Method would be the most accurate. Several of Doris's students were upset with this method, however, because the curvy line on the top and bottom of the parallelogram they constructed was not straight. They were concerned that the formula for the area of a parallelogram would not work. The idea of a limit, and how it might function in a mathematical problem, seemed inaccessible to them. Doris's students liked the Displaced Objects Method best but were concerned about its accuracy. Several students were bothered by the spaces between the dried beans that they used. They thought that the area could not possibly be correct because of all the small spaces that were unaccounted for, even though the same spaces existed in the square as existed in the circle and even though this method gave a close approximation to π. Several students had difficulty generalizing their findings and seeing the power of the algebraic expressions that they were supposed to discover during this activity. For example, one student wrote of the Displaced Objects Method that, "This method was one of the most accurate, but how would you use it to measure the area of a large circle like a field?"

Exhibit 7.17   Sample Worksheets for the Displaced Objects Method

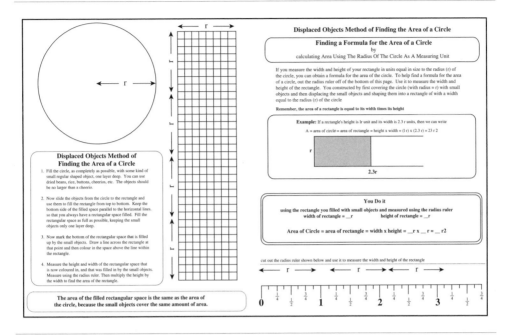

When the discussion is over, Doris has her class vote on which method Maria and Regi should recommend to An-Nab as the best. Each student writes a short note about their conclusions so they can transmit their thoughts to Maria and Regi, and then Doris continues the story.

> After a while An-Nab returns to his office beaming with delight. He loves the calculator. He asks Maria and Regi, "Which method of finding the area of a circle do you think is best?"

Doris now has her class transmit their recommendations to Maria and Regi using the clap-rap-clap method.

> As soon as Maria and Regi receive our recommendations they tell them to An-Nab in ancient Egyptian. He listens attentively, reflects for a while, and then responds that he will have to think about what they said.
>
> Suddenly there is a great commotion outside of An-Nab's office as children pour out of their classrooms. Isi bursts into her father's office and yells, "Maria, Regi, school is over for today! Let's go home."
>
> While following Isi home, Maria nudges Regi and points to her amulet. It has a new purple gem glowing brightly in it.

Doris ends the story by having her students remove their amulets, color in one of its circles orange and another purple, and then put their amulets in their desks.

DAY 11

This session of the story often takes 2 days to complete, for Doris's students take great care with their artistic creations.

When her students are settled in their seats with amulets around their necks, Doris continues the story.

> When we last left Maria and Regi, they were following Isi home to An-Nab's house. When they reach An-Nab's house, Isi's sister Jeanna greets them and offers them some bread and dates for a snack. While eating, Jeanna admires Maria's red and white checked shirt.
>
> Maria says that almost all of her shirts have many colors.
>
> Isi exclaims, "You're lucky! All we have is white clothes. Boys wear white linen loincloths and girls wear baggy white linen dresses. But we women can dream of beautiful patterns. Jeanna makes paddle dolls that she sells in the market. She dreams up all sorts of beautiful patterns for the dresses that she paints on the dolls. Sometimes I help her, and we have loads of fun."
>
> "What are paddle dolls?" Maria asks.
>
> "Let me show you!" says Jeanna as she leads the children to a small mud building that she calls her factory. In it are about twenty colorful painted dolls with hair made of strings of clay beads. Here are three examples of paddle dolls that have come out of ancient Egyptian tombs. [*Doris holds up a drawing of three paddle dolls and then thumbtacks it to her bulletin board.*]

Exhibit 7.18   Egyptian Paddle Dolls, Dating to About 2000 BCE

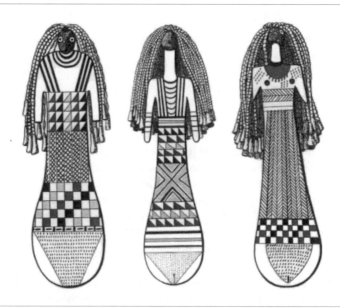

In Jeanna's paddle doll factory there are also containers of red, blue, green, black, and white paint; a pile of paint brushes; a large bin of clay beads to make hair; and several stacks of wood paddles to make dolls. Some of the paddles have bead hair on their heads, faces drawn on them, and patterns of squares outlined on their bodies. There is also a large sandbox of the type used in the scribe school for writing.

Jeanna tells Maria and Regi how the dolls are made. First, you buy the paddle bodies from a carpenter. Then you string clay beads to make hair and attach the hair, draw the faces, and outline grids on the paddle bodies. You then use the grids as guides to help you invent and paint clothing patterns on the dolls. Jeanna points to a doll and says, "Notice how this doll's body is covered with a square grid. I always draw a grid on a doll's body before I start to color in clothes. I fit my patterns in the grids sometimes by coloring whole squares and sometimes by drawing lines from one corner to the other and coloring in half squares. From looking at the squares and half squares, I have discovered all sorts of puzzles. Let me show you one."

Jeanna walks over to the sandbox, smoothes out the sand in it with her hand, and then draws a single square in it and says, "This is one square." [*As she speaks, Doris draws this on her blackboard.*]

Exhibit 7.19

Jeanna then smoothes out the sand again and draws a 2-by-2 grid like this, and asks, "How many squares are there here?" [*Doris draws this on her blackboard.*]

Exhibit 7.20

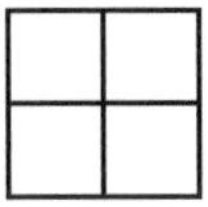

Now, class, you must help Maria and Regi figure out how many squares there are, for they cannot speak ancient Egyptian mathematics.

Doris puts her students into groups of two students. She then has them decide on writers and speakers, draw the grid on a sheet of paper, count the number of squares, write the number on the paper, have a short class discussion, and then send their answer back to Maria and Regi using the clap-rap-clap method of transmission.

As soon as we send the message, Maria and Regi yell out "5!"

Doris now repeats this same scenario three more times with the following grids, transmitting answers back to Maria and Regi after the numbers of squares in each grid are counted.

Exhibit 7.21

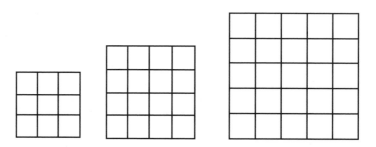

When students work on the 4-by-4 grid and the 5-by-5 grid, Doris has them first discuss and then send back to Maria and Regi a description of a number pattern that relates the number of squares in a grid to the size of the grid, as well as to the total number of squares. (Finding number patterns like this is an activity students have engaged in before in Doris's class.) During whole-class discussions students describe different number patterns they discover.

Several groups of students notice this pattern: in a 4-by-4 grid there is 1 square of size 4-by-4, 4 squares of size 3-by-3, 9 squares of size 2-by-2, and 16 squares of size 1-by-1. The total number of squares is thus $1^2 + 2^2 + 3^2 + 4^2 = 30$. Doris asks her students if they think the pattern holds up with other-sized grids. They confirm that it works with a 1-by-1 grid that contains 1^2 squares, a 2-by-2 grid that has $1^2 + 2^2$ squares, and a 3-by-3 grid that has $1^2 + 2^2 + 3^2$ squares. They make the hypothesis that an n-by-n grid contains $1^2 + 2^2 + 3^2 + 4^2 + \ldots + (n-1)^2 + n^2$ squares.

Other students put numbers in a table and notice a different pattern. This is the table they create that compares the number of squares on each side of a grid to the total number of squares in the grid, for grids up to 5-by-5.

Exhibit 7.22

size of grid	number of squares
1	1
2	5
3	14
4	30
5	55

They notice that the difference between 1 and 5 is 4, which equals $2 \times 2 = 2^2$, that the difference between 5 and 14 is 9, which equals $3 \times 3 = 3^2$, that the difference between 14 and 30 is 16, which equals $4 \times 4 = 4^2$, and that the difference between 30 and 55 is 25, which equals $5 \times 5 = 5^2$. Doris's students say they believe that this pattern will continue with larger grids, and it relates to the previously described pattern.

When discussion of the 5-by-5 grid is complete, Doris has her students send their answers and thoughts about numerical patterns back to Maria and Regi using the clap-rap-clap method of transmission.

As soon as we send the message, Maria and Regi yell out "55!" and then describe your observations about the number patterns.

Jeanna is impressed with their number pattern observations. [*See the accompanying CD for a second problem Doris gives her students before continuing.*]

Isi has had enough of square patterns and says, "I think that Maria and Regi get the idea of the type of puzzle that we have invented. Now let's see how they do at designing paddle dolls. Let's give them some of our paddle doll design puzzles and see what they come up with."

Jeanna says, "OK. Here is one of our clothing design puzzles. It has two parts. Here is a paddle doll that is complete, except for coloring the clothing patterns. Notice that there are two different grids on the pattern doll's body, one for a blouse and one for a skirt. Follow these instructions to create the clothing designs."

Exhibit 7.23

For the Blouse

Color in the squares using two different colors in such a way that no two squares of the same color touch on a side but so that every square touches four other squares of the same color at its corners.

For the Skirt

Draw diagonals through the squares to make many triangles, as in the following diagram. Diagonals should make up-and-down zigzag lines. Color in the triangles using two different colors to make lots of bands of zigzags across the skirt (that look like mountains and valleys going up and down).

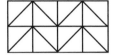

Now, class, you must help Maria and Regi. In groups of two students, you are going to have to figure out how to make the designs, and then you are going to have to color them in on the copies of the paddle dolls I am going to give you. First, I am going to give you some graph paper. Use it and colored pencils to figure out how to create the designs. When you have created the designs, raise your hand and I will give you a paddle doll to color. When you are done, we will share our designs and then send them back to Maria and Regi.

Doris's students go to work. As each group finishes their blouse and skirt designs on the graph paper, Doris gives them two paddle dolls to color in. When all groups complete their paddle dolls, Doris has them share them with the class, and then they send them back to Maria and Regi using the clap-rap-clap method. Sample paddle doll templates are shown in the accompanying exhibit. (Templates ready for children's use are on the accompanying CD.)

Exhibit 7.24   Sample Paddle Doll Templates

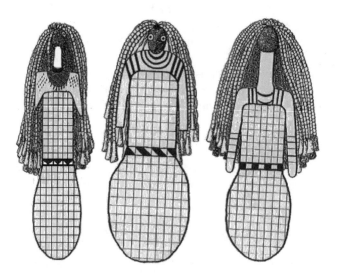

As soon as Maria and Regi get our message, they each take a paddle doll and work quickly to create the designs we sent them.
   "Super!" say Isi and Jeanna.

Doris then gives her class a second problem before continuing. (See the accompanying CD-Rom.)

Jeanna now says, "Let's have them create any clothing design that they want to, and let's see what they create. They might create something new."
   "OK," says Isi, "but first show them some of our designs, so they know some possibilities." Jeanna shows Maria and Regi some clay shards with designs on them. Then Jeanna gives them each a paddle doll so they can each invent their own clothing design.

Maria and Regi need your help. I am going to give you some ancient Egyptian designs to examine and some graph paper. Examine the designs to see the way ancient Egyptians thought. Then use the graph paper and your colored pencils or crayons to create your own designs. When you have created blouse and skirt designs that you like, raise your hand, and I will give you a paddle doll to color in. When you are done, we will share our designs and then send them to Maria and Regi.

Doris distributes to each group graph paper and designs from ancient Egyptian tomb paintings and pottery that she got out of a book (Wilson, 1986), has them examine the patterns, has them create their own patterns, and then has them copy their patterns onto paddle dolls. Students then share their completed pattern dolls and transmit their ideas back to Maria and Regi using the clap-rap-clap method.

Exhibit 7.25   Samples of Ancient Egyptian Designs

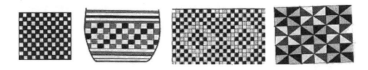

As soon as Maria and Regi get our message, they each take a paddle doll and work quickly to create the designs we sent them. They both finish their dolls at the same time. Regi looks at Maria and nudges her. He points to her amulet. It has a new pink gem in it.

While Isi and Jeanna admire their designs, Maria's amulet begins to behave strangely. First the whole amulet glows bright yellow. Then its stones start to flash on and off with bright bursts of light, each in its own color. A low-pitched humming sound starts to come from the amulet as the colored light grows in size until it engulfs Maria and Regi. Maria yells, "No, I want to stay longer! Goodbye Isi! Goodbye Jeanna! Say goodbye to An-Nab!"

And that was it. The next thing Maria and Regi knew they were in An-Nab's tomb in the museum, with the tomb door closed. They yelled and banged on the door. The museum custodians and I answered them.

All we knew was that the tomb door suddenly closed, and that it was closed for about an hour with no noise coming from inside. For an hour, no matter what we did, we could not get a single stone in the tomb to move. But right after we heard Maria and Regi yell, we pushed on the door and it easily slid open. Something strange had clearly happened.

I could not believe what Maria and Regi said about their adventure. That is, I couldn't believe what they said until several days ago when π^3 visited me and told me what we had to do to save them. We have done it and the story is now complete.

All that remains for you to do is to get a pink crayon out of your crayon box, take your amulets off of your necks, and color in the last circle pink.

ENDNOTES

1. Traditionally, Egyptian numbers are written somewhat differently from the way they are presented here. The difference is that if there are more than two ones (or tens, hundreds, etc.) that exist in a number, they are presented half size and stacked in two rows, one above the other, as in some of the problems on Regi's notes.

2. Traditional views of the ancient Egyptian number system indicate that it had no symbol for zero. Recent research, however, seems to refute this. (Lumpkin, 1997, pp. 101-117).

3. This is a free translation of two British Museum documents: "Satire of the Trades" (Olivastro, 1993, pp. 32-33) and "Teachings" (Stead, 1986, p. 21).

4. The games described here are discussed in greater detail in *Sports and Games of Ancient Egypt* (Decker, 1992).

5. This is discussed in *Mathematics in the Time of the Pharaohs* (Gillings, 1972, pp.16-18).

6. This discussion of the area of a circle comes from the *Rhind Mathematical Papyrus,* problems 41, 42, 43, 48, and 50. (Chace, Bull, Manning, & Archibald, 1927).

7. These numbers are actually one sixth of the numbers that exist on a memorial tablet of Pharaoh Narmer.

8. "Think of a number" magic tricks such as these existed in ancient Egypt. Two examples can be found in the *Rhind Mathematical Papyrus,* problems 28 and 29. Most ancient Egyptian tricks had problems involving multiplication and division by 3 and 9. More magic number tricks can be found in *Mega-Fun Math Puzzles* (Schiro & Cotti, 1998).

Chapter 8

An Interview With Doris Lawson About "The Egypt Story"

This interview with Doris P. Lawson took place on June 28, 2003. It is about practical aspects of her experiences while teaching "The Egypt Story" to her sixth graders five times between 1998 and 2003. It has been edited for such things as "umms," digressions, and juice breaks.

MS: *Doris, you brought two milk crates full of materials with you. What's in them?*

DL: *They're all the materials I need for "The Egypt Story." One box contains my teaching materials. Each day has a separate folder, and in the folder is all of the stuff I need to tell the story for that day. The other box has posters that go on the bulletin board, booklets for children to read, hieroglyphic stamps for the children to use, and such.*

MS: *Tell me about the things in the second box.*

DL: *I have two sets of hieroglyphic ink stamps that children use to write their name and An-Nab's name in the tomb. I have a disk with a hieroglyphic font that I bought for my computer, but I don't let my children use it until after they have written their names in hieroglyphics. I have this hieroglyphic phonics/alphabet chart to help children figure out how to write their own names in hieroglyphics. I also have a little poster that the children made of An-Nab's name because it's An-Nab's tomb, although they make their own. This is just a sample. This is an Egyptian punch out mummy tomb. This is real papyrus, genuine papyrus paper. I have a couple of books. This one is called* Growing Up in Ancient Egypt *by Rosalie David. It has extra information for the children. This is a magazine called* The Egyptian News: The Greatest Newspaper in Civilization. *It has articles about things going on in ancient Egypt. I have a card game called* Mummy Rummy, *an additional game they play that is not in the story. The children in my class love to play games, and there are a lot of games in "The Egypt Story." Here is a sarcophagus and mummy with a book about them that tells how to mummify a body. I have a pen that looks like a mummy, some Egypt stickers, and several more books on mummies.*

MS: *And what is that around your neck?*

DL: *This is an amulet from the story. I enlarged it to about 5 inches in diameter. I print it on card stock, and the children cut it out. I go around punching a hole in one of the circles, and I give them some string so they can tie it around their necks. I let them color in the amulet, except the circles. We color in the circles during the story.*

MS: *You use a lot of things like the amulet with your class. What do they feel about things like the amulet?*

DL: *They love it! I thought at first that the boys might say this is baby stuff and they wouldn't go for it, but every year they do. They have absolutely no problem. Sometimes the string breaks, and I have to go scrounging around for more string. But I have plenty of string in my classroom. I learned my lesson there.*

MS: *What do they feel about other things, like the messages they send back in time?*

DL: *They love to do that. I tell the children, "On the count of three clap your hands three times, knock on the desk three times, clap your hands three times." In fact, it's not just knock on the desk; they have to knock on the information to be sent back. And this year, for the first time—it's never happened before—we haven't been synchronized. I don't know what it is, but if somebody claps an extra time or they're slow, I'll say, "It didn't work. Have to do it again." We've done it as often as maybe three times until finally, the kids get annoyed with each other because they want to get on with the story, so, you know, they say, "Come on, let's get with it." I will not continue with the story if we're not all synchronized. And they don't have a problem with that. In fact, they love it. Usually it gets to be very loud. I mean you have thirty children knocking on their desks just as loudly as they can. They think that's wonderful, and then we continue on with the story.*

MS: *What do your children think of all the fantasy, all the impossible things in the story like time travel and sending things back to the past? Do they believe it's real, or do they just enjoy it as a story?*

DL: *I don't know. No one ever in all the years that I've told "The Egypt Story" has ever said that they don't believe. I've never had a problem that way. As with many good stories the children begin to identify with Maria and Regi. In fact, my sixth graders think of the Egyptian children in the scribe school as real people. My children know from their social studies chapter on ancient Egypt what a scribe is and a little bit about what life in ancient Egypt was like. Many of the things they have already learned about ancient Egypt are paralleled in "The Egypt Story." When my sixth graders talk about the kids in the scribe school, it is not a fantasy to them because in their minds those kids actually existed.*

MS: *You integrate together social studies and math. Why do you do that?*

DL: *I am a firm believer in integrating subjects. I don't believe that in real life you do 20 minutes of math and 20 minutes of reading. In my class there is reading and math, there's writing in math, there's math in social studies. It's too bad that we have to have separate subjects. It's too bad we can't teach it all together. I am a total believer that our brains aren't compartmentalized the way school subjects are.*

MS: *Let's go back to the boxes of materials you brought with you. Tell me more about the teaching materials.*

DL: *All right, in my box of teaching materials I have what I will say on each day of the story in a separate folder. With each day's story I have the things that go with that particular day. I have to mention that I very rarely finish one day of the story in a day. I usually leave about an hour per session, sometimes a little more, sometimes a little less. Look, these are Regi's notes on ancient Egyptian numbers. I found some paper that had an Egyptian theme border—I found it in one of those teacher stores—and I copied the ancient Egyptian numbers from your original story onto the paper, and I laminated them. See, I have fifteen of them in the folder for Day 2 and these are very old. They've held up very well. I pass these out when Regi and Maria are trying to figure out how Egyptian numbers work. Then I pass them out several more times because my students need this information to help them figure out some of the games and the tomb contents problem.*

MS: *So you have a folder for each day with things in each folder such as the template for your amulet and the handout on Egyptian numbers?*

DL: *Right, and here in the Day 2 folder, I have The Snake Game. And here I have bags with problems in them.*

MS: *And you save the bags from year to year so you can reuse them?*

DL: *Right, and they're all folded up neatly in the folder, and The Snake Game has also been laminated. My students are fascinated with the information at the bottom of the game where it says that variations of this game board were found in ancient Egyptian tombs and it gives the dates. And here is a worksheet that I made up for students to fill in to help them figure out how the ancient Egyptian number system works, which is from the story. I pass out this worksheet, and I tell the children I'm not going to correct it. It's not for a grade. It's so they can understand how the number system works, so they can send the information back to Maria and Regi. And you know, sometimes you think the kids will only work for a grade and if you tell them that you're not going to grade it they will not take it seriously. Well they take this very seriously because when I say, we need this information so we can send it back to Maria and Regi, I know they don't really believe it, but they act like they do. You know what I'm saying. It's like they really get into it. They want to send the information back to Maria and Regi.*

MS: *You use cooperative groups rather than having children work alone. Why?*

DL: Oh, I always do. I always have cooperative groups. The children do everything in
cooperative groups except take tests and write journal entries. I think they can learn so
much more from each other if they help each other. Two (or more) heads are better than
one. When you do anything with somebody else, it is just much easier, much more pleasant. Sometimes you can't think of something and your partner(s) can. My students pretty
much talk about everything they do and share ideas with each other.

MS: How much time do you spend preparing each session of the story? Is that amount of
time different from when you first told the story? Did you have to spend hours and hours
in the beginning getting prepared?

DL: Hours and hours? No way. It was kind of easy just to take the story and break it up day
by day. And I read the story over a couple of times. Then I said, OK, I need The Snake
Game, so I made copies of The Snake Game and I laminated them. Now there's virtually no preparation time except possibly making copies of something. Right now, the
preparation time is virtually none except to make sure that I have the copies because
everything is in the folders ready to go.

MS: And when you started?

DL: When I started, it didn't take long to prepare. However long it took to make
fifteen copies of The Snake Game, laminate it, collect the game pieces, copy the problems, cut them up, put them in a paper bag, and fold up the paper bag. However long
that takes. I'd say maybe a half hour to an hour per day.

MS: You've taught "The Egypt Story" many times by now. What have you changed about
how you tell the story? Can you think back to the first time you taught the story and how
was it different from maybe the second or the third or the fourth time you taught it?

DL: The first time I told the story, I read the story word for word. Then I changed the word-
ing of the story. That was probably the second year. Now I skim it as I am telling it. I
do not read it word for word, and I'll put in my own words, like I'm reading the story
but as I'm going I'm ad-libbing the story. The story is in my hand and I'm ad-libbing.
I read some parts, like Tuauf's Scolding. But even then I may digress, look at the
children, and say something like, "Remember last summer when it was really, really hot
and your mother had you out weeding the garden and there was no pool to jump into
afterwards? Well, it was like that all the time for the kids in ancient Egypt who did not
get to go to the scribe school." You can see them nodding their heads. They understand.
I explain to my sixth graders that the children in ancient Egypt that were allowed to go
to school to become scribes knew they didn't have to do things like weed gardens, so it
was something the children felt privileged about. It was a privilege rather than a right
to be able to go to school. I will digress because I feel it's important for the children to
understand that part of the story.

MS: And in the beginning?

DL: *I never did that in the beginning. Now I'm much more comfortable with putting me into the story, and my own philosophy, and my own thoughts, and my own feelings, and my own emotions. So I put in myself in lots of places.*

MS: *What is the effect of putting your emotions and your fantasy and you into the story as compared to teaching from a mathematics textbook?*

DL: *Well, it certainly isn't a math textbook! It kind of makes the story mine even though you wrote it. But I think the fact that I put myself into it, it makes the story ours. I think that because I'm engaged, it engages the class. It's not like I'm reading a story, which kind of puts the story, literally, between the teller and the audience. I think that telling the story personalizes it and helps the children engage with the story a lot more.*

MS: *What has been the effect upon you to be able to personalize your instruction in that way?*

DL: *Well, it's put me into the story, and I'm much more comfortable with it. In the beginning I felt as though in order to be true to the story or to get the correct information, I had to follow the story the way you wrote it.*

MS: *How has putting yourself into the story changed you as a teacher?*

DL: *It would be nice if everything could be taught in a story format, and I make every effort to do that, even when I teach algebra. I do know the strength of helping children understand something through a story, whether it's an epic tale or whether it's just a one-day story. If I know, for example, children are having trouble comparing fractions, I make up a short little story about Gus and Erika, my own children, and how they had to solve a similar problem. I know that has more of an impact than if I just review how to do a problem with them. I think if you put anything in the context of a story, it's like rays of sunshine. You wouldn't see those rays if there wasn't dust in the air. The light has to bounce off the dust in the air for you to see the rays of sunshine. A story is like the dust. It allows kids to latch on to something with which they can associate abstract math ideas.*

MS: *Has telling math stories made teaching more enjoyable for you?*

DL: *Oh yes! Absolutely! Because when I say I'm going to tell a story, the kids immediately pay attention. I don't have to ring my bell. I don't have to do anything to get kids' attention. In fact, in my pre-algebra class where I have some kids that do struggle and it's sometimes hard to hold their attention, if I say, "I'm going to tell you a story," the class leaders will say, "Shut up! She's telling us a story." They'll do that to each other and immediately I have their attention. Any chance I have to tell a story I take. It definitely has changed my method of teaching. And it's a lot of fun because you get the response from the kids. It's no fun teaching to a bunch of kids that just sit there like statues.*

MS: *So you make up and tell your own stories. Have you started doing this more often since you first told "The Wizard's Tale"?*

DL: *Yes, absolutely. A lot of times I'll bring my own kids into a story, or sometimes I'll use children from my class in stories. And I'll borrow stories from children's literature, history, and biographies of famous mathematicians.*

MS: *And the story comes from you rather than just reading the story.*

DL: *Right, that's right. I will make up the story.*

MS: *So you're much better at creating and telling stories now than before?*

DL: *Right. The one I'm the most comfortable with that I totally made up myself is about Erika and Tinkerbell's bakery and fraction multiplication. But it's a fifth grade story. So on one of my free periods, I will go into the fifth grade and I will tell that story and teach that lesson. I even tell the teacher not to introduce multiplication of fractions, but to let me know when she wants it done so I can come in and tell the story about Erika and Tinkerbell's bakery. And then, with the sixth, seventh, and eighth graders I'll say, "Do you remember that story about Erika and Tinkerbell's bakery?" Oh yes, they remember, and they remember fraction multiplication.*

MS: *Your school gives students achievement tests. Does oral storytelling influence children's scores on those achievement tests? Think back to before you started telling stories. Do you think there has been any gain on achievement test scores?*

DL: *I do. Yes. Absolutely. And I think the storytelling is part of it.*

MS: *Remember back 10 years ago. Do you think the scores, from your memory, were lower or higher?*

DL: *I think the scores were lower because math was scary, and if you make math seem more fun then the scores are going to be affected. When math is more fun, it becomes more attainable, more accessible, more doable. That makes the scores go up.*

MS: *Think back to before you started telling oral stories. Did anyone ever tell you you needed to work harder to get achievement test scores in math up?*

DL: *Oh absolutely, absolutely!*

MS: *Do they do that anymore?*

DL: *No! They haven't done that in a long time. In fact, usually they look at it in amazement because the scores are creeping up higher every year, depending of course on the class. Sometimes you have a class that really struggles, but for the most part, maybe one or two points, not a big significant amount, but they seem to be creeping up. I'm the* testing coordinator for the school, and I keep all of this information, and the principal comes to me every year and asks how we compare to last year. I have a place in my classroom where I have that information. The scores are creeping up slowly, and I know storytelling is a big part of it, but it also has to do with the fact that the children are seeing math as something not so scary, and oral storytelling is a big part of that. It makes math a lot more approachable and fun, and so children learn it better.

MS: *How do your students respond to "The Egypt Story"?*

DL: *Oh they love the story. In fact, Thursday, the day I told "The Egypt Story" last year, they would come into the classroom and someone would say, "It's Thursday. Are we doing 'The Egypt Story' today?" "Yup, if we get to it," I respond. Well, that motivates them. I have to teach the science and math lessons first. They'll sit quietly, they'll work in their groups, and they don't digress or start fooling around because they know that when they finish the science and math lessons, then I'm going to get out the box and the folder and we're going to do "The Egypt Story."*

MS: *Do you do anything with parents related to "The Egypt Story"?*

DL: *Yeah, a lot of times, after they built the tombs, I display them at one of the PTO meetings. The children use the hieroglyphics stamps and put their names on their tomb so the parents can find them. Parents seem to be very supportive of the story.*

MS: *"The Egypt Story" is an epic tale.*

DL: *Right.*

MS: *And you've said that you tell stories a lot, but they're not epic tales. What is the difference between an epic tale and a story that lasts only one day, in terms of the influence on your children?*

DL: *Well, the children love the epic tale, you know. I should have an epic tale going all year long. The first thing that comes to mind is the enthusiasm for "The Egypt Story." However, my children love any story. I think it's a matter of degree with "The Egypt Story" or "The Wizards Tale." They love to have epic tales continued from week to week. It's like in the old days when kids used to go to the movies and watch those serials in the movies or wait for the next episode of whatever exciting adventure tale. It's the anticipation that is exciting, which isn't there in a story that has closure in one telling. It's that whole anticipation thing, and anticipation is exciting.*

MS: *Do you and your students have favorite parts of "The Egypt Story"?*

DL: *I think the students' favorite activity is building the tomb. They love to build the tomb. That's my least favorite activity because it takes so long. I think they lose the train of the story because I cannot continue that story until the tomb is built, and it takes hours and hours to build the tomb. Another of their favorite parts is the clapping, knocking, clapping to send information back to Maria and Regi—they really seem to get into that even though they know it's not true. I know it sounds kind of silly, but the banging on the desks engages the children and they have a part in the story, and if it weren't for them the story couldn't continue. They also really enjoy playing the games. I like "Tuauf's Scolding," when I can tell them why school is like the House of Life. Both the children and I like making the paddle dolls. At first I thought the boys wouldn't like the paddle dolls, but even they thoroughly enjoy making the designs on the little squares.*

MS: *What are some of your favorite activities and problems?*

DL: *I personally like the multiplication. Many of the children do also because they immediately see the doubling. When I say that the Egyptian kids didn't have to learn their multiplication tables, oh wow! My sixth graders think that's pretty good. My kids do tell me that the Egyptian kids had to do the adding. I like that they play The Palm Tree Game that goes along with the multiplication. It gives the children practice in the new skill.*

MS: *How do students do when they have to do things like compare ancient multiplication and current-day multiplication?*

DL: *Well, they usually have a slow start, because they've never been asked to do that. They always understand the math, but to critique it is something that they are not used to. So I'll start out with a suggestion. For example, I might say, "You know those kids in ancient Egypt never had to learn multiplication tables. That is one difference." It's not like I'm giving them information, because Maria and Regi talk about that in the story, and so it's like priming the pump. Then they get going. They work in cooperative groups, and I have the groups set up so that there is a struggler in every group and a bright kid in every group. Somebody usually comes up with something else, and then they talk about it. When I notice they're beginning to get off task as I'm circulating around the room, I can tell that they're pretty much depleted and can't think of anything else, so then I'll say, "OK, group one, what did you come up with?" I ask each group what they thought of. This helps the other groups think of more comparisons. Then I tell the groups to keep working. After they finish, they write down everything so we can send it back to Maria and Regi. But talking about it in their groups, giving them an idea, letting them talk about it some more, having groups share ideas, then letting them discuss some more, usually gives them lots of ideas.*

MS: *So when you're working with the groups, you do a lot of circulating among groups and priming the pumps.*

DL: *Yes. Getting one group to share with the rest of the class in order to get the other groups moving a little bit further.*

MS: *Doris, thank you for participating in this interview.*

DL: *You're welcome.*

Chapter 9

PROBLEM SOLVING

Mathematical and Multicultural

"The Egypt Story" is a *multicultural, problem-solving* oral story. This chapter examines both its multicultural and problem-solving dimensions, with the major focus on problem solving. It proceeds by discussing the story's mathematical problems. In doing so it describes a model for understanding mathematical problem solving, as well as introducing multicultural issues that will be discussed later.

Teachers have given children mathematical problems to solve for centuries, but it is only since about 1950 that mathematics educators have explored how to teach problem solving as an independent topic separate from the content learned in the mathematics curriculum. And it is only since about 1980 that the teaching of problem solving has become popular. The National Council of Teachers of Mathematics (NCTM) dedicated the decade of the 1980s to problem solving (Krulik, 1980, p. xiv) and then made it the first of its new mathematics standards that it promoted during the 1990s (NCTM, 1989). Some mathematics educators have almost made the topic into an object of reverence, often equating it with the way mathematicians think (Schoenfeld, 1992, pp. 334-335) and sometimes valuing it more than the knowledge and algorithms discovered and accumulated by mathematicians over the centuries.

THE GENERATIONS PROBLEM (DAY 1)

The first problem in "The Egypt Story" is to calculate the number of generations from An-Nab (3,500 years ago) to Maria (today). Every year I ask Doris if she continues to use this problem, for it is a problem that I think could be dropped from the story. But Doris insists upon keeping it. She says her students love it and that after giving it, she hears them talking about cultural issues such as the age ancient Egyptians got married, when they had their first baby, how many children they had, whether they or their parents chose their spouse, and when they died—all in comparison to today. Doris says that this is part of what multicultural mathematics instruction is for her: seeing how mathematics can be used to gain insight into both another culture and your own culture.

Learning in the Context of Our Lived Lives

Multicultural oral storytelling floods students with cultural information by immersing them in an adventure in another culture. This occurs when Doris's students, through the eyes of Maria and Regi, confront comparative cultural data in the generations problem.

Not only do multicultural issues naturally arise out of the story, seemingly accidentally, but the mathematics that children learn also arises naturally out of a situation that appears not inherently mathematical in nature. The students must learn mathematics and accomplish mathematical feats to help a story's characters proceed through their adventures, not just to meet the demands of the teacher. Mathematical activity occurring in the context of a story is not just an exercise for building understanding and skills but an endeavor that allows Doris's students to understand and care for others by helping them negotiate their adventures as they project themselves into the lives of a story's characters and live their adventures with them.

Children need to experience using mathematics in the context of their lives—to find answers to mathematical questions that have their origins outside of strictly mathematical endeavors—because that is the way mathematics will be useful to them in most of their endeavors outside of school. Doris wants her students to learn to recognize, in their own lives, real-life problems they might be able to solve with mathematics, and she wants her students to acquire the initiative and confidence to try to solve them.

Open-Ended Problems

To solve the generations problem, Doris's students must make decisions about the numbers they will use within it. Most mathematics problems provide students with a single set of numbers to use in solving them and have a single correct answer. This is not the case in the generations problem. There is not a single set of correct numbers to use in the problem or a single correct answer. Sometimes the phrase *open-ended* is used to describe this type of problem, in which children have to decide what data to use in a problem that can be solved in a variety of ways or have several different answers. Students need to encounter this type of problem in school, for many problems they meet outside of school are this type.

Looking Back and Looking Forward

An important aspect of the generations problem is that Doris's students share their answers with each other and then, after considering everyone's solutions, make a joint decision about which answer is best to send back through time to An-Nab. Doris thinks that the process of recording how a problem was solved and then explaining the solution strategy to others helps her students better understand what they accomplished in solving the problem. It also helps them discover the nature and value of mathematical proof. This is called the *looking back* phase of problem solving. For Doris the process of looking back, seeing that there are sometimes different solutions to a problem, comparing different solutions to see the advantages and disadvantages of each, and making judgments about the adequacy of different solution strategies are all important problem-solving endeavors for her students to engage in.

An important part of the looking back process that is usually not highlighted in problem-solving models involves *looking forward* to examine how the information acquired during the solution of a problem and the solution strategies used while solving it might be used in one's life when one moves beyond that problem. After solving the generations problem, looking forward involves applying to one's life the information gained while solving the problem, raising questions about one's life as a result of the information acquired, and gaining insight into one's own life as a result of what was experienced while solving the problem. For Doris's students this involves such things as questioning marriage ages, arranged marriages, and life spans. It could also mean gaining insight into the future application of mathematics, such as when to round up or down (when dealing with something like half a generation). The looking forward aspect of problem solving requires raising the issue of how activity involved in a particular problem-solving endeavor might relate to a person's life beyond that endeavor. It involves issues of relevancy to and application to the learner's life; it involves raising the question, "What new insights into my life and what new power over my life can the process of solving the problem give me?"

Looking back should really be called the "looking back and forward" phase of problem solving. In this book, however, the more traditional label of "looking back" is used, even though the activity is given the broader meaning of looking back and forward.

Finding a Problem

One might wonder what happened to the problem of finding how many descendants An-Nab had up until the time that Maria was born. Doris does not have students solve this problem, although she says that occasionally students solve it on their own. Why might a teacher mention a problem to students, in passing, and then not have them solve it?

One reason is that part of our job as teachers is to help children learn to find problems in their lives that they want to solve and learn to take the initiative to solve the problems they discover. This is called *finding a problem* to solve. Finding problems to solve is an important phase of the problem-solving endeavor. It is what professional mathematicians, in fact, do all the time. While working on one problem, they frequently generate others that need to be solved. Children need to learn to do the same. They need to learn to identify mathematical problems in their world that might be worthy of solution; while solving one problem, they need to learn how to identify other interesting problems that might arise as a result of their endeavors to solve the initial problem.

THE PROBLEMS OF WRITING EGYPTIAN NUMBERS (DAY 2)

Two Approaches

Multicultural curriculum materials that present ancient Egyptian numerals to students usually do so by first showing a picture of each hieroglyphic numeral next to its modern equivalent, then asking students to translate hieroglyphic numerals into modern place value numerals, and finally asking students to translate current-day numerals into hieroglyphics (Lumpkin, 1997b; Krause, 2000). Here mathematics is viewed as consisting of information and procedures, and learning mathematics is viewed as mastering the information and procedures.

Doris goes beyond the traditional practice when presenting hieroglyphic numerals to her students. She introduces hieroglyphics by asking students to make sense of Regi's notes, notes that contain a series of hieroglyphics laid out in a pattern. By figuring out the mathematical pattern, Doris's students figure out how hieroglyphic numerals are constructed. Once they figure out how hieroglyphics work, they then play The Game of Snake to practice their knowledge of hieroglyphics. While playing the game, students translate between hieroglyphics and current-day numerals to check answers to problems.

Underlying these two approaches to teaching are two different conceptions of the nature of mathematics and mathematics learning. Schoenfeld (1992) describes them this way:

> At one end of the spectrum, mathematical knowledge is seen as a body of facts and procedures dealing with quantities, magnitudes, and forms, and the relationship among them; knowing mathematics is seen as having mastered these facts and procedures. At the other end of the spectrum, mathematics is conceptualized as the "science of patterns," an (almost) empirical discipline closely akin to the sciences in its emphasis on pattern-seeking on the basis of empirical evidence. (pp. 334-335)

When Doris's students examine Regi's notes to figure out how hieroglyphic numerals are constructed, they take a *pattern-seeking* approach to mathematics. Later, when they play The Game of Snake they take a *mastering-facts-and-procedures* approach to mathematics. All too often mathematics educators take an extreme position and assume that only one or the other end of the spectrum is worthy of pursuit. Both approaches are present in "The Egypt Story."

Parallel views of multicultural education exist in "The Egypt Story." At certain times—for example, when Doris's students compare the ancient Egyptian hieroglyphic number system to our modern-day place value number system—students take a pattern-seeking approach to learning about cultures, much as an anthropologist involved in fieldwork might. At other times—for example, when Doris's students learn about different ancient Egyptian measuring units—students take a master-the-facts-and-procedures approach to multicultural studies.

"The Egypt Story" includes both a pattern-seeking and a master-the-facts-and-procedures approach to mathematics education and to multicultural education. In addition, these different approaches to mathematics education and multicultural education can be combined in a variety of ways. Sometimes "The Egypt Story" uses a pattern-seeking approach to mathematics while taking a master-the-facts-and-procedures approach to cultural studies, while at other times it uses different combinations of these approaches.

For example, from a mathematical perspective, when Doris's students play The Game of Snake, they are practicing writing and calculating with hieroglyphics. At the same time, from a cultural perspective, they are getting a feel for the patterns inherent in ancient Egyptian life and their relationship to life today. This is because The Game of Snake, an authentic ancient Egyptian game, is used to illustrate to students that ancient Egyptian children engaged in endeavors similar to those of children today. The game board for The Game of Snake was found painted in an ancient Egyptian tomb dating from the Third Dynasty (c. 2868–2613 BCE) and actual boards were found in later tombs (Bell, 1979). The similarity of the cultural endeavors of ancient Egyptian children and children of today is not lost on Doris's students. Doris herself uses a similar spiral game with her class to get them to practice math facts, and many of them play more recent versions of the game (such as Snakes and Ladders) (Love, 1978; Love, 1979; and Bell, 1979).

Curricular Integration

The literature on curricular integration written by mathematics educators often speaks about providing children with a cultural experience that acts as a jumping-off point for a mathematical exploration. In this type of curricular integration, children are introduced to a mathematical problem through a cultural experience, and then, as work on the problem progresses, involvement in the cultural experience disappears. This is not what occurs in "The Egypt Story." Here, to the degree possible, the cultural and mathematical dimensions of the experience are intertwined for the duration of children's work. Here multicultural mathematics is seen as integrating the study of mathematics and culture in such a way that children learn both simultaneously. It is not the use of one as a pretext for studying the other, or the use of one as a tool to catapult the child into the study of the other.

Contextualization

When Doris's students interpret Regi's notes and play The Game of Snake, they construct mathematical and cultural meaning in the context of events they imagine taking place in ancient Egypt. Building an intellectual context in which students learn is an important part of oral storytelling. Doris's students do not learn about ancient Egyptian mathematics and culture from the perspective of outsiders who are not involved in the events of the story. Rather they learn from the personal perspective of insiders involved in an adventure that takes place in the context of ancient Egyptian life. They live the story just as Maria and Regi would have if the fantasy actually occurred, finding patterns in Regi's notes and playing The Game of Snake as if they were Maria and Regi in ancient Egypt. Contextualizing mathematics and cultural study provides learners a personal perspective on what they are learning.

Social Context of Learning

In both the problem of Regi's notes and The Game of Snake, Doris has her students problem solve in groups. During this story she emphasizes the social construction of meaning, in comparison to individual construction of meaning.

During "The Egypt Story" Doris wants her students to learn mathematical problem solving as a cooperative social endeavor. She believes her students will acquire greater mathematical and multicultural knowledge and have greater success solving problems if they share their insights and their problem-solving endeavors with each other rather than if they work alone. She also wants her students to experience problem solving with others so that they build the behavioral repertoires that lead to constructive group problem-solving behavior. When her students encounter mathematical problems in their everyday life outside of school, she wants them to feel that it is acceptable to ask for help, give help, and problem solve with others.

It is important to note that children construct mathematical meaning in a social context in every mathematics class. Even if students work in isolation and the norms of the classroom do not condone sharing of problem-solving solution strategies or answers, this is still a social context. Social contexts that are built on the assumption that "each of us is on our own—sink or swim by yourself" are quite different from those built on the assumption that "we are all in it together—help others and you help yourself." Teachers must carefully consider the social context in which mathematical learning takes place and decide if it does or does not work to their benefit. The question for Doris is not "Do we view mathematical learning as taking place in a social context or not?" Rather it is "How do I want to manipulate the social context in which my students learn in order to accomplish my goals?"

THE PROBLEM OF AN-NAB'S TOMB (DAYS 3 AND 4)

The problem of An-Nab's tomb consists of two related subproblems: deciding what to place in the tomb and building a scale model of the tomb.

Artifacts

The problems relating to An-Nab's tomb represent an attempt to introduce ancient Egyptian artifacts into the classroom, artifacts that children can physically manipulate and by so doing get to know about ancient Egypt. Since real artifacts are not available, pictures and scale models of artifacts are provided. Providing children with the ability to physically manipulate multicultural artifacts takes into account that many sixth graders are still primarily in what Piaget has called the concrete operational stage of development: they learn best by physically acting (or intellectually operating) on concrete objects (or visual representations of concrete objects). In this case, Doris's students physically manipulate (operate on) the tomb cards (visual representations of concrete objects) and actually construct (operate on) a scale model of An-Nab's tomb to satisfy mathematical specifications given in the story. Manipulating artifacts also allows students to utilize a variety of mathematical problem solving, thinking, and learning styles (such as motor, visual, and artistic).

Contextualized Learning

Doris's students encounter mathematical problems and learn about ancient Egyptian culture in the context of Maria's and Regi's Egyptian adventures, under the assumption that contextualized knowledge that is grounded in a larger web of ongoing personal experiences is more meaningful to them than decontextualized information. The two mathematical problems related to An-Nab's tomb are also placed in the context of An-Nab's life and the ancient Egyptian religious belief system. To give further meaning to cultural information about ancient Egyptian beliefs needed to solve these two problems, that information is placed in the context of "The Play of the Tomb" (an artistic form of choral drama used thousands of years ago in Mediterranean cultures). The play not only provides the cultural information needed to solve the problems of the tomb, but it also sets the stage for the problems of the tomb. In addition, it is exciting for Doris's students to perform and involves them intellectually, emotionally, and socially in its cultural information as they read its lines and rhythmically chant its chorus. This places Doris's students in the frame of mind in which they see themselves—to the degree possible—acting in ancient Egypt doing the types of things that ancient Egyptians did. Within a classroom it is impossible for children to authentically project themselves into another culture and experience it as members of the culture. During multicultural mathematics instruction, however, we can try to come as close as possible by immersing students in experiences in which—to the greatest extent possible—they imagine themselves in another culture, imagine themselves accepting the values and beliefs of that culture, and imagine themselves encountering mathematical problems that are important to members of that culture.

Problem Solving

A model for conceptualizing mathematical problem solving will now be introduced. How the cultural backgrounds of problem solvers influences their problem-solving endeavors will be considered later. Note that multicultural mathematical problem solving is multicultural both because problems exist in a cultural context and because the influence of the cultural knowledge base of problem solvers on their endeavors is taken into account.

The way in which Doris's students solve the problem of what to put in An-Nab's tomb provides a model for mathematical problem solving. This is how groups of students proceed.

First, they discuss the list of items that must go into An-Nab's tomb in light of what they learn from "The Play of the Tomb" and Maria and Regi's discussions with An-Nab in his office. This helps them understand the nature of the problem and what they must accomplish in order to solve it. Next they make a plan for how to solve the problem. The plan usually consists of compiling an initial list of contents for An-Nab's tomb, a list that meets his specifications. Students then execute their plan by calculating how much they spent. Then they look back (a) to see how close they have come to spending 2,000 debens and (b) to see if they have acquired all of the necessary items for the tomb. Usually their review indicates that they are not close to spending 2,000 debens.

As a result, Doris's students review their initial list of tomb items in light of An-Nab's specifications and what they know about ancient Egypt and discuss additions to and substitutions for items on their initial list. This provides additional understanding of the cultural and mathematical dimensions of the problem. Based on their discussions, a new plan—in the form of a new list—is formulated. Students then carry out the second plan by calculating the price of items on the revised list. As they execute the plan they keep in mind the problem's specifications while monitoring (by looking back at their endeavors) their progress toward solving the problem and altering the plan while in the process of carrying it out. They alter their plan by doing such things as adding or dropping an item from their list of tomb contents as a result of how quickly the cumulative cost of the items adds up. When students finish executing their second plan, they look back to see how close they have come to adequately solving the problem (spending 2,000 debens). They then tinker with their solution by adding, deleting, or substituting items so they spend as close as possible to 2,000 debens while monitoring their endeavors as they look back at the consequences of their actions.

This cycle of understand the problem, make a plan, execute the plan, and look back continues until students are satisfied with their solution to the problem, with each tentative conclusion reached during each phase in the process informing activity that takes place during later phases in the process. This all takes place while students discuss the advantages and disadvantages of including different items in the tomb, check each other's calculations, and monitor each other's speculations.

Exhibit 9.1   Polya's Phases of the Problem-Solving Process

This description of how Doris's students solve the tomb contents problem is similar to a model for problem solving proposed by George Polya (1957). Polya's four-phase model involves the phases (or steps) of understanding the problem to be solved, devising a plan to solve the problem, carrying out the plan, and looking back to see the effectiveness of the plan. Polya's four-phase method does not offer a prescribed set of problem-solving strategies or an algorithm for obtaining solutions to problems. Rather it is a model for understanding the problem-solving process, which in turn has implications for how to approach problems in a systematic manner. The four major phases of Polya's model are presented in Exhibit 9.1 and described below.

Understand the problem. For Polya (1957), understanding a problem involves being able to "repeat the statement" of the problem, "state the problem fluently," and "point out the principal parts of the problem, the unknown, the data, the conditions" (pp. 6-7). It involves acquiring necessary background knowledge about the context in which the problem arises, for as Polya says about devising a plan, "it is hard to have a good idea if we have little knowledge of the subject, and impossible to have it if we have no knowledge. Good ideas are based on past experience and formerly acquired knowledge" (p. 9). It also involves analyzing the problem and if possible breaking it into component smaller problems.

Devise a plan. To solve a problem the nature of the problem must be explored and a plan must be devised to guide one's endeavors. A number of educators have offered strategies designed to facilitate mathematical problem solving for use at the stage of exploring a problem and devising a plan (strategies also useful at other stages of problem solving). Polya offers suggestions such as "draw a figure," "introduce suitable notation," and examine "a related

Exhibit 9.2 Popular Problem-Solving Strategies

Polya	Baroody	Burns	Hoogeboom & Goodnow	Ewen
introduce suitable notation	write an equation	write an equation		specification without loss of generality
		use objects		
draw a figure	act out the problem, make a model, draw a picture, or draw a diagram	act it out	act out or use objects	use a computer
		make a model		
		draw a picture	make a picture or diagram	visual representation
	organize data in a list, table, or chart and look for patterns	construct a table	use or make a table	sequencing
		make an organized list	make an organized list	
	look for a pattern by examining specific examples	look for a pattern	use or look for a pattern	find a pattern
	use logical reasoning		use logical reasoning	deductive reasoning
	work backward	work backward	work backward	work backward
examine a related problem	simplify a problem and look for patterns	solve a simpler (or similar) problem	make it simpler	solve a simpler analogous problem
	relate new problems to familiar problems			consider extreme cases
				account for all possibilities
	guess and check	guess and check	guess and check	intelligent guess and test
			brainstorm	
				adopt a different point of view
				determine necessary or sufficient conditions

problem" (1957, pp. 7–9). Other educators offer strategies such as: write an equation, draw a picture, construct a table, act out the problem, look for a pattern, relate a new problem to familiar problems, work backwards, use logical reasoning, guess and check, make a model, account for all possibilities, consider extreme cases, and brainstorm. The categories of problem-solving strategies presented by Baroody (1993), Burns (1992), Hoogeboom and Goodnow (1987), and Ewen (1996) are presented in Exhibit 9.2, with similar strategies juxtaposed next to each other.

Carry out the plan. To conceive a plan and to carry it out are two different things. Devising a plan requires that the child construct a method for solving a problem. Carrying out a plan requires that the child engage in working through the details of actually doing the calculations, graphing, manipulations, or other tasks necessary for carrying out the plan. While carrying out a plan, children should monitor their endeavors in order to determine if their plan is having the desired effect, if a new point of view or perspective on the problem is needed, or if an easier or more elegant way of accomplishing their goals might be discovered. Evaluating one's success while implementing and revising a plan is an important part of successfully carrying it out.

Look back. Once children have reached a tentative or final solution to a problem, it is important for them to look back and see what they have accomplished. Polya (1957) describes this "looking back" phase in this way:

> Even fairly good students, when they have obtained the solution of the problem and written down neatly the argument, shut their books and look for something else. By looking back at the completed solution, by reconsidering and reexamining the result and the path that led to it, they could consolidate their knowledge and develop their ability to solve problems. (pp. 14-15)

As previously discussed, "looking back" should probably be called the "looking back and looking forward" phase of problem solving.

If children simply put aside their work upon completing it, without engaging in the process of looking back to see what has been accomplished and looking forward to see how what was learned might be relevant to their everyday lives, they are likely to miss many of the benefits of their endeavors. Reflecting upon what has been accomplished often provides a sense of perspective, greater understanding, and a set of advanced organizers useful when similar problems are faced in the future. Reflecting upon what has been experienced while solving a problem can also provide increased insight into and understanding of one's life, increased perspective on one's life, and increased power over one's life.

From the previous discussion it is necessary to add an additional phase to this model, which in the discussion of the generations problem was called "finding a problem." This phase might be described as follows.

Find a problem. During mathematics instruction teachers usually give students problems to solve. It is also important to ask children themselves to discover mathematical problems they feel need to be solved, to define the nature of those problems and their solutions, to commit to solving them, and then to go on to solve them. This includes having students make value judgments about which problems are or are not worthy of being solved and which are within their reach to solve. Finding their own problems to solve and solving their own problems are important endeavors for children to undertake (Brown & Walters, 1983; Schiro, 1997).

From the description above of how Doris's students solve the problem of furnishing An-Nab's tomb, it is clear that they do not proceed through the problem-solving process in a linear manner, visiting each stage once and only once. Rather they visit each phase multiple times and use feedback from looking back at previous phases to plan future activities. To

Exhibit 9.3   Problem-Solving Model Adjusted to Account for Cyclic Activity and Feedback
Between Phases

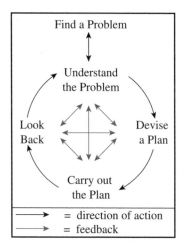

incorporate these elements into our model, the linear nature of the model needs to be altered
to make it more cyclic, and a mechanism for allowing feedback between phases needs to be
introduced.

A revised model for mathematical problem solving is presented in Exhibit 9.3 in which
solid arrows show the general direction of action during problem solving and shaded arrows
show feedback from one type of activity to another.

Several additional elements need to be added to this problem-solving model. But first,
some observations about problem solving need to be introduced.

Problem-Solving Knowledge Base

Alan Schoenfeld (1989, 1992) has examined how novice and expert problem solvers
progress through the different phases of problem solving when solving difficult nonroutine
problems. In his research Schoenfeld uses a slightly different set of phases than the ones used
here. His phases are read, analyze, explore, plan, implement, and verify. His observations can
be easily transposed onto the phases being used here, with his read and analyze phases corresponding to our understand phase, his explore and plan phases corresponding to our plan
phase, his implement phase corresponding to our carry-out-the-plan phase, and his verify
phase corresponding to our look-back phase.

What Schoenfeld found is that novices and experts spend their time solving problems
differently. Novice problem solvers, as illustrated in Exhibit 9.4, quickly read and gain an
initial understanding of a problem, then proceed to quickly select a strategy for solving the
problem, and finally struggle to try (often unsuccessfully) to get the strategy to work—
without ever abandoning the initial problem-solving strategy selected or altering the plan for
how to proceed, even when it does not prove useful in solving the problem under consideration.

Exhibit 9.4   Time Graph of a Novice's Progress in Solving a Nonroutine Problem

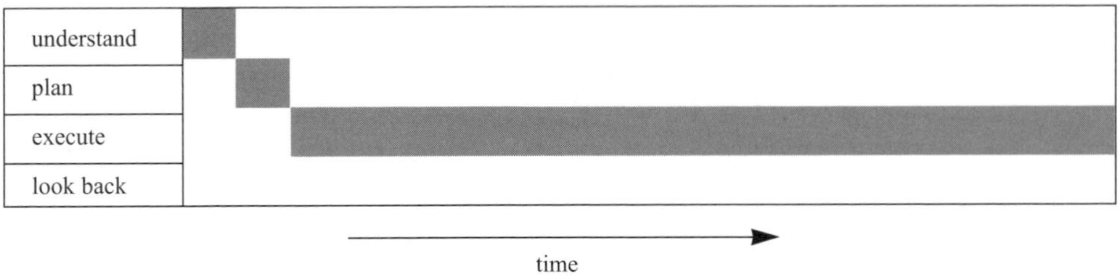

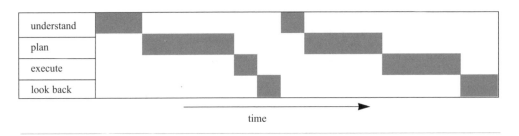

Exhibit 9.5   Time Graph of an Expert's Progress in Solving a Nonroutine Problem

Schoenfeld (1992, p. 356) describes this strategy thus: "Read, make a decision quickly, and pursue that direction come hell or high water."

In contrast, the expert problem solver spends a great deal of time understanding and planning how to solve a problem, usually reviewing and assessing the value of multiple strategies for solving a problem at hand before selecting a strategy to use. The expert problem solver then executes the strategy chosen for use while constantly monitoring the usefulness of that strategy and abandoning it if it does not produce the desired results. After looking back to see what was thus far accomplished, the expert problem solver returns to try to understand the problem in order to gain additional insight into it, to again explore different strategies that might produce a solution, and to choose another strategy to use in solving the problem. The expert problem solver continues this cycle of understand, plan, execute, and look back until a solution is found or the problem is abandoned. (See Exhibit 9.5.)

There are major differences between novice and expert problem solvers noted in Schoenfeld's research: the range of different problem-solving strategies explored before one is selected for use in solving a problem, the degree of self-monitoring that takes place with respect to determining whether or not a particular strategy is proving useful in producing a solution, and the speed with which a strategy that is not proving useful in solving a problem is abandoned so that other possibly more useful strategies can be explored and put into use. These behaviors are closely related to the ability of problem solvers to monitor, have personal control over, and self-regulate their mathematical thinking processes.

Important to note here is that the knowledge base of expert problem solvers contains more than just knowledge about the problem to be solved. It includes knowledge of different problem-solving strategies and facility in using them. It includes self-regulating problem-solving functions that allow problem solvers to do the following types of things: to explore different problem-solving strategies before embracing one to execute, to be frequently looking back on their progress in solving a problem, and to abandon a chosen strategy that is not producing the desired results so that other strategies can be explored and a new one chosen and executed. The knowledge base of problem solvers also includes beliefs, attitudes, and affects (not yet spoken of) about their ability to solve mathematical problems, think mathematically, and learn mathematics.

Multicultural mathematics educators ask many important questions about the knowledge base of learners that relate to their different genders, socioeconomic status, or cultural backgrounds.

At one level are questions about such things as the different amounts and types of information that students from different cultural or socioeconomic backgrounds might bring to solving problems, because they are more or less intimately familiar with the information needed to understand a particular problem. For example, what advantages might students who have played little league baseball have over students who have never heard of baseball in solving problems about baseball players' batting averages?

At another level are questions about such things as the range of and facility with different problem-solving strategies that students of differing genders, cultures, or socioeconomic backgrounds might bring to solving problems because of exposure to or use of different strategies in their families or communities. For example, research has indicated that females have a greater tendency to use verbal and articulatory problem-solving strategies while males tend to have a greater tendency to use visual and spatial problem-solving strategies (Casey, Nuttall, Pezaris, & Benbow, 1995). What is the effect of this on males' versus females' ability to solve different types of problems?

At another level are questions about such things as children's facility with the use of language (and particularly abstract, deductive, logical mathematical language and linguistic structures) in the case of children who come from different socioeconomic backgrounds or cultures. For example, what problem-solving strategies are available to children from more oral families, communities, and cultures compared to the problem-solving strategies available to children from highly literate families, communities, and cultures—because of the mathematical structures embedded in the very nature of the language they learn in their families and communities? And what is the effect of children's culturally learned ways of communicating (with themselves and others) on their ability to succeed in learning to think mathematically?

At still another level are questions about such things as differences in children's experiences with, orientations toward, and inclinations to use different metacognitive problem-solving structures depending on their culture and socioeconomic backgrounds. For example, are certain groups of students taught in their families and communities to be more or less impulsive in their thinking as opposed to self-monitoring and self-regulating of their thinking? And what is the effect of children's culturally learned ways of monitoring their thought processes on their ability to solve mathematical problems and succeed in becoming powerful users of mathematics?

These are the types of questions about the knowledge bases of learners that interest multicultural mathematics educators. They will be incorporated into our problem-solving model shortly and explored in greater depth in later chapters.

THE PROBLEM OF COMPARING NUMBER SYSTEMS (DAYS 3 AND 4)

Multicultural Assumptions

Day 4 highlights three multicultural mathematics assumptions:

- Different mathematical systems exist.
- Different cultures can have different mathematical systems.
- A culture's mathematical system can reflect its underlying social, artistic, political, economic, scientific, and religious beliefs.

"The Egypt Story" presents these assumptions and then asks students to act in accordance with them when comparing ancient Egyptian and our current-day number systems.

The story presents these assumptions by first noting that ancient Egyptian mathematics contained two different numeration systems (hieroglyphic and hieratic); that one was for royalty and the other was for the common people; and that an underlying social, religious, and political doctrine of ancient Egypt was the belief in a dualistic society with different laws, privileges, burial grounds, and mathematical systems for each group. ("There are the Pharaohs and nobles who are related to the gods, and then there are the rest of us who are common people.") This is very different from mathematical and cultural beliefs in the United States today where, as Maria says to An-Nab,

In the future we believe that all people should be treated equally. We don't have any royalty. There is only one social class, even though some people are richer than others. Everyone is buried in the same burial grounds, and everyone has to obey the same laws. And we have only one number system.

The presentation of these multicultural assumptions continues when An-Nab states his belief about the relationship between a culture's indigenous mathematical system and its indigenous underlying beliefs when he says, "The essence of a culture is reflected in its number and writing systems."

Being a Mini-Mathematical Anthropologist

"The Egypt Story" does not stop with highlighting these three multicultural assumptions. It goes on to ask students to behave as though they were mini-mathematical anthropologists (multicultural mathematicians) whose job it is to uncover the links between a culture's mathematical system and its underlying cultural beliefs.

Underlying this instructional practice is the assumption that children learn multicultural mathematics not just by observing the results of the research of multicultural mathematicians, but also by thinking and behaving as though they are multicultural mathematicians themselves.

Accompanying this instructional practice is the belief that multicultural mathematics is not just a body of content. It is also the way in which mathematicians view, communicate, think about, construct meaning about, learn about, and solve problems in their world. Here mathematics is seen as a mini-culture with its own social, scientific, cultural, artistic, political, linguistic, and communication beliefs and practices. Here it is assumed that the way that children learn about multicultural mathematics—the way that they become enculturated into the discipline of multicultural mathematics—is both by doing multicultural mathematics themselves (as though they were mini-multicultural mathematicians) and by learning content knowledge created by multicultural mathematicians.

From these pedagogical beliefs it follows that a type of problem is needed that gets children to behave as multicultural mathematicians. The problem of comparing number systems is such a problem. When Doris asks her students to compare the numeration systems of ancient Egypt and the current-day United States and see if it is possible to determine how those systems reflect beliefs of their respective cultures, she is asking her students to behave as mini-multicultural, mathematical anthropologists.

Mathematics problems do not usually ask children to do this. Usually multicultural mathematics problems ask the following of children:

- Use the mathematical system of another culture once they are shown how to do so (as Doris's student do after being shown the ancient Egyptian method for finding a circle's area).
- Figure out how the mathematical system of another culture works (as Doris's students do when they figure out how the ancient Egyptian numeration system works by examining Regi's notes).
- Appreciate the differences between the mathematics of different cultures (as Doris's students do when examining the mathematical designs in ancient Egyptian textiles).
- Use current-day mathematics to find out about people living in different cultures (as in the case of the generations problem).
- Use current-day mathematics to discover inequities between cultures, and to make value judgments about those inequities (as when using mathematics to discover infant mortality rates of different nations and to conclude that some cultures are healthier and thus better to live in than others).

Children need to have the chance to work problems that ask them to behave as mini-mathematical anthropologists if we want them to learn multicultural mathematics (which is herein taken to consist of the cultural behaviors, attitudes, and content knowledge of mathematicians from other cultures). Asking students to uncover the links between a culture's mathematical system and its social beliefs, and asking students to compare and contrast the paired mathematical and cultural systems of two different groups of people, is an example of this type of problem.

A Mathematical Problem-Solving Model

This discussion raises issues of how the culture of students who solve mathematical problems relates to the problem-solving model thus far proposed. Will not students' cultural assumptions about such things as the nature of mathematics, the nature of the types of mathematical problems it is worthwhile to solve, the types of problem-solving strategies it is acceptable to use, and even the nature of the numeration systems and algorithms used—all of which are influenced by their family and community culture—influence the way in which they solve problems? Will not children raised in a highly literate culture and children raised within a culture in which literacy rates are very low have different mathematical problem-solving knowledge bases? Will not the child from the as yet undiscovered Native American village in the rain forests of Brazil have a different mathematical knowledge base than the highly literate child raised in a suburb of San Francisco? And might not a child from a highly literate family in the suburbs of Boston have a different mathematical knowledge base than a child of the same racial and religious background but different socioeconomic class who comes from a primarily oral family in urban Boston? Every community's view of mathematical problem solving is influenced by its underlying social, economic, artistic, cultural, political, and religious beliefs, just as every culture's view of these is reflected in its mathematical problem-solving knowledge base. How culture influences children's ability to do mathematics will be examined in later chapters.

The problem we confront now is finding a way to indicate, within the problem-solving model thus far proposed, that when a child does mathematics, the child does it in a cultural context, and that there are different cultural contexts from which children can do mathematics. To incorporate this viewpoint into the problem-solving model thus far proposed requires that we individualize that model. We do this by surrounding the problem-solving model previously presented with a closed curve. The closed curve will designate an individual's zone of proximal development. A person's *zone* is often thought of as containing those things the person can learn as a result of their own endeavors and interactions with a teacher or other more knowledgeable person (Vygotsky, 1978; Davis, 1996; Albert, 2000). That individuals have different zones of proximal development—or different things that they are capable of learning at any point in their mathematical development—will thus be indicated by different-shaped closed curves.

To indicate an individual's culturally influenced mathematical knowledge base, we will then shade the interior of the closed curve. Different shadings within the closed curves will then indicate that children have different culturally influenced knowledge bases. Exhibit 9.6 portrays the problem-solving model thus far proposed, individualized to adjust for a child's zone of proximal development in the context of the child's cultural background and knowledge base.

LEARNING ANCIENT EGYPTIAN MULTIPLICATION (DAYS 5 AND 6)

During Day 5 Doris's students learn ancient Egyptian multiplication in the same way that they learned about hieroglyphic numerals. They are shown a mathematical pattern, and as a result of analyzing it in small cooperative-learning groups, they figure out how the operation works. What could have been a didactic lesson in learning an algorithm is thus turned into a problem-solving activity. Afterward Doris's students play The Palm Tree Game on a game board found in ancient Egyptian tombs. As before, Doris points out interesting problems that she does not follow up on in class, in the belief that students need to learn how to find and solve their own problems (in this case whether or not it is possible to write every positive integer as the sum of multiples of 2).

Exhibit 9.6   Problem-Solving Model Individualized to Account for an Individual's Zone of
Proximal Development in the Context of That Individual's Cultural Background and
Knowledge Base

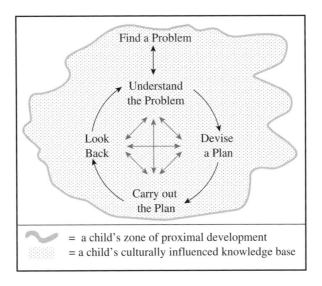

= a child's zone of proximal development
= a child's culturally influenced knowledge base

Informal Learning

Doris's students are informally flooded with information about ancient Egyptian culture
and mathematics as they listen to "The Egypt Story." They learn about ancient Egyptian measurement units, how these units of measure were linked to Pharaoh's body, and the types of
things measured in ancient Egypt. They play a mathematics game on an ancient Egyptian
game board, learn about ancient Egyptian children's sports, and hear "Tuauf's Scolding."
"Tuauf's Scolding" is a free reconstruction of two ancient Egyptian documents in the British
Museum titled "Satire of the Trades" (trans. 1993) and "Teaching" (trans. 1986). It is
designed to illustrate both the different types of trades practiced in ancient Egypt and how
scribes 3,500 years ago tried to convince their students of the benefits of their trade in comparison to other trades, using arguments similar to those used by modern-day teachers to convince students of today to learn academic subjects.

All of this cultural knowledge could have been summarized in a few carefully crafted,
abstract, formal, didactic statements, and could have been conveyed directly to students as objective knowledge to be committed to memory. Students then could have been tested on their
ability to represent on an objective test their memory of the content of these statements shortly
after they were presented. But this is not what occurs. Instead students are informally flooded
with information about ancient Egyptian culture and mathematics, they are each given the

opportunity to construct their own personal meaning from the information-rich environment in which they are immersed, and no formal testing of the information presented looms on the horizon.

Cooperative-Learning Groups

When Doris's students engage in problem solving, they work in small cooperative groups. In their groups, students help each other solve problems, and together they prepare a report on their endeavors with one (or more) student(s) acting as the recorder(s) and the other (or others) acting as the presenter(s) of their findings to the whole class. The dynamics of these groups were discussed in an earlier chapter.

Learning problem solving in small cooperative groups is not what one usually conceives of occurring in the traditional mathematics class. Usually one imagines students working alone, doing their own work. Usually one also imagines that this is the way that mathematicians solve problems—secluded in their individual offices working alone. Mathematicians frequently, however, work together on mathematical problems. And during the last 30 years educators have begun to ask students to work together on problems, mirroring the similar practice among mathematicians. In the process they have discovered the value of having students learn to solve problems in cooperative groups (as well as having them learn to do so individually).

There are several interrelated reasons why educators think that cooperative learning is a powerful instructional tool for helping students learn mathematical problem solving.

- Cooperative learning improves mathematical achievement. In fact,

  > studies comparing cooperative learning with competitive and individualistic learning have demonstrated that cooperative learning promotes higher achievement in mathematics than the other two methods. Not only do students solve math problems more successfully and learn and retain mathematical concepts, but cooperative learning also results in more use of higher-level thinking, more frequent discovery, more new ideas and solution strategies, and more transfer of what is learned in groups about problem solving to individual problem-solving situations. (Hartman, 1996, p. 403)

- Cooperative learning enables students to exchange mathematical ideas with each other, ask questions of each other, monitor each other's behavior, compare the appropriateness of problem-solving strategies for different types of problems, justify their thinking to each other, accept and endure frustration while continuing to persevere, and offer each other constructive criticism. It places emphasis on student control over their own learning and fosters increased self-reliance, self-monitoring, and self-esteem on the part of problem solvers as they "make, detect, and correct their own and each other's errors" while solving problems (Hartman, 1996, p. 402). In so doing, it provides at a group level a model for self-monitoring, higher-level thinking, perseverance, and independent decision making that can be internalized by individuals and later emulated when they work alone.
- Solving problems in groups in which one observes and participates with one's peers in struggling with and successfully solving problems "can demystify the problem-solving

process and reduce math anxiety . . . [which] . . . can contribute to poor mathematics self-concepts and can inhibit success in mathematical problem solving" (Hartman, 1996, p. 403).

- The social nature of cooperative problem solving can make it fun and motivating. It can draw students into active involvement with learning.

- Being taught by a peer whose knowledge base, language, and ways of thinking are similar to one's own can facilitate learning.

- Teaching something to someone else is one of the best ways to learn it yourself. It often involves putting into words that another person can understand things only partially or intuitively understood, and, in the process, exploring the ideas being taught in greater depth. It often involves relating the ideas being taught to other ideas in more formal ways than they were previously related, reconstructing mathematical concepts and procedures at a higher level of understanding, exploring one's own meanings from additional perspectives, and more systematically organizing one's thoughts about what is being taught (Pressley, Wood, Woloshuyn, King, & Menke, 1992; Schiro, 1997).

- Cooperative learning can help students appreciate the contributions that peers of different cultural backgrounds and abilities can bring to a joint endeavor (Johnson & Johnson, 1990).

Shared Problem Solving

Students of different genders, cultural backgrounds, or socioeconomic status who solve problems together can enhance each other's (culturally learned) mathematical knowledge bases in ways that contribute to one another's problem-solving ability (as can any students with different knowledge bases). Exhibit 9.7 presents a problem-solving model that portrays two children solving a mathematical problem together who have different zones of proximal development (indicated by the irregularly shaped closed curves) and different (culturally influenced) knowledge bases (indicated by different interior shading of the closed curves). In this model both children benefit from problem solving with someone whose zone of proximal development and mathematical knowledge base is different from their own, because shared access to both knowledge bases is greater than individual access, as well as for the reasons mentioned above.

Let us examine how this might occur. Assume that two students of different cultural (gender or socioeconomic) backgrounds with different zones of proximal development and knowledge bases problem-solve together. Because of their different cultural backgrounds and knowledge bases we will assume that they approach the problem differently. As they work on the problem, they will share their different perspectives with each other. For example, if one student says, "Let me *tell* you what I did," and the other says, "Let me *show* you what I did," they are likely to be sharing different ways of viewing the problem, devising a plan, and finding its solution. The student who says, "Let me *tell* you what I did," might be using problem-solving procedures based on more verbal and articulatory reasoning, while the student who says, "Let me *show* you what I did," might be using problem-solving procedures based on a more visual, spatial, and diagrammatic way of thinking. When these two students share their viewpoints with each other, they are capable of benefiting from two different ways of understanding the problem, planning and finding its solution, and looking back at what was accomplished. These two students' different ways of making sense out of the problem thus

Exhibit 9.7   The Problem-Solving Model Individualized to Two Individuals Working on a
Problem Together Who Have Different Zones of Proximal Development and
Different Knowledge Bases

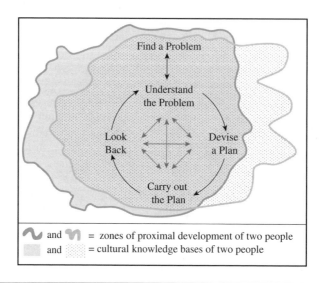

enrich each other's way of making sense out of the problem. This is especially so if (as Doris requires) the two students must listen to each other well enough and understand each other's way of solving the problem well enough so that one can act as recorder and accurately write down both of their different solutions in such a way that the other can read the written notes and accurately explain them to the class.

Two things are important here. First, the two students' different ways of approaching mathematical problems are likely to have been learned within their families and communities and are likely to be correlated to cultural factors. This is why the culturally learned knowledge bases of students are so prominently featured in the problem-solving model depicted in Exhibit 9.7.

Second, Doris's structuring of her students' cooperative problem-solving groups so that students must work together and communicate together well enough so that one can act as recorder and the other can then read the recorder's notes and explain them, is a group-structuring element that forces the sharing of knowledge bases. This structuring element facilitates sharing in such a way that one student's mathematical problem-solving knowledge base can influence the knowledge base of another student.

WHICH IS BEST? OUR MULTIPLICATION OR THE ANCIENT EGYPTIANS' (DAY 7)

Knowledge >> Assessment >> Values >> Action

During Day 7 Doris Lawson's students solve two problems given to Regi and Maria by An-Nab: "Which is better, the twenty-first century, modern-day way of doing multiplication or the ancient Egyptian multiplication algorithm?" and "Should or should not An-Nab, and other ancient Egyptians, be taught our modern-day multiplication algorithm?"

To answer these questions, Doris's students engage in four types of mathematical endeavors that both define an approach to multicultural mathematics instruction and introduce an important type of mathematics problem that is infrequently found in mathematics curricula.

First, they learn both ancient Egyptian and modern-day multiplication (acquire an understanding of two mathematical algorithms, elements, or systems), compare them, and understand the similarities and differences between them.

Second, they assess the advantages and disadvantages of each algorithm (or mathematical element) in the context of the cultural background and societal knowledge bases within which it was used.

Third, they make a decision based on their personal values—such as what is most humane, fair, kind, or just—about whether or not to introduce our modern-day multiplication algorithm (or other mathematical element) into ancient Egyptian culture (or some other culture). This value decision is based on their analysis of the possible impact of modern-day multiplication on ancient Egyptians (or the impact that any innovation might have on the lives of those living in a culture).

Fourth, they make a commitment to act based on their value decisions and, if possible, actually act on their decisions to improve the lives of people (in this case, ancient Egyptians).

Let us examine these four types of mathematical endeavors.

Knowledge. To solve the problems posed, Doris's students must understand ancient Egyptian and modern-day multiplication. During Day 6 they learn ancient Egyptian multiplication. They already know modern-day multiplication. They now compare the two multiplication algorithms, noting similarities and differences. Differences are noted, such as the fact that in our modern-day system we directly multiply by each of the digits from 0 to 9, while in the ancient Egyptian algorithm the only multiplier used is the number 2.

Assessment. Doris's students then assess the advantages and disadvantages of each algorithm in the context of their cultures. They do so by acting as mini-mathematical anthropologists. The modifier "in the context of their cultures" is of critical importance. This view of multicultural mathematics sees mathematics as part of a larger cultural endeavor and not as an objective body of truths independent of the culture in which it exists. Here Doris's students note that ancient Egyptian children did not have to memorize very many multiplication facts, while today children must memorize many facts.

Values. Doris's students now must make a value decision: should they introduce modern-day multiplication into ancient Egypt? This decision is based on an analysis of the innovation's possible impact on ancient Egyptians. Making a value decision about what is better for people is important in this type of multicultural problem solving. Here the criterion of "better" relates to quality-of-life issues. Here Doris's students note that modern-day multiplication can be done more quickly and with less writing than the ancient Egyptian algorithm, and that means less work. They also note that memorizing lots of multiplication facts is "torture."

Action. Finally, if possible, Doris's students would make a commitment to act based on their value decision and do what they determined to be in the best interest of ancient Egyptians. In this type of multicultural problem solving, action to improve the lives of people, based on some vision of a better life, is required. Educators who use this multicultural approach have taught indigenous South Americans new mathematics so that they can acquire ownership of their ancestors' native lands and preserve their way of life (Knijnik, 1997) and have helped urban children mount political-action campaigns to clean up neighborhood pollution (Ladson-Billings, 1995; Frankenstein, 1995).

It is important for children to be exposed to this approach to multicultural problem solving. Once they complete school and become participating members of society, it is one of the ways in which they will be able to use mathematics to improve their own lives and the life of their community.

THE AREA OF A CIRCLE AND MATHEMATICAL PROOF (DAYS 8, 9, AND 10)

During Days 8, 9, and 10 Doris focuses on how, using the technology of 3,500 years ago, one might determine the area of a circle. In doing so, Doris presents a sequence of four activities that define one type of problem-solving endeavor (that can be used in many different instructional scenarios).

First, Doris asks her students to calculate the area of a circle that is 9 rods in diameter, without using current-day formulas or technology. (Students try to solve a problem prior to instruction using methods they themselves invent.)

Second, Doris introduces an ancient Egyptian algorithm for finding the area of a circle. Doris's students use this algorithm to help Maria and Regi do problems. (Instruction takes place and students practice what they learn in order to develop understanding and skill.)

Third, a proof of the algorithm is presented—an actual proof from the *Rhind Mathematical Papyrus*. In a humorous passage Regi discovers two errors in the proof. Doris asks her students to discover the errors and to discuss the differences between ancient Egyptian mathematical proof and current-day mathematical proof (as it is presented in their mathematics textbook). (Proof and analysis of what was taught take place.)

Fourth, Maria and Regi discuss with An-Nab some methods that he collected from different parts of his world of determining (and proving) the area of a circle, methods and proofs that existed 3,500 years ago. Doris's students then explore several ancient methods of finding the area of a circle to determine which they like best. In the process they struggle with the question of what makes a good proof in different cultural contexts. (Students compare alternatives and analyze differences in order to acquire perspective and deeper understanding.)

Mathematics and Culture

Mathematicians have worked in many different cultures. Have all of them thought in the same objective, deductive, and logical manner that current-day mathematicians supposedly think, or do their cultures influence the way they think?

As the phrasing above hints, we have to stop and consider two myths: that current-day mathematicians think in an objective, deductive, and logical manner and that their proofs and solutions to problems are truths for all times.

The activities of problem solving and constructing proofs are creative endeavors. When engaging in these endeavors, mathematicians frequently use a wide range of creative methods that are not always rational or logical, involving intuition, fantasy, and analogy (Hadamard, 1945). Recently mathematicians have begun to let us in on the secret that, as Epp says,

> the kind of thinking done by mathematicians in their own work is distinctly different from the elegant deductive reasoning found in mathematics texts. In this era of public candor people freely admit things they might once have seen as compromising their dignity. When discussing the process of mathematical discovery, mathematicians now openly acknowledge making illogical leaps in arguments, wandering down blind alleys or around in circles and formulating guesses based on analogy or on examples that are hidden in the later, formalized exposition of their work. (1994, p. 257)

If the way in which mathematicians solve problems and construct proofs is not logical, deductive, and rational, then what does this say about the content of mathematics, the facts and proofs that mathematicians create?

We need to acknowledge that the validity of mathematical facts and proofs is determined by the community (or subculture) of people who call themselves mathematicians. Unfortunately the members of such mathematical communities form a subculture that shares the same cultural orientation toward mathematics. Frequently, over short periods of time, their collective judgment is incorrect, and frequently, over longer periods of time, their cultural orientation changes and evolves. As a result, what is taken to be an acceptable mathematical proof or fact today in our culture may not necessarily be seen as adequate tomorrow or in another culture. As Schoenfeld (1994) sums this up, "What is accepted as mathematical truth is in fact the best collective judgment of the community of mathematicians, which may turn out to be in error."

For example, at one level, just recently a widely accepted proof of the Jordan curve theorem was found to be inadequate, while a recent proof of the four-color theorem, over which there was a great deal of controversy, has been accepted (Schoenfeld, 1994, p. 60). At another level, we are coming to accept that just as science goes through paradigm shifts in its views of scientific truth (Kuhn, 1962), so too may mathematics. As Schoenfeld says in comparing mathematics to science,

> Now the stereotype is that it's different in mathematics: It appears that you start with definitions or axioms and all the rest follows inexorably. However, . . . that isn't the way things really happen. The "natural" definition of polyhedron was accepted by the mathematical community for quite some time and was used to prove Euler's formula—until mathematicians found solids that met the definition but failed to satisfy the formula. How did the community deal with the issue? Ultimately, by changing the definition. That is, the grounds for theory—the definitions underlying the system—were changed in response to the data. That sure looks like theory change to me: New formulations replace old ones, with the base assumptions (definitions and axioms) evolving as the data come in. (1994, p. 59)

This is a surprise: Mathematics is not necessarily created through what we would call an objective, deductive, and logical process. Mathematical endeavors, proofs, and truths are inherently social activities and are given acceptance by a group of mathematicians living and working in a particular cultural context. The cultural orientation of mathematicians influences what they accept as truths and proofs. And the truths and proofs that we today accept as infallible and universal are, in fact, cultural constructs that members of other cultures might not be able to comprehend or accept as meaningful.

The importance of this for us now is that it begins to allow us to see the extent to which mathematics is a cultural endeavor and to accept that different cultures, as well as a single culture at different times in its evolution, may view mathematics from different perspectives, both in terms of what they accept as its truths and what they accept as its ways of creating and proving those truths.

Knowledge and Proof in a Cultural Context

Doris's students explore similar issues when they discover that ancient Egyptians proved mathematics differently and had different formulas than we do today, just as they dressed differently, spoke a different language, wrote differently, and had different religious beliefs. (They proved things by arguing from concrete particulars rather than from generalizable definitions and axioms, and their formula for the area of a circle was different from ours.)

Cultural differences continue to be emphasized when Doris's students try out different methods for finding the area of a circle (many of which existed 3,500 years ago) and decide which they like best. Deciding which method they think is best, when faced with several competing mathematical demonstrations that support slightly different conclusions, is an important type of problem-solving endeavor for students. It raises issues about the standards that different groups use for mathematical proof and reasoning, as well as issues about the types of "beauty" mathematicians prefer in their proofs, demonstrations, and algorithms.

When Doris's students compare different proofs, formulas, and algorithms and consider issues of mathematical beauty, they are engaging in the phase of problem solving called "looking back." Doris works hard to encourage her students to look back at their mathematical endeavors.

This is part of the reason why she has her students record their reflections in writing and orally present them to their classmates, just as mathematicians might review their problem-solving endeavors and record them in a mathematically beautiful proof that is reported to peers in written form in a journal or verbally at a conference. If we want children to behave as mathematicians might, by looking back at their work after solving a problem and presenting the results of their endeavors to their colleagues (classmates) in a clear and convincing way (a quasi-proof), then they need to be given the chance to do so.

PADDLE DOLL PROBLEMS (DAY 11)

During the last day of "The Egypt Story," Doris has her students explore ancient Egyptian clothing, pottery, and tomb designs that were created on grids of squares. Their explorations culminate in each student designing clothing patterns for paddle dolls (an ancient Egyptian toy similar to Barbie dolls) and transferring those patterns onto paddle doll replicas.

Mathematics and Patterns

Visual patterns were everywhere in ancient Egypt. Visual, numeric, algebraic, and other types of patterns are also everywhere in modern-day mathematics. Patterns are such an important part of mathematics that some educators even claim that mathematics is the science of patterns and that mathematical problem solving is an endeavor involving the uncovering, exploring, analyzing, and understanding of mathematical patterns.

On the surface it looks like Doris's students are solving problems involving geometric patterns. But to solve the geometric problems, her students must analyze the numerical patterns underlying them. To solve the numerical problems, students have to construct numerical tables and look for algebraic expressions that describe the numerical relationships. Taken together, this involves the exploration of mathematical functions, an important mathematical topic.

Cultural Patterns

Noticing the visual patterns that surround the lives of people of different cultures is one of the easiest ways in which the novice observer can perceive differences between cultures. It is easy to observe the distinctiveness and uniqueness of geometrical patterns in a culture's clothing designs, rug designs, pottery designs, religious designs, and other such artistic expressions. That there are mathematical patterns and functions underlying these designs is not as widely known. That these mathematical functions might relate in profound ways to the manner in which members of a culture conceptualize mathematics is even less frequently explored. And still more rarely examined is the way in which those patterns and functions might provide information about the ease with which children from different cultures can learn mathematics. For example, the idea that circular patterns might relate to a culture's sense of time being circular while linear patterns might relate to a culture's sense of time being linear is an important cultural difference. And it is extremely important for teachers working with children from different cultures to understand that a culture's view of time as circular or linear might influence children's ability to learn the Western concepts of measurement taught in most of today's schools.

Future Explorations

This is where the theoretical discussions in the following chapters will take us: They will lead us into an exploration of how the cultures that children experience in their families and communities can influence their knowledge bases and ways of knowing. They will take us into an exploration of how children's knowledge bases and ways of knowing can facilitate or inhibit their learning of school mathematics—and in particular the current-day abstract, deductive, linear mathematics taught in most schools since the middle of the last century. They will lead us into an exploration of what we can do about the inequities that children must deal with because of the families and communities in which they are raised. And they will take us into an exploration of how we can value mathematical ways of knowing and knowledge bases that are different from ours, and nurture the unique talents, insights, and problem-solving styles that children who come from cultures different from our own bring with them.

Chapter 10

MATHEMATICS AND CULTURE

When Doris Lawson suggested that I create an interdisciplinary mathematics and social studies oral story about ancient Egypt for her sixth graders because ancient Egypt was part of her social studies curriculum, I started to read about ancient Egyptian mathematics.

I soon discovered that studying the mathematics of other cultures was not new. Traditionally it was reported in books on the history of mathematics where the intent was often to glorify the successes of Western mathematics and culture by showing how superior they were to the endeavors of more primitive cultures. In fact, until recently, many histories of mathematics seemed to deny that non-Western cultures made significant mathematical contributions (Nelson, Josephs, & Williams, 1993). I also discovered, however, that recent studies have constructed a new view of the relationship of mathematics to culture, and in particular the significance of the mathematics developed by non-Western cultures. Terms such as *multicultural mathematics, indigenous mathematics, sociomathematics, spontaneous mathematics, oppressed mathematics, folk mathematics, culturally relevant mathematics,* and *ethnomathematics* are but a few that I discovered that have been coined in the endeavor to highlight non-European mathematical contributions.

Fundamental to endeavors to highlight the value of non-Western mathematical contributions is the view that mathematics is best understood in the social, economic, religious, and cultural context in which it was created, used, and valued, rather than as an abstract objective set of facts that exists free from any social context. This view of mathematics as a sociocultural construct was first discussed by Keyser (1932) and Wilder (1950, 1968, & 1981). Recently, as the multicultural view of education has displaced others such as the "melting-pot" and "superior-race" orientations, a wide range of endeavors have taken place worldwide to nurture people's appreciation of the power of mathematics in their ancestral cultures (Powell & Frankenstein, 1997c). This had a profound effect on "The Egypt Story."

In general, there currently seem to exist at least three major groups of educators pursuing multicultural mathematics endeavors. The fact that Western academic mathematics has become the mathematics taught in schools around the world greatly influences their endeavors.

One group primarily explores the nature of the non-Western mathematical systems of traditional peoples (Ascher, 1991, p. 1). This group is also concerned with the relationship of those mathematical systems to the cultures in which they exist or existed, and with difficulties that participants in those cultures can have in learning the Western academic mathematics currently taught in their schools (difficulties that arise because of discrepancies in cultural assumptions underlying their community culture and school mathematics). Recently these educators have begun studying the mathematics practiced among identifiable cultural groups both inside and outside of Western societies who have developed mathematical systems different from school mathematics. This includes labor groups, children of a certain age bracket, poor urban dwellers, and reservation Navahos (D'Ambrosio, 1985). Their merging of anthropological, mathematical, and educational explorations is typified by the work of Marcia Ascher (1991).

Another group is concerned with teaching mathematics to people living in non-Western cultures who are having difficulty learning the Western mathematics taught in their schools. The problem they confront is that many non-Western cultures have mathematical knowledge bases (linguistic, conceptual, informational, logical, and metacognitive systems) that make learning Western mathematics difficult for their members. The intent is to help members of these cultures learn both school mathematics and their indigenous mathematics in such a way that they become powerful users of mathematics who can liberate themselves from Western world views by embracing the value of their own culture. This merging of liberation pedagogy and mathematical instruction is typified by the work of Fasheh (1982) in Palestine.

Another group is concerned with teaching mathematics in European and American cultures that contain people from non-European cultures. Here we find British educators concerned with helping Indians and U.S. educators concerned with helping Hispanic Americans to learn both school mathematics and the mathematics of their indigenous ancestral cultures, become proud of themselves as budding mathematicians who originate from cultures that created original mathematical ideas, and feel powerful in their world as users of mathematics in a way that is consistent with the culture from which they originated and the culture in which they now find themselves. The work of Nelson, Joseph, and Williams (1993) in England and Zaslavsky (1996) in the United States is typical of this group. "The Egypt Story" is representative of this third type of endeavor.

CULTURALLY FREE OR CULTURALLY BOUND MATHEMATICS

While reading about ancient Egyptian mathematics, I discovered that I needed to confront three myths that relate mathematics and culture:

- Myth 1: Mathematics contains universal truths and a reasoning system that exist free of any cultural constraints.
- Myth 2: Contemporary mathematics is a creation of the people of Europe and North America.
- Myth 3: Contemporary school mathematics is consistent with the underlying social, political, religious, linguistic, and conceptual traditions of every world culture, and children from all cultures can with equal ease learn and use that mathematics.

These myths will now be examined.

Myth 1. Mathematics contains universal truths and a reasoning system that exist free of any cultural constraints.

This myth is highlighted in "The Egypt Story" numerous times. Doris's students discover that, unlike our current-day number system, the Egyptian number system had two sets of numerals (one for Pharaoh and his family and another for the rest of the population) and that this was a natural extension of their economic, social, political, and religious beliefs that saw Pharaoh as a god. They discover that the Egyptian measurement system was based on the length of Pharaoh's body parts, that our formula for a circle's area is different from the ancient Egyptian formula, that our multiplication algorithm is different from theirs, and that our methods of mathematical proof are different from those used in ancient Egypt (applying deductive methods to generalizable abstractions versus arguing from concrete particulars). When children discover these things, they are learning that different mathematical systems have existed and that the mathematical system of a culture can be an extension of its religious, social, political, economic, and cultural beliefs—that mathematics is not a set of universal truths free of any cultural constraints, but an extension of the underlying culture in which it exists.

How could this be? In mathematics are not answers correct or incorrect, unlike in history where observers' perspectives and interpretations make a difference? Is not the sum of the interior angles of any triangle equal to 180 degrees, $1 + 1 = 2$, and $7 + 5 = 12$ in France, China, and on the moon?

But is the sum of any triangle's interior angles always equal to 180 degrees? Is it true on the Earth's spherical surface? Think about one triangle, with one vertex at the North Pole and two vertices on the Equator, two sides of which run through San Francisco and New York. Compare it to a second triangle, with one vertex at the North Pole and two vertices on the Equator, two sides of which run through San Francisco and London. The base angles of both triangles, on the equator, are the same, but the sizes of their angles at the North Pole are different. Surprise! The sum of the three triangles' interior angles is neither the same nor equal to 180 degrees!

And do $1 + 1 = 2$ and $7 + 5 = 12$ in all circumstances? What about in ancient cultures that did not have a base ten number system? What about in current-day specialized mathematical systems—such as computer languages that use a binary number system (where $1 + 1 = 10$) or a base twelve number system (where $7 + 5 = 10$)? And why is it that in military time, which uses a 24-hour clock, 11:00 plus 2 hours equals 13:00 while in our normal time, which uses a 12-hour clock, it equals 1:00?

Unfortunately, there is not a single universal mathematical system that contains a single set of undeniable truths that are valid for all cultures, all times, and all situations. And things are even more complicated. For example, given the power of our Hindu-Arabic base ten number system, why might people want to use, let us say, Roman numerals rather then Hindu-Arabic numerals? Yet medieval Europeans between about 1200 and 1350 CE called the Hindu-Arabic base ten system the "work of the devil" and avoided using it, presumably because the Vatican denounced Hindu-Arabic numbers, viewing "the widespread use of an easy way to calculate as a means by which European merchants and craftsmen would become even more independent of the Church" (Anderson, 1997, p. 301). The mathematical truths and reasoning systems that we have considered to be "universal absolutes" do not exist free from any cultural, religious, political, economic, and technological constraints.

Even more important for our multicultural purposes, people during their everyday lives may come in contact with inconsistent mathematical systems. For example, Carraher, Carraher, and Schliemann (1985, 1987) identified two distinct mathematical subcultures that many Brazilian working-class children function in daily. One involves working in their parents' shops where they use mental addition and subtraction calculations that involve money. Here mathematical accuracy and calculation speed is critical, and mathematics is situated in a concrete social context. These same students also attend school where they learn different addition and subtractions algorithms. Their school mathematics is a paper-and-pencil endeavor that is intentionally decontextualized and generalized. These two subcultures of home and school coexist, and children add and subtract in both. However, the mathematical algorithms, attitudes toward the uses of mathematics, ways of construing mathematical meaning, level of generality at which the calculations take place, and media used for calculating (mental versus paper-and-pencil) are dramatically different (Carraher, Carraher, & Schliemann, 1985, 1987; Carraher, 1988; Nunes, Schliemann, & Carraher, 1993). In addition, both mathematical systems are equally viable even though they are psychologically incompatible.

What is important to recognize is that mathematics does not consist of universal truths that exist free of any cultural constraints. In mathematics we start with assumptions, and slight variations in assumptions can create very different mathematical systems. Unfortunately, or fortunately, slight variations in cultural assumptions about mathematics can create large variations in the mathematical knowledge bases of different cultures (and the knowledge base of children who grow up within them).

Myth 2. Contemporary mathematics is a creation of the people of Europe and North America.

A related myth is that mathematics was created during two time periods: in ancient Greece between about 600 BCE and 300 CE and in Europe and America since about 1400 CE, with a period of stagnation called the Dark Ages separating them.

"The Egypt Story" confronts these myths by portraying ancient Egyptian mathematics prior to the time in which Greek mathematics flourished.

The inaccuracy of these myths begins to become apparent when it is noted that the earliest proofs of the Pythagorean theorem are found in the ancient Chinese text *Chou Pei* and the ancient Indian texts of the *Sulbasutras,* which are conservatively dated between 1000 BCE and 600 BCE— prior to the birth of Pythagoras (Nelson, Joseph, & Williams, 1993, p. 13). In addition, many of the great Greek mathematicians (including Euclid, Ptolemy, Heron, Diophantus, Theon, Hypatia, Thales, Pythagoras, and Plato) studied and worked in Egypt, not Greece, with many attributing the origins of their creations to Egyptian mathematics (Bernal, 1992, p. 88; Lumpkin, 1997b, pp. 106-107).

In fact, the history of mathematics has its origins in Egypt, India, Babylonia, and China. Greeks, Indians, Chinese, Persians, and Arabs made later significant contributions. Their creations were brought to Europe by Moslem cultures through Africa, entering Europe by way of Sicily and Spain. And it is only within the last several hundred years that the contributions of western Europe were at all significant (Nelson, Joseph, & Williams, 1993, Ch. 1). Current-day mathematics is the result of the endeavors of peoples from many different cultures; it is truly a multicultural subject.

One of the goals of multicultural mathematics educators is to broaden our understanding of the history of mathematics and extinguish myths that inaccurately portray its evolution. Inaccurate beliefs about the evolution of mathematics include the following: that it evolved from primitive, non-Western cultures containing only a simple counting system to Western cultures with rich mathematical systems; that it evolved from cultures that deal with mathematics using concrete ways of thinking to those that use abstract thought; that it evolved from mathematically pre-logical cultures to those that are logical; and that it evolved from cultures that contextualize mathematics to those that decontextualize it. These Eurocentric myths no more accurately describe the history of mathematics than the idea that the Earth is the center of the universe accurately describes current views of astronomy.

When students finish "The Egypt Story," they have a good sense that mathematicians were active outside of Europe prior to the rise of the famous ancient Greek mathematicians who would, perhaps, be more accurately remembered for formalizing and extending the work of many great mathematicians from earlier cultures.

Myth 3. Contemporary school mathematics is consistent with the underlying social, political, religious, linguistic, and conceptual traditions of every world culture, and children from all cultures can with equal ease learn and use that mathematics.

Children learning "The Egypt Story" confront this myth when they decide whether or not Maria and Regi should teach ancient Egyptian children our multiplication algorithm. Thus far Doris's students have not had them do so because of their perception of the intellectual difficulties that would result from differences between our culture and that of ancient Egyptians.

This myth is problematic because recent research indicates that certain cultures do nurture in their members languages, systems of logic, world views, and ways of viewing spatial and temporal relations that are dramatically different from those of contemporary school mathematics. In addition, research indicates that such differences can make the learning of contemporary academic mathematics (that is based on Western religious, linguistic, philosophical, logical, and conceptual traditions) difficult for children from non-Western cultures (Atweh, Forgasz, & Nebres, 2001; Powell & Frankenstein, 1997b; Trentacosta & Kenney, 1997).

Reflect on how meaningless the following activities might be for the designated students: South Americans who have never heard of baseball solving statistics problems about baseball; Africans who live in round single-story houses solving volume problems about rectangular skyscrapers that they have never seen; children who have never played a game of chance learning probability by using dice. Asking children to build mathematical knowledge on a foundation of unfamiliar cultural information can hinder their construction of new understanding from existing meaning.

The level of abstraction of different cultures' referents that vary from concrete to abstract can also influence children's ability to learn school mathematics. For example, Waqainabete (1996) points out the effect of the level of abstraction of contextual cues on her fellow Fijians when she says,

> The mathematics curriculum . . . in the Fijian education system is too abstract and very much geared toward a Westernized culture. Generally, the Fijian student fails or achieves poorly in the Mathematics examination because there is no correlation between the Mathematics learnt in school and the life lead at village level. (p. 315)

What this means for Waqainabete is that school mathematics is more difficult for Fijians because of the level of abstraction of its referents than it is for children from cultures where the norm is to think in terms of the level of abstraction of the curriculum's referents. Waqainabete wants the objects, actions, and knowledge referred to in the curriculum to be connected to familiar concrete elements of indigenous Fijian culture, such as Fijian measuring systems, Fijian "wood carving, weaving, . . . cloth dying, pottery, canoes, . . . decorations of household objects," and "house building activities" (Stillman & Balatti, 2001, p. 315).

In addition, the degree to which the semantic and syntactic structure of a culture's language is consistent with that of school mathematics can affect the ease with which children learn and use mathematics. For example, in China students with certain dialects "experience difficulties reading multi-digit numerals, such as 7,612,439, without first pointing and naming from right to left the place value of each digit before knowing how to read the '7' in the millions place and the rest of the numeral" (Powell & Frankenstein, 1997a, p. 251). Powell (1986) suggests that the reason is because the semantic and syntactic structure of their dialect imposes numerical delimiters at intervals of every four digits, which is quite different from the Western linguistic structure of imposing numerical delimiters at intervals of every three digits. How might you function if you had to read 5678,5678,5678 using someone else's place value language (made up of groups of four digits), as compared to reading 567,567,567 using your familiar Western place value language? And what conceptual difficulties might you experience if you had to accurately represent the first number (with its four-unit place value structure) with base ten blocks that only have three shapes, cube, long, and flat? This is an example of how a culture's linguistic structure can cause its members cognitive and linguistic difficulties while learning Western academic mathematics.

Let us also examine an example from geometry. Harris (1991) studied certain subcultures of Australian aborigines to discover how they determine orientation and location. In Western mathematics we use a relativistic *local* system of orientation involving right, left, front, and back and a relativistic *global* system of orientation involving Cartesian coordinates with positive and negative directions on the x and y axes. Aborigines use only an absolute north, south, east, west system of orientation, even when dealing with objects only a few feet from them. (A person might be 3 feet to the *north* of them, never 3 feet *in front* of them.) Their indigenous language and culture do not support a relativistic local or global system of orientation and location. When they enter a mathematics class, they have great difficulty with the relativistic system supported by Western school mathematics and only want to use their absolute system.

At a deeper level there can exist major conceptual differences between the knowledge bases of a culture and that of school mathematics. For example, Navaho concepts of time and space are inconsistent with the Western concepts taught in school mathematics. Even though we Westerners know that 5 minutes may feel shorter when we are excited than when we are bored, we assume that mathematical time is truth and psychological time is just a figment of our imaginations. Similarly, even though we Westerners know that walking 5 miles may seem shorter when we are energetic than when we are tired, or when we know where we are than when we are lost, we assume that mathematical distance is truth and psychological distance is just a figment of our imaginations. We assume that time and distance are measured by a consistently calibrated measuring device (a mechanical clock that operates independently of location or time of day, and a ruler whose length and units do not increase or decrease depending upon where one is located). But this is not the case in Navaho culture in which time and distance are calibrated by where you are located and what you are doing and feeling and not simply determined by an inhuman machine that you wear on your wrist or carry in your pocket (Pinxten, 1997, p. 394). For Navahos, 5 minutes and 5 miles may be different when they are near home versus far from home because time, space, and distance are circularly defined in terms of each other rather than arbitrarily defined in terms of absolute standards. What happens to Navahos, who learn Navaho concepts in their family and community, when they have to learn school mathematics? According to Pinxten, overlaying Western and Navaho mathematics leads to such cognitive confusion that the result is mathematical "misunderstanding and sociocultural and psychological alienation of Navaho children and adults." (1997, p. 394).

When we consider culturally learned metacognitive problem-solving strategies, it is also possible to see that school mathematics is not compatible with every world culture and how discrepancies can make mathematics easier or more difficult for children depending on which metacognitive problem-solving and thinking strategies they learn in their family and community. As discussed in a previous chapter, a major difference between expert and novice problem solvers is the degree to which they can self-regulate and self-monitor their thinking. Research of Heath (1983) on three communities in the same American town indicated different approaches to self-regulation. In one community children were taught to be highly self-regulating, in another to be moderately self-regulating, and in the other to be impulsive, spontaneous, impetuous, and passionate in their thinking and behavior. If the appropriate degree of self-regulation and self-monitoring (in such things as exploring different problem-solving strategies before embracing one to execute) is a prerequisite for success in mathematics, and if these things are learned from birth as part of family and community culture, then how can we expect children who have learned to be "excessively" self-regulating or "excessively" impulsive (in comparison to what is required for success in mathematics) to do as well in school as children raised in communities where the levels of such metacognitive skills match the levels required for mathematical success? In fact, Heath's research points out that children raised in communities whose cultures emphasized either extreme self-regulation or extreme impulsivity did far less well in school than other children.

The Western interpretation of mathematics that is taught in schools around the world is not consistent with the underlying social, political, religious, linguistic, and conceptual traditions of every world culture. In fact, it can be so incompatible with certain cultures that the differences can severely interfere with children's ability to learn mathematics in school and can interfere with their normal intellectual functioning outside of school (Gerdes, 1997b, p. 225).

Cautions

Five cautions need mention with respect to the above and future discussions. First, some people believe that if teachers are culturally, socioeconomically, and sexually blind so that they cannot see student differences, then they will teach all students identically and all students will learn mathematics equally well. This belief coexists with the assumption that the reason why all students do not achieve equally well is because of preferential treatment of certain students by teachers. Research indicates, however, that factors related to equal access to mathematics are not so much correlated to the preferential treatment of students by teachers as they are correlated to the very nature of school mathematics and schooling conditions (Ambrose, Levi, & Fennema, 1997). Rather than blinding themselves, educators should sensitize themselves to student attributes and hidden cultural biases of school mathematics and school environments. Then, perhaps, they can figure out how to adapt schooling to the nature of their students.

Second, the correlation between the student culture and the culture of school mathematics is not the only factor affecting mathematical achievement. There are hidden biases in the social and political environment of schools that can make mathematics more difficult for some students to learn than others. Social and political assumptions underlying students' family and community cultures can also be incompatible with assumptions underlying the social and political environment of schools.

Third, this chapter has addressed the relationship between culture and mathematics. However, people are products of both their cultural upbringing and biologically inherited characteristics. Both affect children's ability to learn.

Fourth, educators need to be wary of stereotyping students and assuming that all students fit a particular profile. During the last 30 years researchers provided profiles of socio-economic and cultural groups that relate to student achievement. For example, Shade (1989), Hilliard (1989), Stiff (1990), and Stiff and Harvey (1988) argued that the African American culture is incompatible with the culture of school mathematics because of the following attributes of African Americans: learning by working in social groups that nurture interpersonal relationship, telling spontaneous stories that may not seem to relate to the task they are working on, needing to be mobile and physically active while learning, and learning through oral discourse rather than reading and writing.[1] In contrast, school mathematics is viewed as requiring student attributes such as working independently, working in a very structured, orderly, and sedentary manner, and learning through literate media of instruction such as reading, writing, and diagramming. There is danger in stereotyping students and assuming that all students who belong to a particular group conform to its profile. We need to be aware that "generalizations about a *group* of people often lead to naïve inferences about *individual* members of that group" that do the individual members a great disservice because "within a group, the variations among individuals are as great as their commonalities" (Guild, 1995, pp. 17, 19).

Fifth, consequences of discrepancies between the students' culturally influenced mathematical knowledge base and that of school mathematics are more complex than herein presented. For example, scholars worry that many African Americans (to continue the previous example) suffer emotional dysfunction as a result of these discrepancies because their culture (supposedly) nourishes loyalty to social-group norms. The consequence is that many African Americans who can perform well in mathematics choose not to do so in order to maintain affiliation with peers who have difficulty with mathematics, while those who choose to do well in mathematics are seen as disloyal to peers who perform poorly in mathematics and as a result suffer social rejection, isolation, and alienation (Moody, 2001).

MANY MATHEMATICAL SYSTEMS EXIST TODAY

Many mathematical knowledge bases exist in our world today. Just as health care workers, lawyers, accountants, and police within a single society have specialized ways of communicating among themselves—each with a specialized language, knowledge base, and world view that allows them to give meaning to their world—so do mathematicians have rather unique ways of speaking to each other about mathematics. In addition, if we just consider health care workers, we discover that many distinct subgroups of health care workers exist, each with its own subculture. For example, the views of general practitioners, surgeons, physical therapists, psychologists, Christian Science nurses, acupuncturists, and herbalists are quite different from each other. Similarly, so too do there exist within most modern-day cultures multiple subgroups of people who view mathematics from very different perspectives and who have different mathematical knowledge bases. That two or more ways of communicating and thinking about mathematics can exist within a single culture or between cultures is of critical importance to this discussion.

As previously mentioned, Carraher, Carraher, and Schliemann's research highlights two different mathematical knowledge bases that currently exist in Brazil. One involves practical mathematical endeavors that take place in marketplaces and occupations where orally guided mental calculations are the norm. Here mathematics is highly intuitive, crucial to economic survival, and tied to particular circumstances in which it arises. Its canons of beauty rest on criteria of accuracy and ease of use. Another mathematical knowledge base is taught in schools. It is primarily a decontextualized paper-and-pencil endeavor in which logical relationships internal to the mathematical system itself are of prime importance. Its canons of beauty rest on deductive derivation from abstract axioms and consistency within a larger mathematical system (Carraher, Carraher, & Schliemann, 1985, 1987; Carraher, 1988; Nunes, Schliemann, & Carraher, 1993).

Just as these two different approaches to mathematics exist in Brazil, they also exist in many other places in our world. Accepting this leads to three points that we must deal with:

- Many very different culturally based mathematical systems have existed in the past and currently exist in our world.
- Each of these mathematical systems has inherent within it both a knowledge base and an accompanying set of cultural values.
- It is currently the practice to promote and value only one of these many possible mathematical systems within schools.

These points, which have already been introduced, need further elaboration because many of us who have been exposed to only one mathematical system (the one recently taught in schools) may need the points more directly related to our knowledge base. To do so, we will describe five subtraction algorithms used during the last century and present the history of why we use our current subtraction algorithm. The purpose here is to illustrate the abovementioned three points. However, also observe how the mathematics we learned in school can trap us into conceptualizing the subject in only one way when several viable options exist.

Models of Subtraction

The presentation of each subtraction algorithm that follows begins with an example of the type of written work a child might record while using the algorithm and the type of utterances a child might make that accompany the written work. The words in parentheses that are part of the utterances have been added to help the reader follow what is occurring and are unlikely to be uttered by a child.

Trading Model

Exhibit 10.1 Trading Model

$$
\begin{array}{cccc}
\begin{array}{r} 6\ 5\ 2 \\ -\ 2\ 7\ 6 \\ \hline \end{array}
&
\begin{array}{r} 6\ \overset{4}{\cancel{5}}\ {}^{1}2 \\ -\ 2\ 7\ 6 \\ \hline 6 \end{array}
&
\begin{array}{r} \overset{5}{\cancel{6}}\ \overset{14}{\cancel{5}}\ {}^{1}2 \\ -\ 2\ 7\ 6 \\ \hline 6 \end{array}
&
\begin{array}{r} \overset{5}{\cancel{6}}\ \overset{14}{\cancel{5}}\ {}^{1}2 \\ -\ 2\ 7\ 6 \\ \hline 3\ 7\ 6 \end{array}
\end{array}
$$

Subtract 276 from 652. First I need to take 6 from 2. I can't do it, so I have to trade from the tens. Cross out the 5 (tens). Make the 5 (tens) into 4 (tens) and then trade so the 2 (ones) become 12 (ones). Now I can take 6 from 12, and I have 6 left. Record the 6. Now I need to take 7 (tens) from 4 (tens). I can't do it, so I have to trade (from the hundreds). Cross out the 6 (hundreds). Make the 6 (hundreds) into 5 (hundreds) and then trade so the 4 (tens) become 14 (tens). Now I can take 7 (tens) from 14 (tens), and I have 7 (tens) left. Record the 7 (tens). Now I can take 2 (hundreds) from 5 (hundreds), and I have 3 (hundred) left. Record the 3 (hundred).

The *trading model* is the most common subtraction algorithm taught in schools today. In it all *trades* (decompositions, rearrangements, and recompositions) take place within the 652, which is understood to be 6 hundred + 5 tens + 2 ones, which in turn (by mathematicians) is assumed to be equal to $6 \times 10^2 + 5 \times 10^1 + 2 \times 10^0$. This (in the abstract generalizable form of $A \times 10^2 + B \times 10^1 + C \times 10^0$) is the standard way mathematicians write numbers so that they can use generalized algebraic proofs to demonstrate that this method of subtraction works, and, in fact, relate the proof of subtraction to those of the other arithmetic operations. The proof that it is possible to trade (decompose, rearrange, and recompose) between columns within a number such as 652 while maintaining the value of that number (which is offered in more generalized algebraic terms than presented here) goes something like this:

$$652 =$$
$$6 \text{ hundreds} + 5 \text{ tens} + 2 \text{ones} =$$
$$6 \times 10^2 + 5 \times 10^1 + 2 \times 10^0 =$$
$$6 \times 10^2 + (5 - 1) \times 10^1 + (2 + 10) \times 10^0 = \quad \textit{(trade 1 ten for 10 ones)}$$
$$6 \times 10^2 + 4 \times 10^1 + 12 \times 10^0 =$$
$$(6 - 1) \times 10^2 + (4 + 10) \times 10^1 + 12 \times 10^0 = \quad \textit{(trade 1 hundred for 10 tens)}$$
$$5 \times 10^2 + 14 \times 10^1 + 12 \times 10^0$$

In a more abstract and generalizable form (preferred by mathematicians), the notation looks like this:

$$A \times 10^2 + B \times 10^1 + C \times 10^0 = (A - 1) \times 10^2 + (B - 1 + 10) \times 10^1 + (C + 10) \times 10^0$$

What has made this subtraction algorithm popular among mathematicians and educators is the power of this type of algebraic notation and these types of abstract axiomatic deductive proofs to prove in a single consistent manner all of the methods of arithmetic we currently use in schools. Being able to do this has been one of the great accomplishments of mathematics within the last several hundred years. The method's popularity among mathematicians and mathematics educators for these reasons is what led them to convince the educational community that it should be the only method taught in schools. Following the advice of mathematicians, educators promoted this method over others, and in less than 60 years it became a standard part of the school curriculum—and a tradition that many of us erroneously believe has been part of the school curriculum for centuries.

Equal Addition Model

Exhibit 10.2   Equal Addition Model

$$
\begin{array}{ccccc}
\begin{array}{r} 6\;5\;2 \\ -\,2\;7\;6 \\ \hline \end{array}
&
\begin{array}{r} 6\;5\;\overset{1}{2} \\ -\,2\;\overset{8}{\cancel{7}}\;6 \\ \hline 6 \end{array}
&
\begin{array}{r} \overset{1}{6}\;\overset{1}{5}\;\overset{1}{2} \\ -\,\overset{3}{\cancel{2}}\;\overset{8}{\cancel{7}}\;6 \\ \hline 6 \end{array}
&
\begin{array}{r} \overset{1}{6}\;\overset{1}{5}\;\overset{1}{2} \\ -\,\overset{3}{\cancel{2}}\;\overset{8}{\cancel{7}}\;6 \\ \hline 3\;7\;6 \end{array}
\end{array}
$$

Subtract 276 from 652. First I need to take 6 from 2. I can't do it, so I add 10 to the 2 (in the ones column, top number) to get 12, and I add 1 (ten) to the 7 (tens, in the tens column, bottom number) to get 8 (tens). I cross out the 7 (tens) and put an 8 next to it (in the tens column), and I put a 1 next to the 2 to show it is 12 (ones). I can now subtract 6 (ones) from 12 (ones) and I have 6 left. Record the 6. Now I need to take 8 (tens) from 5 (tens). I can't do it, so I add 10 (tens) to the 5 (tens, in the tens column, top number) to get 15 (tens), and I add 1 (hundred = 10 tens) to the 2 (hundreds, in the hundreds column, bottom number) to get 3 (hundreds). I cross out the 2 (hundreds) and put a 3 next to it (in the hundreds column), and I put a 1 (ten) next to the 5 (tens) to show it is 15 (tens). Now I can take 8 (tens) from 15 (tens), and I have 7 (tens) left. Record the 7 (tens). Now I can take 3 (hundreds) from 6 (hundreds), and I have 3 (hundred) left. Record the 3 (hundred).

The *equal addition model* was a very common model of subtraction taught until about half a century ago. It was revived briefly in some school districts during the 1980s, under the belief that the equal addition process was easier for children to understand than the trading process because it more closely corresponds with their natural intellectual processes. Underlying this subtraction algorithm are the simple provable assumptions that adding the same amount (in this case 10 or 100) to the subtrahend and minuend of a subtraction problem leaves the problem unchanged $[a - b = (a + x) - (b + x) = a + x - b - x = a - b]$.

and that when doing the adding of 10 you can add 10 in the ones place of the minuend and 1 in the tens place of the subtrahend, and that when doing the adding of 100 you can add 10 (tens) in the tens place of the minuend and 1 (hundred) in the hundreds place of the subtrahend. This subtraction algorithm requires no more writing than the trading model and no more intellectual work than the trading model. However, the trading model displaced it because it did not correspond with the new ways in which mathematicians proved the basic arithmetic operations in a consistent manner using algebra.

Left-Handed Model

Exhibit 10.3   Left-Handed Model

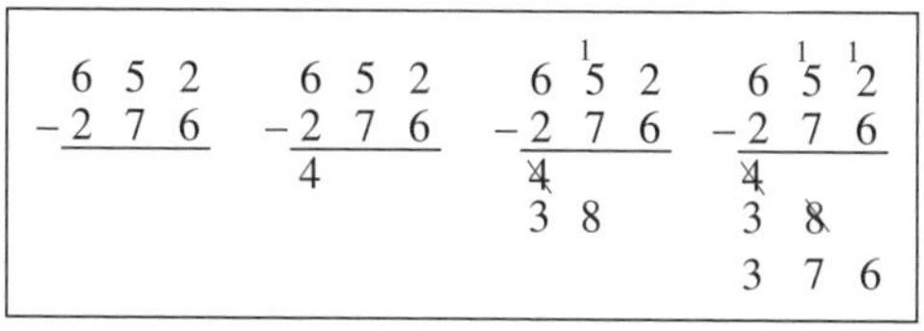

Subtract 276 from 652. First I need to take 2 (hundred) from 6 (hundred). I have 4 (hundred) left. Record it. Now I have to take 7 (tens) from 5 (tens). I can't do it, so I decompose 4 (hundred) into 3 (hundred) and 10 (tens). I record the 3 (hundred) under the 4 (hundred) and add the 10 (tens) to the 5 (tens) to get 15 (tens). Now I can take 7 (tens) from 15 (tens). I have 8 (tens) left. I record the 8 (tens) next to the 3 (hundred). Now I have to take 6 (ones) from 2 (ones). I can't do it, so I decompose 38 (tens) into 37 (tens) and 10 (ones). I record the 37 (tens) under the 38 and add the 10 (ones) to the 2 (ones) to get 12 (ones). Now I take 6 (ones) from 12 (ones), and I have 6 (ones) left. I record the 6 (ones) next to the 37 and my answer is 376.

The *left-handed model* is a close relative to the trading model. The difference is that it deals with the digits with the greatest value first. This seems to make more sense than starting with the digits of least value. For example, in the real world of money one would always be more concerned with the number of dollars one has than with the number of pennies. This sensible way of doing subtraction has recently been revived by educators who noticed that children, when left to their own devices, invent a left to right subtraction algorithm similar to this. It was replaced by the trading model in schools because its procedures do not correspond with the abstract algebraic methods of proving modern mathematics that operate only on the minuend. Again, the values of mathematicians that reside in "modern mathematical methods of generalizable proof" won out over values concerned with a sensible way of proceeding or consistency with children's invented mathematical structures.

Shopkeeper's Model

Exhibit 10.4　Shopkeeper's Model

```
  6 5 2       6 5 2       6 5 2
- 2 7 6     - 2 7 6     - 2 7 6
                  4             4
                2 0           2 0
              3 0 0         3 0 0
                5 2           5 2
                            3 7 6
```

In this subtraction problem I need to find out what has to be added to 276 to get 652. Adding 4 to 276 will get me up to 280. Record 4. Adding 20 to 280 will get me up to 300. Record 20. Adding 300 to 300 will get me up to 600. Record 300. Adding 52 to 600 will get me up to 652. Record it. I have reached 652, so now add the numbers recorded. 4 + 20 + 300 + 52 is 376, which is my answer. Record the 376.

The *shopkeeper's model* is a popular model throughout the world. One need only enter any store in which employees do not use automatic cash registers or paper and pencil and listen to them make change to hear it at work. You will hear things like this as first pennies, then dimes, and finally dollars are handed to the customer, "You gave me $5.00 and your bill is $2.76 so here is your change: $.01 + $.01 + $.01 + $.01 makes $2.80 + $.10 + $.10 makes $3.00 + $1.00 + $1.00 makes $5.00."[2] The shopkeeper's model of subtraction is a very practical and efficient way of doing subtraction that primarily uses oral methods of calculation. It is usually used in practical problems involving the exchange of goods where merchants make change. It is the type of oral method described by Carraher, Carraher, and Schliemann's research (1985, 1987) in Brazil, the type that children learned in the marketplace rather than in school. It has been replaced by the trading model because its calculation methods do not correspond with the more abstract algebraic methods of modern mathematics that unify the way in which all arithmetic algorithms are approached in a single consistent manner. Here the value of ease of use has been subjugated to the value of approaching all arithmetic operations in a single consistent, abstract, algebraic manner that corresponds with recently developed methods of mathematical proof.

Complementary Model

Exhibit 10.5　Complementary Model

```
  6 5 2
- 2 7 6
  3 7 6
```

Subtract 276 from 652. $10 - 6$ is 4, $4 + 2$ is 6, and record 6 (in the ones column). Now, $9 - 7$ is 2, $2 + 5$ is 7, and record 7 (in the tens column). Finally $9 - 2$ is 7, $7 + 6$ is 13, throw away the ten and 3 is left, and record the 3 (in the hundreds column). The answer is 376.

The *complementary model* is more efficient and less subject to errors than most other models. The internal parts of the problem are all done without paper and pencil, either by quietly uttering to oneself or by vocalizing aloud. In addition, one need only know how to subtract the numbers from 0 to 9 from the number 9 or the number 10, and need not memorize any of the subtraction facts involving numbers greater than 10 (for example $13 - 5$).

What is going on during the process? The user of the complementary model visualizes (without writing) the digits 9, 9, and 10 to be located between 652 and 276, as in the diagram below. To do the problem the user then, within each column, subtracts the subtrahend from the middle number, adds the difference to the minuend, and records the result at the bottom of the column. For the given problem, in the ones column the user thinks: "$10 - 6$ is 4, $4 + 2$ is 6, and record the 6 below."

Exhibit 10.6   Complementary Model Dynamics

$$
\begin{array}{r}
6\ \ 5\ \ 2 \\
{\scriptstyle 9\ \ \ 9\ \ 10} \\
-\,2\ \ 7\ \ 6 \\
\hline
3\ \ 7\ \ 6
\end{array}
$$

In the tens column the user thinks: "$9 - 7$ is 2, $2 + 5$ is 7, and record the 7 below." While in the hundreds column the user thinks: "$9 - 2$ is 7, $7 + 6$ is 13, throw away the ten and 3 is left, and record the 3 below." Very simple, and it works no matter what size the number: one need only imagine a 10 in the ones column and 9s in all of the other columns.

Exhibit 10.7   Complementary Model Proof

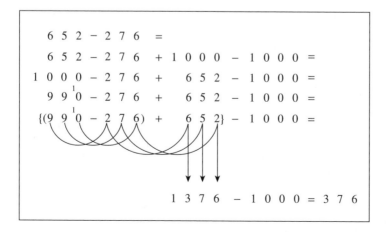

Why does it work? The preceding calculations show what is occurring. In step 2, adding and subtracting 1000 leaves the equation unchanged. In step 3, numbers are now rearranged, which leaves the equation unchanged. In step 4, the number 1000 is rewritten as 99^10 (1000 is decomposed, rearranged, and recomposed until 10 ones reside in the ones column). In step 5, numbers are now grouped and calculations take place, column by column, in accordance with the arrows: $10 - 6 + 2 = 6$ and record it in the ones column; $9 - 7 + 5 = 7$ and record it in the tens column; $9 - 2 + 6 = 13$ and record it in the hundreds column to get 1376; subtract 1000 from the 1376 to get 376.

Three things need to be mentioned about the complementary method. First, this type of proof would have been considered a very adequate proof at one time in our mathematical history. It is a proof for a specific set of numbers and one can understand how to generalize with a little imagination. This type of proof, however, is no longer adequate, for it refers to a specific situation and cannot be easily generalized for all whole numbers; to accomplish that it would be necessary to use abstract deductive methods of proof along with algebraic symbolism. Second, there is a patch that you need to know: if in a problem you get more than 9 as your final sum in a column, you just trade the ten to the next column. (For example, in $6543 - 1828$ you would say "$10 - 8 + 3 = 5$ and write a 5 in the ones column; $9 - 2 + 4 = 11$ and write a 1 in the tens column and trade a 10 into the hundreds column; $9 - 8 + 5 + 1$ (that you traded over) $= 7$ and write a 7 in the hundreds column; $9 - 1 + 6 = 14$ and subtract 10 leaves 4, which is written in the thousands column for a final answer of 4715. Third, the complementary model—even though it is perhaps the least intellectually taxing of all models and the one that produces the fastest answer with the least writing—has been replaced by the trading model because that method corresponds more closely with modern mathematics.

These five models of subtraction need to be discussed in a historical context to more fully understand why the trading model has replaced the others in school mathematics.

Historical Context

The history that needs to be understood goes back to ancient Egyptian times, when any method that gave accurate answers to mathematical problems was probably used. If two different methods were available to solve the same type of problem, the one that seemed to give the best answer was probably used if a demonstration of why it worked could be presented. Demonstrations illustrated specific instances, and then generalizations were made from specifics.

Ancient Egyptians promoted the distinction between "godly" ("scholarly") mathematics and "practical" mathematics—which reflected their distinction between what is suited for Pharaoh (a god) and his scholarly advisors versus the common man. The ancient Greeks continued the bifurcation of mathematics as they distinguished between practical mathematics used by workers versus theoretical mathematics for the ruling elite (D'Ambrosio, 1997b, p. 16). The Greeks also popularized the belief (possibly as an extension of the Egyptian pharaohic distinction) that mathematics was a godly subject, that the world was built on mathematical principles, and that mathematics was a complete, consistent, and understandable subject.

Unfortunately, Greek mathematicians discovered some mathematical imperfections they could not explain, such as their inability to exactly determine the length of the diagonal of a square with a side of length one. (We now call this "irrational" length the square root of two.)

Greek mathematicians also formed secret societies that hid from the uninitiated both mathematical knowledge and mathematical imperfections. One can only speculate that perhaps the reason for hiding mathematical knowledge and imperfections from the uninitiated was to promote the belief among the general public that mathematicians and mathematics should be held in high esteem.

Over time European mathematicians borrowed ideas from many cultures and discovered many things about mathematics that they could not explain—such as imaginary numbers (it could not be imagined how they could exist). But if useful mathematics was discovered that helped solve problems, that mathematics was sanctioned even though it might not be completely explainable.

In Europe the ancient Egyptian practice of accepting and using any information or algorithms that seemed to provide correct answers to problems continued, even if the mathematics being used could not be rigorously proved. Over time European mathematics thus became a collection of disjointed algorithms, information, and conjectures that did not relate to each other in any consistent manner. The ancient Greek practice of allowing the masses to continue to believe that mathematics was a special subject that was perfect, provable, and completely understandable by mathematicians also continued.

By the eighteenth century, European mathematicians became sufficiently distressed by the disjointed collection of not-so-rigorously proved knowledge called mathematics that they set out to reconstruct it. They wanted all of the separate pieces of mathematical knowledge to be related to each other in a single consistent manner using the same methods of rigorous proof, symbolism, and underlying axioms.

By the beginning of the twentieth century, mathematicians were excited because they had made significant progress toward unifying mathematics, rigorously proving it, generalizing it by making it abstract and decontextualized, and relating all mathematical knowledge to all other mathematical knowledge. They had been able to clean up the mess inherited from centuries of mathematical endeavors.

By the middle of the twentieth century, mathematicians thought their job of cleaning up the mess they inherited was almost complete. In their excitement over their new mathematics, mathematicians pushed to revise school mathematics so that its knowledge base, methods, and algorithms reflected the knowledge base, methods, and algorithms of professional mathematics.

Trading subtraction fits into this new consistent system of rigorously proved abstract mathematics. As a result, it became the subtraction model included in the "new school mathematics" that was born during the middle of the twentieth century. As the new school mathematics was implemented worldwide, trading subtraction replaced the other methods that existed.

Mathematics and Values

When one algorithm (and its corresponding mathematical system's knowledge base) replaces another, more is occurring than simply switching algorithms. Profound changes in mathematical and educational value systems are also taking place, changes that are similar to replacing one mathematical paradigm by another. Values based on rigor, consistency, and generalizability replaced other values. These new values (perhaps unknowingly) were held to be of greater importance than other values that emphasize accuracy (shopkeeper's model), efficiency and speed (complementary model), sensible ways of attending to the most important information available before the least important (left-handed model), mental calculations over written calculations (shopkeeper's model), or correspondence with natural intellectual processes (equal addition model).

It is not by accident that in current school mathematics we use trading subtraction. It a result of deliberately (although perhaps unknowingly) embracing a particular knowledge base and a particular set of values—a set of values that holds rigorous proof, abstract generalizable symbolism, and consistency of explanation of a unified body of knowledge to be of the greatest worth from among a variety of other possible values.

These are not values we have to embrace. They are values we have chosen to embrace. (In fact, perhaps one of the reasons why some people may want school mathematics to go back to the basics is that they desire to return to a value system that emphasizes such things as accuracy or efficiency over rigorous deductive mathematical proof.)

The significance of this is that *many very different culturally based mathematical systems have existed in the past and currently exist in our world.* The subtraction algorithms just presented are only one small part of five mathematical systems that have existed during the last hundred years. Most are still used in different parts of the world by millions of people. In addition, within our culture and the rest of the world, many different mathematical systems continue to exist. *Each of these mathematical systems has inherent both a knowledge base and an accompanying set of cultural values.* Frequently the knowledge base and values of school mathematics are inconsistent with those of a particular family, community, or culture. This often presents significant learning difficulties for children from those families, communities, and cultures because *it is currently the practice to promote and value only one of many possible mathematical systems within schools.* Teachers, most of whom have been taught only one set of mathematical algorithms and values, need to understand this if they are to adequately serve the diverse student bodies that populate many of our schools.

ENDNOTES

1. Similarly, Cox and Ramirez (1981) and Vasquez (1991) concluded that Mexican Americans favor interpersonal and global learning styles, while Shade (1989), More (1990), and Bert and Bert (1992) concluded that Native Americans favor visual, reflective, and contextualized learning styles.

2. A variation on this might sound like, "You gave me $5 and your bill is $2.76 so $2.76 (give back 4¢), $2.80 (give back 20¢), $3.00 (give back $1), $4.00 (give back $1), $5.00" or without actions written in, "$2.76, $2.80, $3.00, $4.00, $5.00."

Chapter 11

MULTICULTURAL MATHEMATICS INSTRUCTION

When Doris and I speak about "The Egypt Story," we speak about its content and its method of presentation. When we speak about "content," we discuss such things as ancient Egyptian algorithms and formulas. When we speak about instructional "methods," we discuss such things as its learning activities and its oral mode of presentation.

This chapter addresses issues of how to teach multicultural mathematics. It begins with an examination of methodological dimensions of "The Egypt Story" in comparison to traditional school mathematics, proceeds to a discussion of why it might be difficult for children from certain types of families, communities, or cultures to excel in school mathematics, and concludes with a discussion of pedagogical issues related to multicultural education.

METHODOLOGICAL ISSUES

"The Egypt Story"

When Doris Lawson tells "The Egypt Story," she is telling a multicultural mathematics story that has five features that need elaboration.

First, Doris's method of teaching—through oral storytelling—parallels one of the most important ways that ancient Egyptians passed on their culture from one generation to the next. The major instructional medium of ancient Egyptian culture was probably oral storytelling, which is very different from the highly literate instructional medium of school mathematics. More oral media are characteristic of cultures in which the primary modes of daily communication are through oral interactions, as compared to the written word. Ancient Egypt was such a culture.

That Doris's instructional medium is the same as that used by ancient Egyptians in teaching similar content raises questions about the effect of the instructional medium on the ideas being conveyed. What happens to ideas developed in a more oral culture when they are translated into forms deliverable through a highly literate (or visual) culture, if it is desired that those ideas are to be understood in the cultural context in which they were invented or used?

Second, during "The Egypt Story" Doris aligns the primary instructional method she uses with the primary instructional method used in many of her students' families and communities so that she can make mathematics more easily accessible to them than if she used only the highly literate instructional medium of traditional mathematics instruction.

This relates to issues of matching student learning styles and thinking styles with instructional methods and media. From a sociocultural perspective, families, communities, and cultures teach their young learning and thinking styles that facilitate their learning of their family and community culture. The learning and thinking styles they acquire in their home, however, may be both different from and inconsistent with those required during school mathematics instruction. "The Egypt Story" can be viewed as a multicultural endeavor because it provides students with an intellectual bridge between the instructional media of their home and that of their school mathematics classroom. How to create bridges between home and school cultures is one of the concerns of multicultural mathematics educators.

Third, "The Egypt Story" provides a multicultural approach to mathematics because it simultaneously presents mathematics and culture. Many multicultural mathematics curricula only present the mathematics of cultures, without relating it to other aspects of their cultures. For example, stand-alone multicultural worksheets that present the ancient Egyptian numeration system with little mention of ancient Egyptian culture are common. In contrast, while presenting the mathematics of ancient Egypt, Doris presents information about its dualistic society, religious beliefs, architecture, clothing patterns, and games. In "The Egypt Story" mathematics is not treated as something separate from culture but as something that is a part of culture.

Multicultural mathematics educators attempt to maintain a dual focus on both culture and mathematics. Part of what this means is presenting mathematics in its indigenous cultural context (rather than in the foreign context of contemporary school mathematics).

Fourth, "The Egypt Story" provides a multicultural approach to mathematics because Doris asks her students to temporarily suspend their conception of objective reality and use their imagination, fantasy, and intuition to try to experience ancient Egyptian culture in ways that she believes ancient Egyptian children might have experienced it (within Doris's conception of the nature of that culture and the limits of what is possible). She asks her students to project themselves into another culture, to pretend to experience that culture firsthand, and to personally participate in activities that are similar to those that members of that culture might have experienced. Doris does not ask her students to learn ancient Egyptian mathematics through abstract impersonal decontextualized presentations of it. She has her students imagine themselves solving the same problems as ancient Egyptians, playing the same mathematics games as ancient Egyptians (the snake game playing board was found in ancient Egyptian tombs), listening to the same scolding as novice scribes in ancient Egypt ("Tuauf's Scolding" is a free translation of two ancient Egyptian texts in the British Museum, "Satire of the Trades" [Olivastro, 1993, pp. 32, 33] and "Teachings" [Stead, 1986, p. 21]), creating clothing patterns as ancient Egyptians might have, and watching mathematical magicians perform just as ancient Egyptians might have. This helps children in one culture get a better feel for another culture by allowing them to see it as an insider might.

Fifth, "The Egypt Story" is multicultural because Doris helps students learn—to the degree possible—using the objects, artifacts, myths, ideas, customs, beliefs, mathematical processes, and knowledge base that were familiar to ancient Egyptians. She does not only use the highly literate instructional materials of current-day academic mathematics (such as abstract decontextualized paper-and-pencil worksheets). Her students play mathematics games using the same game boards as ancient Egyptians (using the snake game), design paddle doll clothing as ancient Egyptians might have, use the same measuring units that ancient Egyptians might have, study the same proof for the area of a circle as ancient Egyptians might have (from problems 41, 42, 43, 48, and 50 of the *Rhind Mathematical Papyrus* [1927]), and work with religious images familiar to ancient Egyptians (the tomb cards contain copies of actual paintings and statuary from ancient Egypt).

Using familiar objects, artifacts, social practices, and customs of a people to help *others* learn about their culture is one of the instructional methods of multicultural mathematics. This involves contextualizing mathematics within the familiar physical and cultural environment of the people about whom students are learning.

Using familiar objects, artifacts, social practice, and customs of a people to help *them* learn school mathematics, when the knowledge base of school mathematics is discrepant from that of their culture, is also one of the instructional methods of multicultural mathematics. This involves contextualizing school mathematics within the familiar physical and cultural environment of students who will be learning it and by so doing, providing them with a bridge between their indigenous culture and the culture of school mathematics.

Traditional School Mathematics Instruction

More traditional mathematics instruction uses instructional methods very different from those of oral storytelling: presentation, seat work/homework, review, and testing.

During *presentation* either a textbook or a teacher formally presents theoretical mathematical information. The mathematics presented in textbooks usually focuses on abstract symbols and definitions. When teachers present mathematics, they tend to lecture in such a way as to re-present the information found in a textbook in the same abstract, symbolic, and theoretical way as a textbook. Presentations proceed in a very linear, orderly manner wherein explanations given for moving from step to step in the presentation relate to reasons based in deductive logic. The presentations usually move from parts to wholes as they present a picture of mathematics as an objective subject that represents "the truth." They usually proceed without regard for learner characteristics. Contextual issues are usually taken into account after the "real theoretical mathematics" is presented by giving examples of "real-world applications." Real-world examples, diagrams, and pictures focus attention on and highlight the meaning, power, and significance of the "pure mathematics" being presented; take an inferior position in comparison to the "theoretical mathematics;" and are usually mechanical exercises that illustrate applications of the "real mathematics" rather than meaningful mathematical inquiries.

Seat work/homework generally follows a presentation. During seat work/homework children usually engage in a reading and writing activity during which they sequentially solve many separate problems, each of which usually has only one correct answer and frequently only one acceptable method of solution. Seat work/homework typically consists of "exercises" designed to provide "practice" in performing algorithms or clarifying concepts introduced during the presentation. Problems are usually first solved outside of any "real-world" context and then in a series of disjointed real-world applications. Real-world problems are assumed by students to involve direct application of recently presented mathematical material. As Nunes, Schliemann, and Carraher indicate:

> The formal demonstrations are followed by exercises in application of the procedure. In the applications, it is assumed that the procedure just learned is appropriate; therefore students do not concentrate on a discussion of what connections there may be between mathematical models and empirical situations. (1993, p. 86)

During *review* activities students present answers to seat work or homework so that teacher and peers can review it, frequently through written board work. Answers examined are usually checked for both correctness and for a sequence of logical and orderly steps involving written symbols that lead from problem to solution.

Testing is usually a paper-and-pencil activity in which students write answers to problems. Students' tests are generally examined for both correct answers and for correct procedure in solving problems. Correct procedure involves a written record of work that consists of an appropriate sequence of mathematical symbols recorded in a logical and orderly manner that deductively lead from the problem to solution.

The essence of more traditional school mathematics instruction might be summarized as follows: symbolic, written, logical, deductive, analytical, theoretical, abstract, decontextualized, depersonalized, linear, highly literate, assuming separate objective and subjective realities with concern for only objective reality, and assuming that knowledge can be broken into discrete parts that can be objectively presented in such a way that the whole to be learned is the sum of its parts. Cultures with these characteristics are called highly literate (Ong, 1982).

Storytelling, School Mathematics, and More Oral Cultures

The instructional media and methods of oral storytelling and more traditional school mathematics are different. Some of the differences just elaborated are summarized in the leftmost two columns of Exhibit 11.1.

These differences are not important in and of themselves but because the learning, thinking, and problem-solving styles that many children learn in their families and communities are different from, and often inconsistent with, those of more traditional school mathematics. This can inhibit children's ability to learn school mathematics unless they are provided with an intellectual bridge between their home culture and the culture of school mathematics. Oral storytelling is one example of the type of intellectual bridge that can help students make a transition from more oral home and community cultures to the highly literate culture of more traditional school mathematics. Several issues raised by this statement need clarification.

Almost everywhere in our world we now teach school mathematics using the highly literate methods and media of more traditional school mathematics described above. This involves using instructional methods and media that reflect the culturally based learning styles, thinking styles, problem-solving styles, teaching methods, instructional media, and knowledge bases nurtured by Western mathematicians during the last several hundred years. This approach to instruction has been called a "highly literate" approach—an approach that reflects the most literate dimensions of Western culture (and not by any means all of Western

Exhibit 11.1   Attributes of the Instructional Medium of Oral Storytelling, Traditional School Mathematics, and More Oral Cultures

Oral Storytelling	More Traditional School Mathematics	More Oral Cultures
uses oral storytelling, an oral medium of instruction	uses a highly literate medium of instruction, based in the academic textbook or didactic lecture	uses a more oral medium of instruction, based in personalized human interactions
important learning primarily takes place through listening and talking	important learning primarily takes place through reading and writing	important learning primarily takes place through listening and talking
knowledge is created from verbally constructed visual images and experience with concrete physical objects, images, events, and activities	knowledge is drawn from abstract mathematical symbols and theoretical situations	knowledge is verbally constructed from articulations, visual images, and firsthand experience with concrete physical objects, images, events, and activities
learning takes place through involvement with personally engaging experiences that contextualize math in everyday cultural experiences	learning takes place through reflection, analysis, and observation of impersonal, decontextualized, "theoretical" mathematics	learning takes place through personal involvement with contextualized culturally based everyday experiences
learning makes heavy use of fantasy, imagination, and intuition	learning requires deductive thinking, logical reasoning, and systematic analysis	learning makes heavy use of fantasy, imagination, and intuition
values both subjective and objective reality	values objective reality	values both subjective and objective reality

culture) (Ong, 1982). Here the word *literate* refers to the use of reading and writing and the word *highly* refers to very decontextualized, abstract, and symbolic and requiring very logical, deductive, and analytic modes of thinking. (Some educators prefer the phrase *Eurocentric mathematics*. Rather than associating this approach with a particular location, our preference is to associate it with its characteristics.)

Many different types of cultures exist: highly literate ones, more oral ones, more visual ones, and so forth. Within their culture children learn many things from their families and communities, including their knowledge bases, the kinds of knowledge they value, their ways of interacting with and communicating with others, and their ways of thinking, learning, and problem solving. Factors such as these that children learn before coming to school play a significant role in the ways in which children learn and make meaning in school. Just as children acquire the foundations of literacy within their early language and cultural experiences, so too do they acquire their foundations of mathematical understanding, thought, learning, and problem solving within their early home and community culture. When these foundations are significantly different from or partially inconsistent with the highly literate culture of school mathematics, they can have a profound influence on facilitating or inhibiting children's ability to learn school mathematics, unless the cultural differences between children's cultures and the culture of school mathematics are recognized and intellectual bridges are provided that help students make the transition from their home culture to the highly literate culture of school mathematics.

Since this book is concerned with storytelling as an *oral* instructional method, and since many cultures exist whose instructional methods are based in oral-aural media, this chapter will examine some ways in which more oral cultures are different from the highly literate culture of school mathematics. It will also examine how oral storytelling can provide children from more oral cultures with an intellectual bridge between the two cultures, a bridge that makes it easier for them to function within the culture of traditional school mathematics after having learned their own more oral culture in their home and community. What is said here will thus pertain largely to more oral cultures. However, what is presented provides a model for how to think about other types of cultures and how to help children from them make transitions to school mathematics.

The phrase *oral culture* has been used by a number of educators to signify cultures in which most of the population cannot read and write (Ong, 1982; Luria, 1976). Since this chapter will refer to children who come from families in which parents can read and write and to cultures in which the majority of their members can read and write—but whose learning styles, thinking styles, teaching methods, and instructional media are nevertheless more similar to those of oral cultures than to those of highly literate cultures—use of the label *oral* by itself seems inappropriate. Thus to contrast these cultures to highly literate cultures, they will be labeled "more oral" cultures. Here the phrase *more oral* signifies that even though members of a culture know how to read and write, their primary means of communication and instruction are more similar to those of oral cultures than to those of highly literate cultures.

More oral cultures abound in our world. From a global perspective many cultures around the world, until recently, have primarily used oral-aural media of communication for instruction. Many of these cultures are now partially literate: a significant percentage of their members have learned to read and write, but the primary media of communication and instruction used in the family and community are still oral-aural ones. From a local perspective the populations of many large urban centers are comprised of people with a wide range of different cultural and linguistic backgrounds. One of the differences between these urban dwellers is whether they come from homes where communication and instructional methods and media are more oral in nature or more highly literate in nature. Many come from more oral families and communities. The right column of Exhibit 11.1 lists some of the characteristics of the instructional methods and media of more oral cultures. Note how similar they are to the instructional methods and media of oral storytelling, such as those used by Doris Lawson in teaching "The Egypt Story." This is part of the reason why oral storytelling can provide an intellectual bridge between more oral cultures and the culture of highly literate school mathematics.

We will now examine some ways in which more oral cultures are different from highly literate cultures and the effect that these differences might have on their members' ability to learn school mathematics.

Mathematical Knowledge Base of More Oral Cultures

Researchers have examined the knowledge bases of more oral and highly literate cultures. Three examples of this research will be presented: that of Luria (1976) on logical processes, that of Heath (1983) on analytical thinking, and that of Nunes, Schliemann, and Carraher (1993) on symbol systems. This research is important for several reasons. First, it illustrates differences in children's ways of thinking between more oral and highly literate cultures. Second, it illustrates how these differences relate to the ways of thinking required by school mathematics. Third, some of the differences help explain why children from more oral cultures can have difficulty with mathematics. Fourth, if we know how family culture can facilitate or inhibit mathematics achievement, it is then possible to think about how to construct intellectual bridges that help children transition from family to mathematics classroom.

In *Cognitive Development: Its Cultural and Social Foundations* (1976), Aleksandr Luria explored differences between highly literate and more oral people in Uzbekistan. Some of these differences relate to ways in which growing up in highly literate versus more oral families and communities prepares children for school mathematics instruction.

Luria found that persons from more oral families and communities identified geometric figures by assigning them the names of concrete objects found in their everyday world and never as the abstract mathematical entities that we know as a circle, square, or triangle. For example, when shown a picture of a circle, persons from more oral communities always described it as a *plate, bucket,* or *moon.* They described it as representations of concrete real things they personally knew. In contrast, highly literate persons identified geometrical figures by the more abstract and less specific terms of *circle, square,* or *triangle* (1976, pp. 32-39).

Luria found that persons from more oral communities tended to use more concrete situational thinking as opposed to abstract categorical thinking. For example, when shown drawings of four objects, three belonging to what Luria considered to be one set and a fourth belonging to another set, they associated objects with each other differently than persons from highly literate families. When shown drawings of a hammer, saw, log, and hatchet, highly literate persons grouped together the tools and said that the log belonged to a different set of objects. They used more abstract categorical reasoning that focused on the object's attributes, rather than their situational uses. In comparison, more oral people thought of the objects primarily in terms of practical situational groupings, which related to personal endeavors that they had observed or in which they had engaged. When they grouped together log, saw, and hatchet, it was because when cutting logs you use a saw and hatchet. When they grouped together log, hammer, and saw it was because when you are building a house you would rather have a hammer, saw, and logs than a hatchet (because a hatchet chops wood into small, less useful pieces) (1976, pp. 56-74).

Luria also found differences in people's ability to use formal deductive, syllogistic, inferential logic, in which reasoning operates in a self-contained, closed system where conclusions are derived from premises without reference to real-world experiences. For example, Luria gives the following problem. *In the Far North, where there is snow, all bears are white. Zembla is in the Far North and there is always snow there. What color are the bears in Zembla?* The typical response of a person from a more oral family was "I don't know. I've seen a black bear. I've never seen any others. . . . Each locality has its own animals"

(1976, pp. 108-109). Here the reasoning is in terms of personal experience and not in terms of deductive syllogistic logic. A more literate person responded, "To go by your words, they should all be white" (1976, p. 114). Here the insecurity of dealing with logic ("by your words") in comparison to personal practical experiences highlights the more literate person's ability to use deductive syllogistic logic while still distrusting reasoning that does not directly reference and connect to his personal real-world experiences. The highly literate person who was raised in a family and community where formal deductive inferential logic is part of the normal everyday discourse among people can complete the inferential problem and reply that the bears of Zembla are white.

Leap (1988) found a similar hesitancy to deal with inferential logic—in which reasoning operates in a self-contained closed system and conclusions are derived from premises without reference to real-world experiences—among middle school children of the Ute tribe of Utah who come from more oral families. For example, when as part of a mathematical problem-solving class a Ute child was asked to determine how much his brother would have to pay for gas if he drove his pickup truck a certain distance, the child answered simply that "My brother does not have a pickup." In accordance with tribal custom, the child assessed the truth value of statements in the problem before attempting to answer it, and if the statements were not true, the child would not proceed to solve the problem. Part of the Ute culture, according to Leap, is to dismiss from consideration any proposals in conflict with "the way things are" in terms of either tribal conventions or real-world actualities. Having to verify the truth value of statements in mathematical problems before attempting to solve the problems does not make it easy for Ute children to engage in inferential logic or hypothetical thinking, two central elements of school mathematics.

How would children from more oral families and communities in Uzbekistan—or any other place—function in more traditional mathematics classes where instructional methods assume that children can converse and learn using abstractions, decontextualized sets of objects, and deductive logic? Would not the ways in which they were taught to think, learn, and make meaning in their homes have a profound effect on their learning of school mathematics, particularly in comparison to classmates from highly literate homes? If we want children from both more oral and highly literate families to have equal access to school mathematics, we need to think about how to construct intellectual bridges that will allow them equal access.

In *Ways With Words,* Shirley Brice Heath (1983) examines three American communities located in close proximity to each other in the Piedmont area of the Carolinas: a lower-class Caucasian community (called Roadville), a lower-class African American community (called Trackton), and a middle-class Caucasian and African American community (called Townspeople). All three communities are literate, but Roadville and Trackton are more oral, while Townspeople is highly literate.

One of the differences between these communities is the way in which they prepare children to engage in analytical thinking, a thinking process heavily emphasized in school mathematics. Analytical thinking requires that people are able to separate themselves from a piece of (oral or written) text so that they can examine it objectively in a decontextualized context, break the text into "unitary" parts and objectively examine each of the unitary parts as a separate entity, inquire into the effect of altering one part of the text on other parts of the text, return to the text to repeatedly reexamine it, and question the internal consistency and validity of different parts of the text as well as the text as a whole.

Townspeople

For Townspeople, "Both at home and at work, there is an almost continuous use of written material as a topic or backdrop for talk" (Heath, 1983, p. 225). Much of this talk corresponds to highly literate ways of writing and reading that involve the use of analytical thinking. Heath describes how certain aspects of analytical thinking are taught to preschoolers in the home as a natural way of interacting with them:

> Townspeople . . . consciously create on-going social activities in which their children participate, and they also specifically focus children's attention in these social activities. It is as though in the drama of life, townspeople parents freeze scenes and parts of scenes at certain points along the way. Within the single frame of a scene, they focus the child's attention on objects or events in the frame, sort out referents for the child to name, give the child ordered turns for sharing talk about this referent, and then narrate the description of the scene. Through their focused language, adults make the potential stimuli in the child's environment stand still for a cooperative examination and narration between parent and child. The child learns to focus attention on a preselected referent, masters the relationships between signifier and the signified, develops turn-taking skills in a focused conversation of the referent, and is subsequently expected to listen to benefit from and eventually to create narratives placing the referent in different contextual situations. (p. 350)

> In essence, this process enables the child to view each new referent out of its context, and to approach it with decontextualized labels of identification and attribution, rather than only with contextualized responses which link it to specific stated events or situations. . . . Their home life has also given them extensive exposure to stories and situations in which they and adults manipulate environments imaginatively and talk about the effects of changing one aspect of a context while holding all others constant. (p. 352)

> Children learn they should not interpret some oral and written texts literally. . . . Written materials have a context of their own which disengages them from literal linkages to objects, people, and events of the real world. . . . As the children of townspeople learn the distinctions between contextualized first-hand experiences and decontextualized representations of experience, they come to act like literates before they can read. (p. 256)

Here, children of Townspeople, even at a preschool age, learn how to separate themselves from a piece of text so that they can examine it objectively in a decontextualized context, break the text into unitary parts so they can focus on each part as a unitary entity unto itself, analyze each unitary part separately and in relation to the complete text, inquire into the effect of altering one part of the text on other parts of the text, and return to the text to repeatedly reexamine it. "Townspeople carry with them, as an unconscious part of their self-identity, these numerous subtle and covert norms, habits, and values about reading, writing, and speaking about written materials" (Heath, 1983, p. 262) that allows them to pass on to their children analytical ways of thinking, as a natural function of enculturating their children into their family and community.

"For the children of Trackton and Roadville, however, . . . the townspeople's ways are far from natural and they seem strange indeed" (Heath, 1983, p. 262). Although their parents know how to read and write, "Children from neither community have had experience in seeing their parents read or write extended pieces of prose" (p. 348) or use analytical thinking to scrutinize what they read or write.

Roadville

Roadville residents are literate. However, their worldview is highly influenced by oral ways of making meaning.

"When asked what kinds of writing they do, Roadville residents first name letters and notes" (Heath, 1983, p. 216). These letters and notes are not analytical pieces of text but short conversations that are orally constructed in the mind of the writer and then recorded "as though they are parts of oral conversations, using terms such as 'say,' 'tell,' and 'answer' just as they would in referring to talk" (pp. 213, 214). Analytical thinking is not practiced in Roadville as part of the process of writing: "Roadville residents use writing only when they have to, and view it as an occasional necessary tool—to aid their memory, to help them buy and sell things, and sometimes to help keep them in touch with family and friends" (p. 231).

Reading fares no better than writing: "Everyone talks about reading, but few people do it" (Heath, 1983, p. 220). "Within Roadville, the most predictable reading activity in those homes with preschoolers is the bedtime story" (p. 223). As children grow older and "pass their third birthdays, both parents and Sunday School teachers expect them to be able to sit and listen to a story and not to participate—either verbally or physically—during the story" (p. 225). The goal of reading activity is to teach children to "sit and 'learn to listen' passively" (p. 226). When adults do ask children questions about text, adults expect "scripted" answers involving direct recall that includes no analysis, interpretation, or extension of the text. As Heath comments,

> In Roadville, there is a concerted effort on the part of adults to initiate their children both into pre-scripted discourse around printed material and into passive listening behavior. . . . Both mothers and fathers expect their children to answer questions they ask about books, but they also expect them to listen quietly when someone is reading from a book. The questions asked are almost always requests for *what*-explanations, and there is a set answer decided on in the mind of the adult before the child answers. A dog in a book is a *dog*—not a mutt, a hound dog, or Blackie—unless the parent has established one of these terms as the answer to the question. (p. 227)

Roadville children learn that they are not to question the written word. They are to passively listen to what is read and to assume that the written word has an authority beyond themselves. They are not to probe, question, or scrutinize what is written. When they respond to questions about text, they are not to analyze or elaborate but to mirror back to the questioner words presented by the text. As Heath says, "Roadville children . . . are seemingly tutored in pre-scripted performances, in which their parents 'hold book' for them as they learn their parts for labeling, describing, and answering questions" (p. 346).

Not only are children taught to answer questions related to text in a highly scripted manner, they are also taught to live their lives in this same way: "Roadville parents bring up their children in the drama of life by carefully scripting and rehearsing them for the parts they expect them to play" (p. 346). Written text, the authorities one meets in life and school, and life itself is not to be questioned, analyzed, debated, or challenged.

This view of the authority of written text, parents, teachers, and the other authorities in one's life does not leave the child with a sense that text (or authorities in their life) can be probed, analyzed, questioned, disputed, expanded on, elaborated on, or embellished. The very frame of mind that allows children to engage in analytical thinking is thus missing from Roadville society. As Heath elaborates,

> In Roadville, the absoluteness of ways of talking about what is written fits church ways of talking about what is written. Behind the written word is an authority, and the text is a message which can be taken apart only insofar as its analysis does not extend too far beyond the text and commonly agreed upon experiences. New syntheses and multiple interpretations create alternatives which challenge fixed roles, rules, and "rightness."
> (p. 235)

> In Roadville, extension from the authority of the written text is bounded. . . . The young may not interpret the written word in the presence of adults; theirs is to be a passive spectator role in which they may memorize materials or answer specific questions.
> (p. 349)

Trackton

Trackton residents are also literate, but their culture is more oral than literate in nature. Here reading and writing are used "to *substitute for an oral message*" (Heath, 1983, p. 200).

When individuals use text in Trackton, it usually involves short textual fragments not much longer than a few words that substitute for oral cues and that have purely instrumental functions. "Adults and children read what they have to read to solve practical problems of daily life: price tags, traffic signs, house numbers, bills, checks. . . . The most frequent occasions for writing are those when Trackton family members say they cannot trust their memory," and when they write short notes to themselves (Heath, 1983, pp. 199-200). Such uses of text do not support analytical thinking.

Most use of longer pieces of text involves communication with persons not living in Trackton, such as letters or government announcements. These longer pieces of text are not read individually but orally in a group. The Trackton resident who wishes to read a piece of text (for example, a letter) takes it to a group of people and reads it aloud to them, and the group jointly makes sense out of the text by socially constructing its meaning in a process similar to what takes place during improvisational drama. Heath elaborates:

> Community literacy activities are public and social. Written information almost never stands alone in Trackton. It is reshaped and reworded into an oral mode by adults and children who incorporate chunks of the written text in their talk. (p. 200)

> For Trackton adults, reading is a social activity; when something is read in Trackton, it almost always provokes narratives, jokes, sidetracking talk, and active negotiation of the meaning of written texts among listeners. Authority in the written word does not rest in the words themselves, but in the meanings which are negotiated through the experiences of the group. (p. 196)

When text is read, it is transformed into oral language by the reader and then its meaning is constructed through an "improvisational play" enacted jointly by reader and listeners. Here meaning comes not from looking back at the text itself but from the shared experiences of group members. Here there is a shift from text to social interactions:

> The question "What does this mean?" was answered not only from the information in print but from the group's joint bringing of experience to the text. Lillie Mae, reading aloud, decoded the written text, but her friends and neighbors interpreted the text's meaning through their own experiences. The experience of any one individual had to become common to the group, however, and that was done through the recounting of members' experiences. Such recounting re-created scenes, embellished the truth, illustrated the character of the individuals involved, and to the greatest extent possible brought the audience into the experience itself. (Heath, 1983, p. 197)

How can one systematically analyze text when it is abandoned as soon as it is read and when meaning is drawn from social comments inspired by the text rather than from the text itself? Analytical thinking requires that people are able to separate themselves from a piece of (oral or written) text so that they can examine it objectively in a decontextualized context. But this is not how literacy functions in Trackton.

Analytical thinking also involves "freezing text in time" so that it can be repeatedly reexamined. But in Trackton this is impossible because once text is read it takes on its meaning separate from itself as groups interpret it through social interaction. Here each "reading" of text results in different social interactions, and its meaning (in terms of the social construction of meaning) changes with each reading. As Heath (1983) says,

> Trackton children have learned through their long hours in the laps of adults and on the hard church benches, that in the free flow of time . . . [w]ritten words shaped on paper are recomposed in each time and space, created anew in each performance. (p. 349)

Thoughts which were once shaped into words on paper become recomposed in each time and space. Abiding by the written word limits one's performance from being created anew with each audience and setting. To be sure, some of the meaning in the written text remains stable, but as one preacher put it, "the Words must live," and performer and audience alike must therefore integrate the words into their personal experience and express their meaning for them. (p. 233)

Analytical thinking also involves breaking text into unitary parts and decontextualizing it. But Trackton residents do not partition text into unitary segments for analysis. It is part of a holistic performance: "For them there seems a holistic coherency about print which does not depend on its discrete elements." Trackton residents also have difficulty decontextualizing text and separating it from its social interpretation: "They remember print from re-creating its scene and its use," (Heath, 1983, p. 233) with each re-reading of print presenting a new reading task, a new performance, and a new set of social meanings.

In Trackton, analytical thinking (as highly literate cultures know it) simply does not exist.

Heath's research indicates that the highly literate culture of Townspeople prepares its members for analytical thinking through natural processes of enculturation into their families. In contrast, the more oral cultures of Trackton and Roadville do not support analytical thinking. In Roadville, children know their place and are taught from early childhood how to respond to text in very conventional prescripted ways, in which the written word is inaccessible to scrutiny, interpretation, or challenge. In Trackton, meaning is socially constructed from text through an improvisational drama, and text is largely left behind as meaning-making progresses. As a result, children from Roadville and Trackton are often unfamiliar with analytical thinking and view it as an incomprehensible endeavor that is inconsistent with their community cultures. Do children from these three communities have equal access to school mathematics (which requires analytical thinking)? Not according to Heath's research.

In *Street Mathematics and School Mathematics,* Nunes, Schliemann, and Carraher (1993) discuss what occurs when children from more oral working-class Brazilian families learn one method of numerical calculation at home and another in school. Let us examine what they observed. Imagine a 10-year-old who goes to school during the day and works in his father's shop for 2 hours after school and on weekends. Imagine the child calculating $1.75 + $2.58 in his father's shop and at school.

In his father's shop a customer presents the child with two items and asks, "How much?" The child looks at their prices: $1.75 and $2.58. The child then mentally calculates while quietly muttering to himself. This is what he mutters: "One dollar and two dollars gives three dollars, seven dimes and five dimes gives twelve dimes which is one dollar and two dimes, which gives four dollars and two dimes total so far, now five pennies and eight pennies gives thirteen pennies which is one dime and three pennies, which gives four dollars three dimes and three pennies, so the cost is four dollars thirty-three cents." The child also thinks, "That's about two dollars profit for our family if the customer buys the items."

In school the teacher writes $1.75 + $2.58 on the chalkboard and instructs students to solve the problem. The child takes out paper and pencil and records the equation in Exhibit 11.2.

The child now proceeds to add using his pencil without making any utterances. First he adds 5 + 8, writes down a 3 below the 8, and records a 1 above the 7. Then he adds 1 + 7 + 5, writes down a 3 below the 5, and records a 1 above the 1. Now he adds 1 + 1 + 2 and writes

Exhibit 11.2

```
   1.7 5
 + 2.5 8
 ─────────
```

down a 4 below the 2. He next raises his hand. In response the teacher comes to his desk, looks at his paper, and puts a check on it.

In his father's shop the child was probably taught to add by his father, by imitating his father's oral utterances as his father orally coached him on how to add while illustrating the meaning of the utterances with real money. His father also probably emphasized that (a) if he under-calculated his family would lose money or (b) if he over-calculated the customer would call him a thief and never return to the store.

In school the child was probably taught to add by his teacher, who wrote problems and answers on the chalkboard and explained how the answer's written numbers were derived from the problem's written numbers. The child also learned in school that if he made a mistake, his paper would receive a cross rather than a check and that he would be punished if he spoke aloud while calculating.

From such observations, Nunes, Schliemann, and Carraher (1993) learned that working-class children are exposed to two different mathematical systems: oral mathematics (called street arithmetic) and written mathematics (called school arithmetic) (p. 27). The situations in which children use these mathematical systems are different, "the contexts in which these two occur tend not to overlap," and "because the types of symbol systems used in street mathematics and school mathematics are different . . . children structure their [calculation] activities [related to each system] in different ways" (pp. 28-29). In addition, "Analysis of the principles implicit in oral and written arithmetic shows that the radically different performances displayed by the same children in different conditions . . . can be explained in terms of the symbolic systems being used" (p. 45)

Nunes, Schliemann, and Carraher (1993) describe three important differences between the symbol systems of oral (street or home) and written (school) arithmetic this way:

First, oral and written procedures differ in the direction of calculation: The written algorithm is performed working from units to tens to hundreds, whereas the oral procedure follows the direction hundreds to tens to units.

Second, in the oral mode, the relative value of numbers is preserved: we say "two hundred and twenty-two." In the written mode, the relative value is represented through relative position: we write 2 2 2 [. . .] this difference in signifiers is maintained during calculation: Oral procedures preserve the relative values. Written procedures set them aside. (p. 45)

[Third], street mathematics is oral and preserves much of the meaning of the situations at hand. Mathematical practice in school is written and leaves out as much of the specifics of situations as possible in striving for generality. (p. 49)

This third difference in symbol systems is critical. Street mathematics, which is oral in nature, preserves the meaning of the problem-solving situation while children are involved in the process of doing mathematical calculations. (For example, in the problem $1.75 + $2.58 mentioned above, oral calculators retain meaning by constant reference to monetary specifics of dollars, dimes, and pennies.) In contrast, school mathematics, which is written in nature, leaves out as many of the specifics of problem-solving situations as possible in striving for generality. (For example, in the problem $1.75 + $2.58 mentioned above, written calculators obtain generality by dropping any specific meanings related to monetary transactions in terms of dollars, dimes, or pennies.) Expressed slightly differently, the oral arithmetic symbol system is concrete, contextualized, and personalized while the written one is abstract, decontextualized, and impersonal.

Nunes, Schliemann, and Carraher (1993) further distinguish between oral and written symbol systems in the following way:

The picture of street mathematics developed so far shows it to be based on a *semantic* rather than a *syntactic* approach to problem solving. . . . To use a semantic approach means to generate a mathematical model on the basis of relationships in the problem situation. This model of the relations in the situation is then used to guide computations during problem solving. Subjects remain aware of the meanings involved throughout their activities. In contrast, school mathematics represents a syntactic approach, according to which a set of rules for operating on numbers is applied during problem solving. Meaning is set aside for the sake of generality. (p. 103) (Also, see Resnick [1982] for semantic/syntactic distinctions.)

There seems to be a trade-off in oral and written arithmetic as far as preservation of meaning and generalizability are concerned. To a greater preservation of meaning in oral arithmetic procedures correspond restrictions either in the range of numbers or the range of situations that a subject can handle. Similarly, to the loss of meaning in written procedures corresponds a greater range of situations and numbers that can be handled without modification of procedures. (p. 54)

Why, one might ask, don't children abandon street mathematics after they are taught school mathematics? Nunes, Schliemann, and Carraher give two reasons: First, fewer mathematical errors occur when using street mathematics than school mathematics. Second,

It seems that everyday [oral] procedures, which are likely to be already available to students before they are taught the [written] algorithm, compete with the algorithm. The conflict stems from the fact that the everyday knowledge uses calculation procedures in which variables are kept separate. No calculations across variables are carried out. The school-taught procedure violates this principle. Thus it is not easily coordinated with students' previous knowledge.

1993, p. 126

The main issues of this research, for our purposes, are that many Brazilian working-class children learn oral mathematics at home and written mathematics in school, that the symbol systems underlying these two mathematical systems are very different (concrete contextualized versus abstract decontextualized), that the two systems have different real-life uses and advantages (for example, calculation accuracy and infusion of meaning versus generalizability), and that school mathematics is not "easily coordinated with students' previous knowledge" that they learn in their homes and community. In addition, and very important for our purposes, the instructional media and methods used to teach children mathematics in their homes (oral, personalized, and concrete) are different from those used in school (written, impersonal, and abstract).

What Nunes, Schliemann, and Carraher have documented in Brazil has been noted in many parts of the world: the concrete, contextualized, more oral mathematics often taught in homes and communities are frequently different from and inconsistent with the abstract, generalized, highly literate mathematics taught in school.

In summary, the research of Luria; Heath; and Nunes, Schliemann, and Carraher highlight differences that can exist between children's more oral family and community culture and the highly literate culture of school mathematics. Differences include facility with deductive logic, competence with analytical thinking, and flexible use of abstract decontextualized written symbol systems. Their research also hinted that how children are taught and expected to learn in their home and school can be very different. These differences are not trivial and can pose major learning impediments for children. The question we must confront is, "What can be done about the resulting learning problems that so many children from more oral cultures face when they enter the highly literate mathematics classroom?"

CULTURAL DIFFERENCES AND THE MEDIUM OF INSTRUCTION

This section examines two concerns:

- How can educators help children learn school mathematics who come to school having learned how to learn in an instructional environment, through instructional methods, and within the context of a knowledge base that is different from that of school mathematics?
- What instructional methods might help such children learn some mixture of their own culture's mathematics and school mathematics when it is recognized that these two mathematical systems are discrepant and possibly inconsistent?

These concerns about instructional methods arise when educators discover that differences in home and school cultures can have a significant impact upon children's ability to learn school mathematics.

Unfortunately, little has been written about multicultural mathematics instructional methods. The discussion of "The Egypt Story" earlier in this chapter goes beyond much of what is written. To extend that discussion, two perspectives on instructional methods will be examined: First, we will examine the perspective of mathematics educators working in non-Western cultures where the culturally acquired mode of learning for the majority of the population is different in the same way from the mode of learning required in school mathematics. Second, we will examine the perspective of culturally diverse Western nations whose populations bring very different cultural orientations to the mathematics class.

Multicultural Instructional Methods in Non-Western Cultures

Paulus Gerdes (1997a) discusses multicultural mathematics education from the perspective of educators working in non-Western cultures. He discusses how instructional methods "based on rote memory and harsh discipline" lead children to feel alienated from mathematical endeavors and how teaching children mathematics using problems and referents that are alien to their "indigenous" mathematical knowledge base can lead to a situation where "the practical mathematical knowledge that children acquired outside the school is 'repressed' and 'confused' in the school" (p. 225). Gerdes also discusses how the spontaneous mathematical abilities of children can be destroyed by the mathematics learned in school as a result of the psychological blocks that develop as the spontaneous mathematics that has been learned in a cultural context is repressed and forgotten because of the dissonance that comes to exist between the children's own cultural mathematics and the mathematics being learned in school. Gerdes then asks, "How can this 'totally inappropriate education, leading to misunderstanding and sociocultural and psychological alienation' be avoided? How can this 'pushing aside' and 'wiping out' of spontaneous, natural, informal, indigenous, folk implicit, non-standard, and/or hidden (ethno) mathematics be avoided?" (p. 225).

Gerdes answers these "how can" questions by primarily referring to content rather than methods issues. However, while stressing the "need for incorporation of ethnomathematics [content] into the curriculum in order to avoid a psychological blockade," Gerdes (1997a) advocates Gay and Cole's method:

It is necessary to investigate first the "indigenous mathematics," in order to be able to build effective bridges from this "indigenous mathematics" to the new mathematics to be introduced in the school. . . . [T]he teacher should begin with materials of the indigenous culture . . . and from there advance to the new school mathematics. (p. 225)

There are three important elements of this statement of methodology:

First, there is a content component that requires that educators understand the "indigenous mathematics" of their students' culture. This is what most multicultural mathematics educators focus on. Progress is being made in uncovering the indigenous mathematics of many cultures. There is also a second implicit content component of "the new school mathematics." Educators often do not have a deep understanding of the new school mathematics, and without such an understanding it can be difficult to help children meaningfully learn mathematics. Adequacy of teacher knowledge is a problem in many cultures.

Second, there is a methodological construct of starting where the child is as a member of his or her indigenous culture. This requires that educators understand many things. They must understand the materials of the indigenous culture. These "materials" are viewed broadly and include a culture's games, arts and crafts, and technology as well as its mathematical language and symbol systems. Samples of these were highlighted in "The Egypt Story." Multicultural mathematics educators have made progress identifying materials of indigenous cultures and the ways in which mathematics is embedded in and speaks through materials.

But "starting where the child is" means much more than this. It means understanding how a culture's mathematics relates to its cultural assumptions (for example, in "The Egypt Story," understanding that the existence of two numeration systems relates to the existence of Egypt's two distinct social classes). It means understanding how children are taught to think and learn in their indigenous society (for example, comprehending that they think in more oral or highly literate ways, as portrayed in the Brazil example). And it means understanding the instructional methods used in the child's indigenous society (for example, understanding the more personal apprenticeship method versus the impersonal lecture method portrayed in the Brazil example). Multicultural educators have just begun to write about these things.

Third, there is the requirement that educators should build effective bridges from this indigenous mathematics to the new mathematics and that in so doing educators "should begin with materials of the indigenous culture . . . and from there advance to the new school mathematics" (Gerdes, 1997a, p. 225). A number of different types of intellectual bridges need to be constructed between indigenous cultures and school mathematics to help children transition from their indigenous culture to the culture of school mathematics: bridges from one knowledge base to another, bridges from one set of familiar cultural materials to another, bridges from one way of thinking, learning, and problem solving to another, and bridges from one set of instructional methods to another.

Intellectual bridges involving content and materials have been written about. Bridges between pedagogical methods and ways of thinking, learning, and problem solving have just begun to be considered. For example, educators frequently write about the geometrical patterns of clothing, basket, and pottery designs of many cultures and how to relate them to school mathematics, but rarely is anything written about how the *instructional methods* used to teach community members how to make those designs relates to *instructional methods* of school mathematics.

To address issues of building bridges between instructional methods, consideration needs to be given to such issues as how the following types of indigenous instructional methods might be used to help children more easily and meaningfully learn school mathematics:

- oral storytelling, where a character in the story elaborates on mathematics while overcoming some obstacle (as is being advocated in this book)
- apprentice relationships with a parent, skilled adult, or older child while solving a culturally relevant mathematics problem that impacts their economic condition
- observation and then construction of visual sand drawings of mathematical relationships that children demonstrate and explain to an audience as part of a social game or initiation rite
- oral articulation of mathematical relations with a peer, older child, or adult that is part of a larger discussion about political and economic survival in which social standing is conferred as a result of successful oral articulation of mathematical meanings (a method

advocated and used by Gelsa Knijnik (1997) when working with the Landless Peoples Movement in Brazil)

The following questions are important to raise when considering the building of methodological bridges: (1) Are there indigenous instructional methods of teaching and learning? (2) If they exist, do those indigenous instructional methods make the learning of the indigenous culture easier (presumably because they are conceptually consistent with the culture) than other instructional methods? (3) If they exist, do those indigenous instructional methods complement school mathematics and make learning it easier than with other instructional methods for the members of the targeted culture (or other cultures)? (4) Is it pedagogically, socially, politically, and economically feasible to use those methods within the current school context? Little theoretical consideration of such issues currently exists in the ethnomathematical research literature.

This entire book, of course, is about the issue of instructional methods. It is about how epic oral storytelling can facilitate the teaching of mathematics. Part of the power of oral storytelling is its power to provide a "pedagogical bridge" that can help children from more oral families and communities make the transition to learning and thinking in the ways required by highly literate school mathematics.

If we do not figure out how to construct pedagogical bridges, we will make little progress in helping children transition from their indigenous culture to the culture of school mathematics. For example, what might a child really understand about school mathematics if that child studied mathematics without ever learning to use deductive logic, think analytically, or reason using abstract mathematical symbols (as was discussed earlier in this chapter)? Would educators have done much more than train the child to blindly execute mathematical algorithms, automatically recall mathematical facts and formulas, and unthinkingly record mathematical concepts on tests? This is not what we really want for our children. We want much more for them.

Multicultural Instructional Methods in Western Cultures

Many European and American nations are populated by people from numerous cultures, whose children bring different cultural orientations to the mathematics classroom. As a result, the viewpoint of educators from these nations on multicultural mathematics education is different from that of educators in (non-Western) countries where the classroom population is homogeneous. The work of Claudia Zaslavsky from the United States and Nelson, Joseph, and Williams from Europe represent this group of educators.

In *The Multicultural Math Classroom: Bringing in the World,* Claudia Zaslavsky (1996) lets the reader know her agenda in the title of her book. She does not want school mathematics to continue to consist of only highly literate Western academic mathematics. She wants to improve school mathematics by bringing into the classroom real mathematical endeavors of many different peoples from over the span of human history: "Students should realize that real people in all parts of the world and in all eras of history developed mathematical ideas because they needed to solve the vital problems of their daily existence" (p. 29).

Zaslavsky (1996) further clarifies her intentions when she says that she is interested "in equity issues in mathematics education" (p. vii). She believes that "No longer can we be satisfied with cultivating a white-male mathematical elite while the rest of the population lags behind. No longer can we ignore the mathematical heritage of a major segment of the student population: females and people of color" (p. ix). "Multicultural mathematics education is for all people, whatever their ethnic/racial heritage, their gender, or their socioeconomic status" (p. 2).

Since Zaslavsky believes that one way to make classrooms multicultural is by bringing into them the mathematics of many cultures, she introduces readers to a range of different instructional methods and materials from around the world. The following are some of those introduced in *The Multicultural Math Classroom:*

1. Using members of a school's community who bring into the school examples of their indigenous cultural heritage and share with students their culture's ways of thinking mathematically and using mathematics

2. Using indigenous materials, artifacts, and devices of a culture to present its mathematical ideas

3. Using children's (or adult) literature from different parts of the world that let children "feel that they are participating in the lives of people far and near, in the distant past and in the present, in the real world and in the imaginary one" that can act "as a springboard for mathematical investigations" (Zaslavsky, 1996, p. 45)

4. Using games and recreational activities from around the world to teach mathematics and demonstrate how different cultures use mathematical endeavors to enjoy and entertain themselves

5. Using anthropological and archeological investigations that allow children to examine artistic and craft materials from a culture (or family) that have deep mathematical meaning that can be elaborated upon in school

6. Using mathematical data about different families, communities, nations, or cultures and data analysis activities to explore cultures (including their demographics, marriage practices, health practices, and waste treatment facilities)

7. Using interdisciplinary units that simultaneously explore a community's mathematics, science, history, art, literature, and culture

8. Using art activities (such as making murals and constructing architectural models) to explore and present mathematical ideas of different cultures

9. Using classroom discussions that employ mathematics to explore current-day social problems (such as racism) in light of ancient solutions to those problems or solutions found in other parts of the world

This is a wide range of mathematical instructional methods and media. Zaslavsky has taken a giant step in assembling them. In addition, her book provides examples of how these methods can be used to explore a broad range of mathematical content originating from many different cultures.

There are two limitations of Zaslavsky's work (and the work of others who take a similar approach to multicultural mathematics). First, she does not deal with the ways in which the knowledge bases (including ways of thinking, learning, and problem solving) that children learn in their indigenous families, communities, and cultures can facilitate or inhibit their ability to do school mathematics. For example, she does not consider how children's ways of dealing with logic, analytical thinking, or mathematical symbols that they learn in their families and communities can influence their learning of school mathematics (topics that were discussed earlier in this chapter). Second, she does not examine the match or mismatch between the instructional methods she urges we use and either (a) the multicultural mathematics she introduces using those methods, or (b) the cultures from which children come who will be learning from those methods. For example, Zaslavsky never seems to consider what happens when you use visual instructional methods with children from more oral families. Unfortunately, Zaslavsky gives the impression that she has collected all of the instructional methods that have proved powerful during the twentieth century and a wide range of multicultural mathematics content, rather than systematically exploring which methods are best suited to teaching specific content (that originates in certain cultures) to specific children (given their cultural backgrounds).

In fact, if we look at the writings of most multicultural mathematics curriculum developers in the United States and Europe, we discover that they do not seem to have reflected deeply on the instructional methods and media they use to transmit the multicultural content of their curricula. Nelson, Joseph, and Williams (1993) provide an example of this in their work in Britain where children of immigrants from many different cultures are enrolled in schools.

Nelson, Joseph, and Williams have done much to help us understand the mathematical contributions of cultures from around the world and to help us understand the history of our current-day mathematical knowledge base (which developed gradually from early work in Africa and the Middle East to later work in India and China to still later work in Muslim countries in the Middle East and North Africa, until only recently being contributed to by those in Europe and America).

In addition, they have stated, "An important factor in shaping the curriculum is the teacher's command of a range of teaching styles and associated materials" (1993, p. 27). They then list the following different methods for presenting their multicultural ideas:

> (1) direct instruction and exposition, (2) guided discovery and discussion, and (3) pupil-led investigations. . . . To this list we should add cross-curricular initiatives and also projects which involve parents or other members of the local community. (p. 27)

> Another approach is through personalities, not only the leading figures of the past but contemporary figures like Shakuntala Devi, the world's fastest mental calculator. Great events and popular occasions are another possibility. The Olympic games are an obvious source of interesting data. Interdisciplinary work is obviously possible. A study of geometric ornament or rhythm could also involve the art or music department. A study of the mathematics of the Mayas of Central America could be linked to work in history and geography. Finally, a less well known approach with interesting possibilities is the use of original texts. Here the teacher provides the class with a facsimile text of a translation. (pp. 40-41)

What is interesting is how traditional this list is and how most items seem to reflect the methods and media used by academic mathematicians.

Like other multicultural mathematics educators, Nelson, Joseph, and Williams discuss in detail such things as the mathematical content and methods of proof that have existed in different parts of the world at different times in history. They do not, however, take the next step and discuss the methods of instruction used to teach that content. It is as though the multicultural mathematics they discuss becomes trapped in their academic way of thinking, where curriculum content is separated from pedagogical method, and the focus on mathematical truths that make up the curricular content excludes consideration of the methods and media used to present those truths.

For example, in the same chapter as the last quote Nelson, Joseph, and Williams also discuss the mathematical content of Al-Khwarizmi's rhetorical method of algebraic thinking (ninth century CE) and Chu Shih-chieh's visual proof for how to find the sum of the first *n* integers (thirteenth century CE). They spend less space, however, discussing instructional methods than discussing either Al-Khwarizmi's or Chu Shih-chieh's mathematics. In addition, they never explicitly explore in any depth the possible methodical implications of Al-Khwarizmi's rhetorical method or Chu Shih-chieh's visual approach.

One can only wonder what Nelson, Joseph, and Williams would discover if they went beyond the mathematical content of Chu Shih-chieh and Al-Khwarizmi to also ask "What are the methodological implications of Chu Shih-chieh's *method of visual proof* or Al-Khwarizmi's *rhetorical method of algebraic thinking* for the school curriculum, and how might these methods give children who have not been steeped in highly literate mathematical traditions increased accessibility to school mathematics?" For example, their examination of Chu Shih-chieh's methods of visual proof might have led them to ask how methods of visual proof could enrich school mathematics. If they had asked this question they might have discovered that visual proof has recently become popular. This is due in part to educators such as Maria Montessori, who at the beginning of the last century developed visual demonstrations and tactile manipulatives similar to base ten blocks to help poor urban Italian children learn mathematics. What a contribution multicultural mathematics educators could have made if the use of visual proof derived from an exploration of multicultural mathematics rather than from Montessori's attempts to find ways to help culturally deprived special needs children who were disruptive to their communities learn within schools (Lane, 1976).

Certainly there exist other thus far undiscovered or not yet popular instructional methods and materials that can enrich mathematics instruction. A thesis of this book is that oral storytelling is one such method. For much of human history, oral storytelling was probably the major medium through which cultures passed on their accumulated knowledge and traditions to their members. Mathematical epic oral storytelling deserves serious attention as an instructional method, particularly for children who come from more oral cultural backgrounds who have not learned highly literate modes of discourse.

Cultural Diversity and Oral Storytelling

When we look at the mathematics taught in schools around the world, we find a fairly uniform highly literate curriculum in place. When we look at the children in the classrooms around the world we find diversity: linguistic, religious, physical, cultural, and social class diversity, diversity of every kind imaginable. Similarly, when we look at almost any urban school in countries such as the United States and Britain, where a large amount of immigration has taken place over the last century, we also find diversity among school children, diversity almost as great as is found internationally. A problem that educators are confronting is how to deal with the strikingly uniform curriculum that contrasts so dramatically with the diversity of the students learning it.

One answer to this problem comes from examining the indigenous mathematics of the diverse cultures that the children come from and introducing some of that mathematics into the school curriculum in the context of the culture it represents. However, this is only one of several steps that need to be taken in order to accommodate the diversity of children who populate our schools.

Educators must also confront how different the home culture of many schoolchildren can be from the culture underlying school mathematics, and the influence those differences can have on children's mathematical achievement. In this chapter we have examined differences related to facility with deductive logic, analytical thinking, and abstract decontextualized written symbols. Children might also view such fundamental concepts as time and space in different ways than educators, as Pixten has described in the case of the Navahos. And as Nunes, Schliemann, and Carraher's research implies, children from more oral families and communities might also have learned how to learn primarily through oral media of instruction and styles of discourse rather than through the highly literate written instructional media of school mathematics. These types of differences, which result from children's home culture being different from the culture of school mathematics, can have a profound influence in inhibiting or facilitating children's ability to learn mathematics. Some educators have tried to help us understand this.

Other educators have begun to think of ways to construct pedagogical bridges between children's indigenous (home and community) cultures and school mathematics, intellectual bridges that will help children make the transition from their indigenous culture to the culture of school mathematics. This endeavor has been one of the major concerns of this book: how to broaden the instructional methods used during mathematics instruction in order to help children make the transition from their home cultures to the culture of school mathematics.

The range of instructional media used in mathematics classrooms was expanded several times during the last century. It was widened once with the introduction of highly visual and manipulative instructional devices, such as base ten blocks. It was broadened again with the introduction of computers, instructional software, and other electronic media. It was expanded in still another way with the introduction of cooperative learning. Each of these extensions in the instructional media available to mathematics educators has enabled them to provide children from families that nurture more visual, manipulative, and interactive modes of learning, thinking, and problem solving with a bridge that can help them function better within the highly literate culture of school mathematics.

Since many schoolchildren come from more oral home communities, should we not also see if we can find more oral instructional methods and media to help them transition from their indigenous (home) cultures to the highly literate culture of school mathematics? Mathematical epic oral storytelling is offered as an example of one such method of instruction. It has the potential to make mathematics more accessible to children from more oral homes, as well as offering all children an exciting way of learning mathematics.

Hopefully multicultural mathematics educators will be able to discover additional instructional methods and media as they continue to explore the indigenous cultures of people from around the world and over the history of mankind. With any luck they will be able to find the same riches in the mathematical practices of other cultures as medical researchers have been able to find in other cultures' traditional medicines. And hopefully those methods will enable educators to better help all children (whatever their ethnic/racial heritage, gender, or socioeconomic status) to make the bridge from their indigenous mathematics to the new school mathematics.

Chapter 12

STORYTELLING, MULTICULTURAL MATHEMATICS, AND IDEOLOGY

Every book has a story that tells how it came into existence. This book began when I demonstrated to some teachers how to use base ten blocks to teach multidigit addition. I suggested that we pretend to be bulldozers and I demonstrated how a bulldozer would do addition. I followed this up by having them pretend to be bulldozers while using base ten blocks to do some addition problems. Doris Lawson was present when this occurred.

Doris went back to her school and tried bulldozer addition with her fourth graders. It was a success, and Doris reported her success to a group of teachers with whom I periodically met to discuss how to use children's trade books to aid in the teaching of mathematics. The group was excited about Doris's success and suggested that I write a children's book about bulldozer addition. I said I would if they would also create stories that taught mathematics and tell them to their students. I did this as a way of encouraging them to also write stories—the creation and telling of a story being less intimidating than the actual writing of a children's book.

The teachers began creating and telling mathematics stories to their students—and the stories were wonderful. Each month when our mathematics and literature group met, teachers described their stories and reported what occurred when they told them. The stories were told to preschoolers, elementary children, and high school students. Before long we realized that our group had shifted its emphasis from discussing how to use children's trade books in the teaching of mathematics to discussing how to create and tell oral stories that embodied mathematics we wanted children to learn.

Our oral stories solved many of our frustrations with children's trade books. First, they allowed us to tailor stories to the mathematics we wanted our students to learn and to teach that mathematics in the ways we wanted to teach it—in ways that met our students' needs and our own. This was because we were the ones in control of our instruction, rather than an author we had never met and who was unfamiliar with our students. Two of our group's frustrations with children's trade books were that we had difficulty finding books that contained the mathematics we wanted to teach and that they never quite taught the mathematics in the way we desired. Oh, how nice it was to teach what we wanted to teach and in the way we wanted to teach it!

Second, our stories often lasted several days because the mathematics we taught often took our students several days to learn. They were epics. One of our group's frustrations with many children's trade books was that they introduced topics but did not carry children through a sequence of activities needed to bring about mastery. The ability to use stories that lasted several days allowed us to design lengthy instructional sequences. How powerful we felt!

Third, our stories let us speak in our own voices, share our own imagery about mathematics, and express our own personal excitement about the mathematics we were teaching. Another of our group's frustrations with using children's trade books to teach mathematics was that we had to use someone else's words, ideas, and imagery. We always wanted to rewrite children's books using our own words and imagery rather than the author's. Now we could. How liberating!

Fourth, our stories allowed us to look our students in the eye while speaking and to have a far more intimate relationship with them because we looked at each other during the storytelling. Still another of our group's frustrations with using children's books was that the books always sat between us and our students and that while teaching we had to look at the words in the book rather than into our students' eyes. Now we felt so much closer to our students. That feeling of closeness encouraged us and made us feel as if our classrooms were more human places.

Fifth, our stories allowed us to take advantage of events that occurred in our classrooms and to incorporate them into our stories. One of our group's frustrations with using children's trade books to teach mathematics was that no matter what happened in our classroom, we were trapped with a script that someone else wrote that we could not alter. Now, while telling stories, we were free to change them and respond to our students through them. Now we were free to include our students and classroom occurrences in our stories. Such fun! So refreshing it was to share our playfulness with our students in this way.

During our group meetings about the stories that we created and used with our students, we discussed many things: how to use manipulatives in stories, how to structure small-group work during our stories, how to get children involved in helping us tell our stories, how to build different learning and thinking styles into our stories, and possible roles for fantasy and imagination in our stories. Our discussions were exciting, both because we realized that we had discovered a new way of teaching mathematics and because our discussions allowed us to reflect on and share exciting things occurring in our classrooms.

Our mathematical oral storytelling group eventually got me to record "The Wizard's Tale." Doing so pushed me to examine the pedagogical and philosophical underpinnings of mathematical epic storytelling. I discovered and wrote about a number of topics:

- The importance of stories in children's lives
- The power of orally presented stories
- The role of fantasy in children's lives and its power in capturing their interest
- The ability of oral stories to put mathematics in a meaningful context
- The benefits of (epic) stories that continue for several days
- Structural relationships among children, teachers, and mathematics during oral storytelling
- How oral stories can help mold desired classroom cultures through cooperative learning

Several years later Doris Lawson moved from teaching all subjects to fourth graders to teaching mathematics and social studies to sixth, seventh, and eighth graders. Doris and another sixth grade teacher in our group asked me to create a story that integrated mathematical problem solving and ancient Egyptian culture. Both were topics of their sixth grade curriculum.

I started reading about ancient Egypt, which led me to read about the history of mathematics, ethnomathematics, and multicultural mathematics education. What a surprise!

I began to see mathematical epic oral storytelling and mathematics from a new perspective—a cultural perspective.

I began to see how mathematics epic oral storytelling could be used as a multicultural instructional tool because its oral instructional medium could parallel the more oral nature of many cultures as well as the more oral learning and thinking styles of the families and communities of many children; because it could simultaneously present mathematics and culture; because it allows (to the degree possible) children to project themselves into cultures other than their own; and because (to the degree possible) it allows children to learn through the use of the objects, artifacts, myths, customs, and knowledge bases of cultures other than their own.

I also began to see that a highly literate culture underlies school mathematics, to comprehend the nature of the highly abstract, symbolic, and deductive mathematics that we teach in our schools, and to see through the myths about mathematics being a culture-free subject.

In addition, I began to see that the culture of many children's families and communities was different from the culture of school mathematics and that the match or mismatch between the nature of children's indigenous home culture and the culture of school mathematics could facilitate or inhibit children's learning of mathematics. I began to understand how children who came from highly literate families, communities, and cultures could more easily succeed in school mathematics—because the nature of their highly literate families, communities, and cultures provided them at an early age with many of the intellectual skills needed for achieving success in school mathematics. And I began to see how children who came from more oral families, communities, and cultures could have greater difficulty learning our highly symbolic and analytical school mathematics—because the nature of their more oral families, communities, and cultures did not provide them with many of the intellectual skills required for success in school mathematics.

Not only is mathematical oral storytelling a powerful instructional medium for all children, it might also be a particularly powerful instructional medium for allowing children from more oral families, communities, and cultures to make the transition from their more oral home culture to the highly literate culture of the mathematics classroom. This was a major discovery! It was a discovery of how powerful an influence children's home and community cultures could have on their learning of school mathematics. It was a discovery of how profound an influence the culture of school mathematics could have on children's learning of mathematics. It was a discovery of how mathematical oral storytelling might serve as an intellectual bridge to help children whose home and community cultures were discrepant in certain ways from the culture of school mathematics to learn school mathematics. It was a discovery of how mathematical oral storytelling might be a multicultural instructional tool that could help many children who were struggling with school mathematics learn the subject more easily—whether they came from urban or rural communities in highly literate countries or from more oral non-Western cultures.

These multicultural discoveries were important to me for two reasons: First, the theoretical literature on multicultural mathematics education mentions the discrepancies between the culture of school mathematics and the culture of many societies and the intellectual difficulties for children that can result from these discrepancies. This theoretical literature, however, provides few instructional methods that might help children bridge the gap between their indigenous culture and the culture of school mathematics. Mathematical oral storytelling promises to be such an instructional method.

Second, when I speak with K-12 teachers who say they are "multicultural educators," they are very interested in my ideas and the application of my ideas to the students with whom they work. Usually they are primarily concerned with helping recent immigrants to the United States overcome linguistic problems that make the learning of mathematics difficult. Rarely do they speak about conceptual issues, such as those examined in this book. Even more rarely do they speak about how to help children bridge the gap between the conceptual nature of their home culture and the culture of school mathematics. When I direct the conversation to how children whose native language is English can experience the same types of conceptual discrepancies between their indigenous home culture and the culture of school mathematics as children whose secondary language is English, these educators indicate that they have observed similar discrepancies. They always want to know more about the conceptual discrepancies and the methods of mathematical epic oral storytelling. I hope the ideas that I have discovered while writing this book will highlight for teachers the types of cultural problems that both native and nonnative English speakers can have with mathematics. And hopefully these educators will be as excited as I am about finding methods—such as mathematical epic oral storytelling—to help them deal with these types of culturally based conceptual problems.

I was thrilled to be able to contribute to both the theoretical literature on multicultural mathematics education and to the everyday practices of classroom teachers.

This brings me to one final issue. As I read, wrote, and spoke with educators about mathematical oral storytelling and multicultural mathematics education, I noticed something that needs to be addressed. Multicultural mathematics educators—as well as mathematics educators in general—have several very different conceptions about the goals and purposes of education. These different conceptions need to be examined.

MULTICULTURAL INTENTIONS OF MATHEMATICS EDUCATORS

During the twentieth century educators in the United States participated in two great debates about the purposes of schooling. The first debate took place during the first third of the century, and it laid the foundation for the second debate, which took place between about 1960 and 1980. Educators are now reengaging in the same debate as they attempt to determine the purposes of mathematics instruction and how and why multicultural concerns and mathematics instruction should be combined.

During these debates four ideological positions surfaced. I have labeled them the "scholar academic ideology," "the social efficiency ideology," "the child study ideology," and "the social reconstruction ideology" (Schiro, 1978).

Scholar academics believe that over the centuries our culture has accumulated important knowledge that has been organized into the academic disciplines. Our mathematical legacy is embodied in the academic discipline of mathematics. The purpose of education, according to scholar academics, is to help children learn the knowledge of the academic disciplines—in our case, mathematics. While acquiring an understanding of mathematics, children will learn mathematical information, how to prove mathematical conjectures, and the conceptual frameworks of mathematicians. Teachers should be knowledgeable about mathematics (mathematical minischolars) so they can clearly and accurately present it to children, often using direct instruction or guided inquiry.

In the 1890s, the Committee of Ten (National Education Association, 1894) decided that the content of mathematics should be one of the foundations of the school curriculum (along with English, history, science, and foreign languages). During the middle of the twentieth century, organizations such as the School Mathematics Study Group (SMSG) worked to rebuild the school mathematics curriculum so that its content would mirror the most up–to-date mathematical understandings of professional mathematicians. In the last decade of the twentieth century, some states, like Massachusetts, decided that understanding mathematics was so important that children would have to pass a mathematics test to graduate from high school.

Social efficiency proponents believe that the purpose of schooling is to efficiently meet the needs of society by training youth to function as future mature contributing members of society, who can fulfill the many tasks needed by society to help it continue to flourish. Here the goal is to train children in the skills (of mathematics) they will need in the workplace and home in order to live productive lives. Teachers manage instruction by selecting and using teaching strategies designed to efficiently help children acquire the mathematical behaviors prescribed by their curriculum. Instruction is guided by behavioral objectives and reinforcement and may require repeated practice by students to acquire mathematical skills.

Early in the twentieth century, Franklin Bobbitt (1913, 1918) argued that the school curriculum should consist of those skills that children need to function as future contributing adult members of society. During the middle of the century, Robert Gagne (1963, 1965) urged educators to scientifically determine and sequence behavioral objectives that would embody the mathematical process skills that children need to acquire. At the same time, B. F. Skinner provided the behaviorist psychology that guided the endeavors of social efficiency advocates to create competency-based, individually prescribed instruction designed to shape desired mathematical behaviors in children. Recently, social efficiency advocates have refocused the educational debate on skills versus understanding and meanings, as the issue of testing for child, teacher, and school accountability has heated up in the United States.

Child study advocates believe that schools should be enjoyable places where children develop naturally according to their own innate natures. Here the goal of education is the growth of individuals, each in harmony with his or her own unique intellectual, social, emotional, and physical attributes. Child study advocates believe that mathematical experiences should center on children's needs and interests. Given the appropriate instructional environment and encouragement, it is assumed that children will become powerful users of mathematics and constructors of mathematical meanings who will be confident in themselves as mathematicians. Teachers facilitate learning and growth by creating a rich and responsive intellectual, social, physical, and emotional environment in which they use a variety of instructional methods and concrete materials to promote children's construction of mathematical meanings.

In the 1890s, Francis Parker proclaimed, "The centre of all . . . education is *the child*" (1894, p. 383). He wanted to make children, rather than content, the focus of education.

During the middle of the twentieth century, the Education Development Center designed pattern blocks, tangrams, attribute blocks, and geo-blocks to allow children to "mess around" with mathematics in ways that would allow them to enjoy themselves as they created their own mathematical meanings (Elementary Science Study, 1970). Today, child study advocates argue for developmentally appropriate practice, constructivism, and making the child's needs and nature central to instructional planning. They assert that the most worthwhile forms of mathematical knowledge that children acquire in school are those personal meanings that they themselves construct out of their experiences with their environment, whether or not the mathematics they construct corresponds to the traditional mathematical knowledge valued by society.

Social reconstruction advocates are conscious of the problems of our society and the injustices done to its members, injustices such as those originating from racial, gender, cultural, social, and economic inequities. They assume that the purpose of schooling is to facilitate the construction of a more just society that offers maximum satisfaction to all of its members. By learning mathematics children acquire powerful tools that allow them to better understand the problems of society and to more systematically and knowledgeably find ways of acting in order to make it the most just and fair society possible. Teachers collaborate with students during the learning process as they teach mathematics by immersing students in situations in which mathematics can help them confront and improve real social crises.

In the 1930s George Counts (1932) dared teachers to confront and analyze the problems of society, and based on those analyses he dared schools to create a new social order that would be more just and equitable than the existing one. During the middle of the century educators helped children learn mathematics so that they could understand, and act to improve, such social problems as school segregation, the Viet Nam War, environmental pollution, and nuclear proliferation. Teachers attempted to build a better society by teaching children the mathematics they would need to become active social-change agents focused on first understanding and then improving society. Today educators write about the socioeconomic, ethnic, linguistic, racial, and gender inequities of much of mathematics instruction and urge teachers to work to transform their instruction and society to eliminate inequities so that all children will have equal opportunity to succeed in learning mathematics, as one means of attaining a more fair and just society (Zaslavsky, 1996; NCTM, 2000).

IDEOLOGICAL POSITIONS FOR MULTICULTURAL MATHEMATICS

Paralleling the four ideological approaches just described are four similar approaches to multicultural mathematics.

Scholar Academic Position on Multicultural Mathematics

One approach to multicultural mathematics education grows out of the scholar academic ideology. Its concern is with the true nature of mathematical knowledge and the contributions of different cultures to our mathematical knowledge base. From this perspective the purpose of education is to help children learn mathematical knowledge in the most insightful way possible. Here it is assumed that "students have an enormous capacity to learn and will absorb [mathematical] ideas like sponges if properly [taught,] motivated and encouraged" (Keynes, 1995, p. 64).

Currently this endeavor involves reexamining our conception of the nature of mathematics, viewing it not as a homogeneously uniform area of study centering only on Western contributions to the field, but as an area of study that utilizes many different cultures' knowledge bases. The intent is to present an accurate picture of the historical and cultural foundations of mathematics and to enculturate children into the rich heritage of that group of people who study mathematics in all of its diverse dimensions. Here children learn about the mathematical content discovered by many different peoples, as well as the wide range of different methods of proof they employed. For example, they learn about the contextually illustrative methods of proof of the ancient Egyptians, the oral-aural methods of discursive proof of the Persians of a thousand years ago, the visually demonstrative methods of proof of the Chinese, as well as the axiomatically deductive methods of proof popular in Europe during the last several hundred years (Nelson, Joseph, & Williams, 1993, pp. 9-11). Here it is assumed that "knowledge and understanding of other cultures is worthwhile for its own sake. It is argued that an understanding of one's own culture depends upon a knowledge of other cultures, with which it can be compared and through which we can see what is often taken for granted" (Nelson, Joseph, & Williams, 1993, p. 3).

Within this position there are two instructional goals. One is to help children understand and appreciate the mathematical knowledge created by different world cultures. The other is to increase children's understanding and appreciation of the mathematics of their own culture (or cultures) under the assumption that understanding the mathematics of several cultures will enable one to better understand and appreciate the mathematics of one's own culture.

The emphasis on equity is twofold. It involves providing an accurate picture of the mathematical knowledge bases and contributions of a variety of cultures. This first type of equity involves accurately portraying and valuing the knowledge generated by disparate cultures. This includes acting on the belief that "the mathematics curriculum must provide opportunities for all pupils to recognize that all cultures engage in mathematical activity and no single culture has a monopoly on mathematical achievement" (Nelson, Joseph, & Williams, 1993, p. 19). The second type of equity involves providing all learners—independent of race, sex, cultural background, or socioeconomic status—with equal access to mathematical knowledge and the chance to excel in learning that knowledge. This includes making sure that disadvantaged groups are not deprived of equal access to mathematical knowledge because of the way instructional practices might be biased against them. Here it is assumed that children must be presented with rigorous authentic mathematics and that high standards for mathematical excellence must be insisted upon, for "equity for all requires excellence for all, both thrive when expectations are high" (National Research Council, 1989).

Social Efficiency Position on Multicultural Mathematics

Another approach to multicultural mathematics education grows out of the social efficiency tradition. This tradition emphasizes that the purpose of instruction is to help children learn mathematics skills in the most efficient and effective way possible so that as adults they will be able to efficiently solve the problems that arise in their work and home life. The emphasis here is on "student performance" and "the acquisition of mathematical thinking and reasoning skills by students" (Silver, Smith, & Nelson, 1995, pp. 16, 10). From this perspective there are two multicultural concerns:

First, to teach mathematical skills to children efficiently, it is believed necessary to synchronize the mathematical skills that children will need as adults with the variety of different culturally based conceptual frameworks that children come to school with. Here it is believed necessary to determine the nature of children's knowledge bases (acquired from their families and communities) so that mathematics curricula can be scientifically constructed to take into account, accommodate for, and compensate for those knowledge bases, so that mathematics required for future occupational and home life can be efficiently taught and learned. Here the equity concern relates to the efficiency and effectiveness with which children learn mathematical skills.

Second, this approach considers the multicultural neighborhoods in which children live and the multicultural world in which all children will have to live as adults. There is a concern with providing children with the mathematical skills necessary to productively function in both of these environments. Here the belief is that we must identify the mathematics skills necessary for productive functioning in a multicultural society, so that children—who will become adults—can be taught those skills so that they can efficiently and effectively function within society now and in the future. Here mathematics instruction is "seen as part of a broader set of efforts to create a society that offers opportunity to each of its members to be successful and to contribute to the social and economic good" (Silver, Smith, & Nelson, 1995, p. 10).

Here equity issues relate to helping children—children of the poor and working classes, and girls, and in particular the children of cultural, ethnic, and racial groups different from those who are in control of the political, economic, and social functions of the society in which they are located—obtain access to social positions of power and success by learning mathematics skills. Here there is concern because "the potential of this country's cultural diversity has not been fully developed, because all children have not been given reasonable opportunity to learn mathematics and other school subjects that would open the doors to employment and further education" (Silver, Smith, & Nelson, 1995, p. 9). The emphasis is not on learning mathematics as a subject worthy of study in and of itself but on learning mathematics because it is a tool that will provide children with access to good jobs, social prestige, and the ability to productively participate in the activities valued by society.

Child Study Position on Multicultural Mathematics

A third approach to multicultural mathematics education emanates from the child study tradition. It emphasizes that the purpose of mathematics instruction is to help children grow—intellectually, socially, and emotionally—in accordance with their own innate natures and the innate nature of their culture. To accomplish this educators must make sure that powerful social and economic forces within society—forces that want to keep certain social, racial, cultural, economic, and sexual groups in their subservient places through the hidden curriculum of schools—do not inhibit, limit, or pervert the natural growth of the child's mathematical potential or interfere with each child becoming a powerful maker of mathematical meanings who feels good about himself or herself as a mathematician.

Here educators recognize and value the mathematical heritage of cultural and social groups—including minorities within a larger nation, and nations within a larger world culture. They want to help members of those groups recognize, participate in, value, and use their indigenous mathematical cultural heritage. In so doing, educators encourage individuals to make mathematical meanings and develop their mathematical intuition in accordance with their cultural background. Doing so not only builds children's confidence and pride in their mathematical background, but also allows children to develop their own unique mathematical meanings and ways of making mathematical meaning that are consistent with their cultural heritage. It is believed that doing so produces not only a more integrated, holistic, coherent, and powerful view of mathematics within the child but also a more holistic and integrated approach to teaching, curriculum, and knowledge within the instructional arena. For example, knowledge of different academic subjects is seen as related rather than disjointed (as when the mathematics of a culture is seen in relation to that culture's religion, arts, crafts, and history), and knowledge acquired in school and the community is seen as integrated rather than discrepant (as when the mathematics children learn in their parents' markets is seen in relation to the mathematics they learn in school). As Nelson, Joseph, and Williams imply,

> if we accept the principle . . . that teaching should be tailored to students' experience of the social and physical environment in which they live, mathematics should draw on these experiences, including the mathematical heritage of different minority groups. . . . Drawing on the traditions of these groups, indicating that their cultures are recognized and valued, would also help to counter the entrenched historical devaluation of them. (1993, p. 14)

From an equity perspective, this approach encourages children to find their own unique ways of making mathematical meanings that are consistent with their innate and culturally acquired intellectual, social, and emotional natures and knowledge bases. Here the concern is not with accessibility to the mathematical knowledge of the dominant culture or with accessibility to the mathematics skills that will allow the child to be a productive member of society, but with allowing each child to develop in his or her own unique manner in a way that is consistent with his or her individual nature and cultural background.

Social Reconstruction Position on Multicultural Mathematics

The fourth approach to multicultural mathematics education draws on the social reconstruction ideology. It emphasizes that there is a moral and political dimension to mathematics instruction that should be oriented toward providing children with the mathematics skills, knowledge, and social values that will allow them to analyze and reconstruct society in such a way that all of its members have an equal chance for intellectual, emotional, economic, and social success in a society that does not discriminate between people because of their cultural background, racial origins, economic status, social class, or sex.

Fundamental to this approach is the endeavor to place mathematics in a social context and integrate mathematics instruction with a set of social values in such a way that children can (1) see the problems with their current society, (2) envision a more just future society in which those problems do not exist, and (3) actively work to bring about social change that will lead to a more just society. Fasheh (1997) elaborates:

> Math can be used to stress one's own culture with its special and beautiful characteristics. At the same time, math can be used to make one aware of the drawbacks in one's own culture and try to overcome them. . . . Teaching math in a way detached from cultural aspects, and in a purely abstract, symbolic and meaningless way, is not only useless, but also very harmful to the student, to society, to math itself, and to future generations. . . . I came to believe that the teaching of math . . . is a "political" activity . . . teaching math through cultural relevance and personal experiences helps the learners know more about reality, culture, society, and themselves. That will, in turn, help them . . . build new perspectives and syntheses, and seek new alternatives, and, hopefully, will help them transform some existing [social] structures and relations. (pp. 284, 286-288)

Placing mathematics in a social context can take many forms. For people and nations who have had their indigenous mathematics displaced by Western mathematics, it can involve teaching children about their own native culture's mathematical contributions. It can also involve teaching children Western statistics while using problems that provide insight into a culture's economic, social, racial, and sexual inequalities.

Anderson (1997) highlights the need for mathematics educators to help children envision a more just future society when he writes,

> Those of us who are genuinely concerned with educating students for liberation rather than training them for the job market must attack, critique, and dismantle the Eurocentric educational construct while simultaneously planting the seeds for more holistic, in-tune-with-nature, popular, and egalitarian forms of learning. We cannot wait any longer . . . in . . . mathematics . . . to offer an alternative that is genuinely egalitarian. (pp. 305-306)

Powell & Frankenstein (1997b) highlight the social reconstruction assumption that mathematics should be taught in such a way as to encourage children and teachers to actively work toward bringing about social change that will lead to a more just, fair, and egalitarian society when they write that "the cultural action involved in teaching and learning ethnomathematics can play a role in the economic and political action needed to create a libratory society" (pp. 325-326). Knijnik (with respect to her endeavors with the Landless Peoples Movement in rural Brazil) and Ladson-Billings (with respect to her endeavors with urban U.S. students) elaborate:

> Pedagogical practice in mathematical education is fundamentally a political issue. . . . It deals with the interrelations between academic and popular mathematical knowledge in the context of the struggle for land. (Knijnik, 1997, p. 405)

The underlying assumption of multicultural education is that the nation's educational system promotes the status quo and that the status quo is rife with inequity along race, class, gender, and ability lines. . . . [M]ulticultural education assumes that students are social, political, and cultural actors and that through experiences with schoolwide change they can promote social change . . . [that will] ensure . . . that students of diverse race, social class, and gender groups experience equal educational opportunity. (Ladson-Billings, 1995, p. 126)

From this perspective equity issues relate to helping children acquire mathematics skills, knowledge, and social values that will allow them to analyze and reconstruct society in such a way that all of its members have an equal chance for success in a society that does not discriminate against people because of their cultural background, racial origins, economic status, social class, or sex. This goes considerably beyond the goals of helping children acquire mathematical knowledge, become productive members of the existing social structure, or develop in accordance with their own unique personal and cultural potentialities.

Three Considerations

One might not at first notice these multicultural positions, for many educators seem to have difficulty clarifying their beliefs. While most educators seem to teach or create instructional materials in ways that are consistent with one ideological position, their language is often full of confusion and contradictions. For example, educators who claim they promote personal growth (a child study purpose) often create instructional materials that only convey information about the mathematics of different cultures (a scholar academic purpose). To understand mathematics educators' multicultural intentions, it is necessary to ascertain what they are truly endeavoring to accomplish, for frequently lofty articulations do not correspond to concrete actions.

As I read the literature in multicultural mathematics education, at first I did not notice the ideological differences that existed. Once I did notice the differences, several things occurred. First, it became easier for me to understand educators' ideas from the perspective from which they were offered. This, in turn, made it easier for me to make their ideas meaningful to me, from within my current ideological perspective. Second, it became easier for me to understand the purposes of their instructional practices in the context of their ideological perspective. This, in turn, made it easier for me to determine how, when, and if I wanted to utilize their instructional practices in my work.

Those of us who work in the area of multicultural mathematics must each face the difficult task of determining which ideological perspective—or combination of ideological perspectives—we will work from. Determining the nature of our educational beliefs is not a task that educators engage in only once in their lives. It is a continuous process of searching for meaning. Research has shown that we as educators make shifts in our ideologies at the rate of about once every 4 years as we struggle with the realities of classroom instruction, the diversity of our students, and the shifting public pressures on us to pursue different educational purposes (Schiro, 1992). Since becoming interested in mathematical oral storytelling a decade ago, I have shifted my ideological perspective several times. The ideas presented in this book have been meaningful and relevant, in slightly different ways, from within the context of each perspective.

APPLICABILITY OF ORAL STORYTELLING WITHIN DIFFERENT IDEOLOGIES

Mathematical epic oral storytelling is a flexible instructional technique that can be used within the context of each of the four ideologies. In addition, the ideas about multicultural mathematics presented within this book have much to contribute to the beliefs of educators working within the context of each ideology.

Educators' holding the scholar academic ideology should find mathematical epic oral storytelling an ideal tool to help children understand mathematical knowledge. It can convey facts about the history of mathematics in a variety of cultures, as in "The Egypt Story." It can help students understand algorithms, as demonstrated in "The Wizard's Tale." It can be used to help students learn mathematical problem solving, as demonstrated in "The Egypt Story." And it can be used as a way to present mathematical proofs, as was demonstrated in the ancient proofs of the area of a circle in "The Egypt Story."

Educators who hold the social efficiency ideology should find mathematical oral storytelling an ideal tool to help children acquire mathematics skills. "The Wizard's Story" provides an example of how to teach the mathematics skill of multidigit addition. The Game of the Snake, presented in "The Egypt Story," is one type of highly motivating activity that can be used to provide students with skill practice and reinforcement.

Educators who favor the child study ideology will also find oral storytelling quite consistent with their beliefs in constructivism and developmentally appropriate practice. As "The Egypt Story" demonstrates, it is an instructional method that can be used to encourage children to construct their own personal meanings and that can be designed to allow children to make important decisions (such as whether or not to teach An-Nab our current-day method of multiplication). As "The Wizard's Tale" demonstrates, it uses instructional methods that involve the whole child (physical, social, intellectual, and emotional) in learning, that nourish children's fantasies and imagination, and that use approaches and materials (such as base ten blocks) that are consistent with children's developmental levels.

Educators who believe in the social reconstruction ideology should also find mathematical epic oral storytelling a powerful instructional tool. The discussion of ancient Egyptian multiplication in Chapter 9 on problem solving parallels the above discussion of the social reconstruction perspective by highlighting how the stages of knowledge, assessment, values, and action are embedded in Day 7 of "The Egypt Story." The discussion of "The Wizard's Tale" illustrates how a teacher can manipulate social groups in order to teach social values and paint a picture of a world that is better (perhaps kinder and more magical) than our current one. Oral storytelling can also be used to highlight social inequities. Just imagine how the generations problem on Day 1 of "The Egypt Story" could be reconstructed to highlight the inequities of life between ancient Egypt and today—or between any two cultures. In addition, because listeners can become active participants in a story, they can try out (and learn) new behaviors that might allow them to actively confront existing social problems and help build a society that is more fulfilling to more people than the existing one.

IN CONCLUSION

Oral storytelling is a powerful instructional method that teachers can use to aid them in the teaching of mathematics. The perspectives on the relationship between culture and mathematics instruction in this book offer educators new and deeper insights into children's learning of mathematics.

But make no mistake, the instructional methods and cultural insights offered in this book are not limited to the teaching of mathematics. The instructional method of epic oral storytelling is as relevant to the content areas of science, social studies, and the language arts as it is to mathematics. I have worked with teachers who have successfully used it in these areas of instruction. The perspectives on the relationships between culture and mathematics instruction presented in this book are also not limited to the teaching of mathematics. They too are relevant to the other content areas of the school curriculum.

A stage of the currently popular problem-solving model used in mathematics instruction is called "looking back." This book has suggested that this stage be called "looking back and looking forward." The reader of this book is offered a problem-solving challenge: look back on the ideas presented in this book and then look forward to see how its ideas can apply to other areas of instruction and other organizations offering instruction. Applying the ideas on instructional methods and on the relationships between culture and instruction offered in this book to other areas of the school curriculum and other organizations in which instruction takes place will provide intellectual insight and excitement, and has the power to enormously enrich children's learning within school classrooms, community organizations, and families.

REFERENCES

Albert, L. (2000). Outside in, Inside out: Seventh-grade students' mathematical thought processes. *Educational Studies in Mathematics, 41,* 109-141.

Ambrose, R., Levi, L., & Fennema, E. (1997). The complexity of teaching for gender equity. In J. Trentacosta & M. J. Kenney (Eds.), *Multicultural and gender equity in the mathematics classroom.* Reston, VA: National Council of Teachers of Mathematics.

Anderson, S. E. (1997). Worldmath curriculum: Fighting Eurocentrism in mathematics. In A. B. Powell & M. Frankenstein (Eds.), *Ethnomathematics: Challenging eurocentrism in mathematics education* (pp. 305-306). Albany, NY: State University of New York Press.

Anno, M., & Anno, M. (1983). *Anno's mysterious multiplying jar.* New York: Philomel Books.

Ascher, M. (1991). *Ethnomathematics: A multicultural view of mathematical ideas.* Pacific Grove, CA: Brooks/Cole.

Atweh, B., Forgasz, H., & Nebres, B. (Eds.). (2001). *Sociocultural research on mathematics education.* Mahwah, NJ: Lawrence Earlbaum.

Baddeley, A. (1986). *Working memory.* Oxford, UK: Clarendon Press.

Baker, A., & Greene, E. (1987). *Storytelling: Art and technique.* New York: R.R. Bowker.

Baroody, A. J. (1993). *Problem solving, reasoning, and communicating.* New York: Macmillan.

Barrie, J. M. (1982). *Peter Pan.* New York: Bantam.

Beckmann, P. (1974). *A history of π.* New York: St. Martin's Press.

Bell, R. C. (1979). *The boardgame book.* Los Angeles: Knapp.

Bernal, M. (1992). Animadversions on the origins of western science. *Isis, 83*(4): 596-607.

Bert, C. R. G., & Bert, M. (1992). The Native American: An exceptionality in education and counseling. (ERIC Document Reproduction Service No. ED 351168).

Bettleheim, B. (1976). *The uses of enchantment: Meaning and importance of fairy tales.* New York: Knopf.

Bobbitt, F. (1913). Some general principles of management applied to the problems of city school systems. In *Twelfth yearbook of the National Society for the Study of Education. Part I.* Chicago: University of Chicago Press.

Bobbitt, F. (1918). *The curriculum.* Boston: Riverside Press.

Brown, S., & Walters, M. (1983). *The art of problem posing.* Hillsdale, NJ: Lawrence Earlbaum.

Bryant, S. C. (1905). *How to tell stories to children.* New York: Houghton.

Budge, E. A. W. (1894). *The mummy.* Cambridge, UK: Cambridge University Press.

Budge, E. A. W. (1934). *From fetish to god in ancient Egypt.* London: Oxford University Press.

Burns, M. (1992). *Math and literature (k-3).* Sausalito, CA: Math Solutions.

Burns, M. (1994). Arithmetic: The last holdout. *Phi Delta Kappan, 75,* 471-76.

Cambourne, B. (1988). *The whole story: Natural learning and the acquisition of literacy in the classroom.* New York: Scholastic.

Carraher, T. (1988). Street mathematics and school mathematics. *Proceedings of the 12th International Conference on Psychology of Mathematics Education,* Veszprem, Hungary, 1-23.

Carraher, T. N., Carraher, D. W., & Schliemann, A. D. (1985). Mathematics in the streets and in schools. *British Journal of Developmental Psychology, 3,* 21-29.

Carraher, T. N., Carraher, D. W., & Schliemann, A. D. (1987). Written and oral mathematics. *Journal of Research in Mathematics Education, 18*(2), 83-97.

Casey, M. B., Nuttall, R., Pezaris E., & Benbow, C. P. (1995). The influence of spatial ability on gender differences in mathematics college entrance test scores across diverse samples. *Developmental Psychology, 31,* 697-705.

Chace, A. B., Bull, L., Manning, H. P., & Archibald, R. C. (Trans.). (1927). *The Rhind mathematical papyrus.* Oberlin, Ohio: Mathematical Association of America.

Claxton, C. S. (1990). Learning styles, minority students, and effective education. *Journal of Developmental Education, 14,* 6-8, 35.

Coombs, B., Harcourt, L., Travis, J., & Wannamaker, N. (1987). *Explorations 2.* Reading, MA: Addison Wesley.

Counts, G. (1932). *Dare the school build a new social order?* New York: Arno Press.

Cox, B., & Ramirez, M., III. (1981). Cognitive styles: Implications for multiethnic education. In James Banks (Ed.), *Education in the '80s.* Washington, DC: National Education Association.

D'Ambrosio, U. (1985). Ethnomathematics and its place in the history and pedagogy of mathematics. *For the Learning of Mathematics, 5*(1), 44-48.

D'Ambrosio, U. (1997a). Diversity, equity, and peace: From dream to reality. In J. Trentacosta & M. J. Kenney (Eds.), *1997 yearbook: Multicultural and gender equity in the mathematics classroom.* Reston, VA: National Council of Teachers of Mathematics.

D'Ambrosio, U. (1997b). Ethnomathematics and its place in the history and pedagogy of mathematics. In A. B. Powell, & M. Frankenstein (Eds.), *Ethnomathematics: Challenging eurocentrism in mathematics education.* Albany, NY: State University of New York Press.

Davis, B. (1996). *Teaching mathematics.* New York: Garland.

Decker, W. (1992). *Sports and games of ancient Egypt.* New Haven, CT: Yale University Press.

Downing, D. (1989). *Algebra the easy way.* Hauppauge, NY: Barron's Educational Series.

Egan, K. (1986). *Teaching as story telling: An alternative approach to teaching and curriculum in the elementary school.* Chicago: University of Chicago Press.

Elementary Science Study. (1970). *The ESS reader.* Newton, MA: Education Development Center.

Epp, S. S. (1994). The role of proof in problem solving. In A. H Schoenfeld (Ed.), *Mathematical thinking and problem solving.* Hillsdale, NJ: Lawrence Earlbaum.

Ewen, I. (1996). Strategies for problem exploration. In A. S. Posamentier & W. Schulz (Eds.), *The art of problem solving* (pp. 1-82). Thousand Oaks, CA: Corwin.

Fasheh, M. (1982). Mathematics, culture, and authority. *For the Learning of Mathematics, 3*(2), 2-8.

Fasheh, M. (1997). Mathematics, culture, and authority. In A. B. Powell & M. Frankenstein (Eds.), *Ethnomathematics: Challenging eurocentrism in mathematics education* (pp. 281-288). Albany, NY: State University of New York Press.

Frankenstein, M. (1995). Equity in mathematics education: Class in the world outside the class. In W. G. Secada, E. Fennema, & L. B. Adajian (Eds.), *New directions for equity in mathematics education* (pp. 165-190). Cambridge, UK: Cambridge University Press.

Gagne, R. M. (1963). Learning and proficiency in mathematics. *The Mathematics Teacher, 56*(8).

Gagne, R. M. (1965). *The conditions of learning.* NY: Holt, Rinehart and Winston.

Gardner, H. (1993). *Frames of mind: the theory of multiple intelligences.* New York: Basic Books.

Gay, J., & Cole, M. (1967). *The new mathematics and an old culture.* New York: Holt, Rinehart and Winston.

Gerdes, P. (1997a). On culture, geometrical thinking and mathematics education. In A. B. Powell & M. Frankenstein (Eds.), *Ethnomathematics: Challenging eurocentrism in mathematics education.* Albany, NY: State University of New York Press.

Gerdes, P. (1997b). Survey of current work on ethnomathematics. In A. B. Powell & M. Frankenstein (Eds.), *Ethnomathematics: Challenging Eurocentrism in mathematics education.* Albany, NY: State University of New York Press, 1997.

Gillings, R. J. (1972). *Mathematics in the time of the pharaohs.* New York: Dover.

Gregoric, A. F. (1979). Learning/teaching styles: Their nature and effects. In J. W. Keefe (Ed.), *Student learning styles.* Reston, VA: National Association of Secondary School Principals.

Griffiths, R., & Clyne, M. (1991). *Books you can count on: Linking mathematics and literature.* Portsmouth, NH: Heinemann.

Guild, P. (1995). The culture/learning style connection. *Educational Leadership, 51*(8), 16-21.

Hadamard, J. (1945). *The psychology of invention in the mathematical field.* Princeton: Princeton University Press.

Hardy, B. (1977). Towards a poetics of fiction: An approach through narrative. In M. Meek, A. Warlow, & G. Barton (Eds.), *The cool web: The pattern of children's reading* (pp. 12-23). New York: Atheneum.

Harris, P. (1991). *Mathematics in a cultural context.* Geelong, Australia: Deakin University.

Hartman, H. J. (1996). Cooperative learning approaches to mathematical problem solving. In A. S. Posamentier & W. Schulz (Eds.), *The art of problem solving* (pp. 401-430). Thousand Oaks, CA: Corwin.

Heath, S. B. (1983). *Ways with words: Language, life, and work in communities and classrooms.* Cambridge, UK: Cambridge University Press.

Hilliard, A. G., III. (1989). Teachers and cultural styles in a pluralistic society. *NEA Today 7*(6), 65-69.

Hobson, E. W. (1913). *Squaring the circle.* Cambridge, UK: Cambridge University Press.

Homer. (1999). *Iliad.* (A. T. Murray, Trans.). Cambridge, MA: Harvard University Press.

Hoogeboom, S. & Goodnow, J. (1987). *The problem solver 3: Activities for learning problem-solving strategies.* Sunnyvale, CA: Creative.

Hutchins, P. (1986). *The doorbell rang.* New York: Mulberry Books.

Johnson, D., & Johnson, R. (1990). Using cooperative learning in mathematics. In N. Davidson (Ed.), *Cooperative learning in mathematics.* Tucson, AZ: Zephyr.

Johnson, D. W., Johnson, R. T., & Holubec, E. J. (1991). *Cooperation in the classroom.* Edina, MN: Interaction.

Kamii, C. (1987). *Double-column addition: A teacher uses Piaget's theory* [videotape]. Birmingham, AL: Promethean Films South.

Kamii, C., & Dominick, A. (1998). The harmful effects of algorithms in grades 1-4. In L. J. Morrow & M. J. Kenney (Eds.), *The teaching and learning of algorithms in school mathematics* (pp. 130-140). Reston, VA: National Council of Teachers of Mathematics.

Keynes, H. B. (1995). Can equity thrive in a culture of mathematical excellence? In W. G. Secada, E. Fennema, & L. B. Adajian (Eds.), *New directions for equity in mathematics education* (pp. 57-92). Cambridge, UK: Cambridge University Press.

Keyser, C. (1932). Mathematics as a culture clue. *Scripta Mathematica. 1*, 185-203.

Kleiman, G., & Bjork, E. (1991). *My travels with Gulliver.* Scotts Valley, CA: Wings for Learning.

Kliman, M. (1993). Integrating mathematics and literature in the elementary classroom. *Arithmetic Teacher, 40*(6), 318-321.

Kline, M. (1980). *Mathematics: The loss of certainty.* New York: Oxford University Press.

Knijnik, G. (1997). An ethnomathematical approach in mathematics education: A matter of political power. In A. B. Powell & M. Frankenstein (Eds.), *Ethnomathematics: Challenging Eurocentrism in mathematics education* (pp. 403-410). Albany, NY: State University of New York Press.

Krause, M. C. (2000). *Multicultural mathematics materials.* Reston, VA: National Council of Teachers of Mathematics.

Krulik, S. (Ed.). (1980). *Problem solving in school mathematics. 1980 Yearbook of the National Council of Teachers of Mathematics.* Reston, VA: National Council of Teachers of Mathematics.

Kuhn, T. S. (1962). *The structure of scientific revolutions.* Chicago: University of Chicago Press.

Ladson-Billings, G. (1995). Making mathematics meaningful in multicultural contexts. In W. G. Secada, E. Fennema, & L. B. Adajian (Eds.), *New directions for equity in mathematics education* (pp. 126-145). Cambridge, UK: Cambridge University Press.

Lane, H. L. (1976). *The wild boy of Aveyron.* Cambridge, MA: Harvard University Press.

Lawson, D. P. (1995). *Math in boxes, math in books, math in being: Applying a model of literacy learning to fourth grade mathematics instruction.* Unpublished doctoral dissertation, Boston College, Chestnut Hill, MA.

Leap, W. L. (1988). Assumptions and strategies guiding mathematics problem solving by Ute Indian students. In R. R. Cocking & J. P. Mestre (Eds.), *Linguistic and cultural influences on learning mathematics* (pp. 161-186). Hillsdale, NJ: Lawrence Erlbaum.

LeGuin, U. K. (1975). *A wizard of Earthsea.* New York: Bantam.

Love, B. (1978). *Play the game.* Los Angeles: Reed Books.

Love, B. (1979). *Great board games.* New York: Macmillan.

Lumpkin, B. (1997a). Africa in the mainstream of mathematics history. In A. B. Powell & M. Frankenstein (Eds.), *Ethnomathematics: Challenging eurocentrism in mathematics education.* Albany, NY: State University of New York Press.

Lumpkin, B. (1997b). *Algebra activities from many cultures.* Portland, ME: J. Weston Walch.

Luria, A. R. (1976). *Cognitive development: Its cultural and social foundations.* M. Cole (Ed.), M. Lopez-Morillas & L. Solotaroff (Trans.). Cambridge, MA: Harvard University Press.

Ma, L. (1999). *Knowing and teaching elementary mathematics.* Mahwah, NJ: Lawrence Earlbaum.

Madell, R. (1985). Children's natural processes. *Arithmetic Teacher, 32* (March 1985), 20-22.

McLuhan, M. & Fiore, Q. (1967). *The medium is the message.* New York, Random House.

Menten, T. (1978). *Ancient Egyptian cut and use stencils.* New York: Dover.

Merrill, J. (1972). *The toothpaste millionaire.* Boston: Houghton Mifflin Company.

Moody, V. R. (2001). The social constructs of the mathematical experiences of African-American students. In B. Atweh, H. Forgasz, & B. Nebres (Eds.), *Sociocultural research on mathematics education* (pp. 255-276). Mahwah, NJ: Lawrence Earlbaum.

More, A. J. (1990). Learning styles of Native Americans and Asians. (ERIC Document Reproduction Service No. ED 330535).

National Council of Teachers of Mathematics. (1989). *Curriculum and evaluation standards for school mathematics.* Reston, VA: National Council of Teachers of Mathematics.

National Council of Teachers of Mathematics. (2000). *Principles and standards for school mathematics.* Reston, VA: National Council of Teachers of Mathematics.

National Education Association. (1894). *Report of the Committee of Ten on secondary school studies.* New York: American.

National Research Council. (1989). *Everybody counts: A report to the nation on the future of mathematics education.* Washington, DC: National Academy Press.

Nelson, D., Joseph, G. G., & Williams, J. (1993). *Multicultural mathematics.* Oxford, UK: Oxford University Press.

Nunes, T., Schliemann, A. D., & Carraher, D. W. (1993). *Street mathematics and school mathematics.* Cambridge, UK: Cambridge University Press.

Olivastro, D. (1993). *Ancient puzzles.* New York: Bantam.

Ong, W. J. (1982). *Orality and literacy.* London: Methuen.

Parker, F. W. (1894). *Talks on pedagogics.* New York: E. L. Kellogg.

Pellowski, A. (1990). *The world of storytelling.* New York: H. W. Wilson.

Perez, B., & McCarty, T. L. (1998). *Sociocultural contexts of language and literacy.* Mahwah, NJ: Lawrence Earlbaum.

Pinxten, R. (1997). Applications in the teaching of mathematics and the sciences. In A. B. Powell & M. Frankenstein (Eds.), *Ethnomathematics: Challenging eurocentrism in mathematics education.* Albany, NY: State University of New York Press.

Pinxten, R., Dooren, I., & Harvey, F. (1983). *Anthropology of space: Exploration into the natural philosophy and semantics of the Navajo.* Philadelphia: University of Pennsylvania Press.

Piper, W. (1990). *The little engine that could.* New York: Putnam.

Poincaré, H. (1946). *The foundations of science.* (Vols. 1-3). (G. B. Halsted. Trans.) Lancaster, PA: Science Press (Original work published 1913).

Polya, G. (1957). *How to solve it.* Princeton, NJ: Princeton University Press.

Powell, A. (1986). Economizing learning: The teaching of numeration in Chinese. *For the Learning of Mathematics 6*(3), 20-23.

Powell, A. B. & Frankenstein, M. (1997a). Ethnomathematical praxis in the curriculum. In A. B. Powell & M. Frankenstein (Eds.), *Ethnomathematics: Challenging eurocentrism in mathematics education.* Albany, NY: State University of New York Press.

Powell, A. B., & Frankenstein, M. (1997b). Ethnomathematical research. In A. B. Powell & M. Frankenstein (Eds.), *Ethnomathematics: Challenging eurocentrism in mathematics education* (pp. 325-326). Albany, NY: State University of New York Press.

Powell, A. B., & Frankenstein, M. (Eds.). (1997c). *Ethnomathematics: Challenging eurocentrism in mathematics education.* Albany, NY: State University of New York Press.

Pressley, M., Wood, E., Woloshuyn, V., King, A., & Menke, D. (1992). Encouraging mindful use of prior knowledge: Attempting to construct explanatory answers facilitates learning. *Educational Psychologist, 27*(1), 91-109.

The Ramayana. (1927). (Valmiki Krishna Dharma, Trans.). Calcutta, India: Oriental.

Resnick, L. B. (1982). Syntax and semantics in learning to subtract. In T. P. Carpenter, J. M. Moser, & T. A. Romberg (Eds.), *Addition and subtraction: A cognitive perspective* (pp. 135-155). Hillsdale, NJ: Lawrence Erlbaum.

The Rhind mathematical papyrus. (1927). (A. B. Chace, L. Bull, H. P. Manning, & R. C. Archibald, Trans.). Oberlin, OH: Mathematical Association of America.

Root-Bernstein, R. & Root-Bernstein, M. (1999). *Sparks of genius.* Boston: Houghton Mifflin.

Satire of the trades. Translated and referenced in D. Olivastro (1993). *Ancient puzzles* (pp. 32-33). New York: Bantam.

Schiro, M. (1978). *Curriculum for better schools: The great ideological debate.* Englewood Cliffs, NJ: Educational Technology Press.

Schiro, M. (1992). Educators' perceptions of the changes in their curriculum belief systems over time. *Journal of Curriculum and Supervision 7*(3), 250-276.

Schiro, M. (1997). *Integrating children's literature and mathematics in the classroom.* New York: Teachers College Press.

Schiro, M., & Cotti, R. (1998). *Mega-fun math puzzles.* New York: Scholastic.

Schoenfeld, A. H. (1989). Teaching mathematical thinking and problem solving. In L. B. Resnick & B. L. Klopfer (Eds.), *Toward the thinking curriculum: Current cognitive research* (pp. 83-103). (1989 Yearbook of the American Society for Curriculum Development). Washington, DC: ASCD.

Schoenfeld, A. H. (1992). Learning to think mathematically: Problem solving, metacognition, and sense making in mathematics. In D. A. Grouws (Ed.), *Handbook of research on mathematics teaching and learning* (pp. 334-370). New York: Macmillan.

Schoenfeld, A. H. (1994). Reflections on doing and teaching mathematics. In A. H Schoenfeld (Ed.), *Mathematical thinking and problem solving.* Hillsdale, NJ: Lawrence Earlbaum.

Schwartz, D. M. (1985). *How much is a million?* New York: Scholastic.

Shade, B. J. (1989). The influence of perceptual development on cognitive style: Cross ethnic comparisons. *Early Child Development and Care 51,* 137-155.

Sherrill, C. (1994). *Journey to the other side.* Mountain View, CA: Creative.

Sibbertt, E. (1978). *Ancient Egyptian design coloring book.* New York: Dover.

Silver, E, A., Smith, M. S., & Nelson, B. S. (1995). The QUASAR project: Equity concerns meet mathematics education reform in the middle school. In W. G. Secada, E. Fennema, & L. B. Adajian

(Eds.), *New directions for equity in mathematics education* (pp. 9-56). Cambridge, UK: Cambridge University Press.

Smith, F. (1990). *To think.* New York: Teachers College Press.

Snyder, T. (1991). *The wonderful problems of Fizz & Martina.* Cambridge, MA: Tom Snyder.

Stead, M. (1986). *Egyptian life.* Cambridge, MA: Harvard University Press and the British Museum.

Stiff, L. V. (1990). African-American students and the promise of the curriculum and evaluation standards. In T. J. Cooney & C. R. Hirsch (Eds.), *Teaching and learning mathematics in the 1990s* (pp. 152-158). Reston, VA: National Council of Teachers of Mathematics.

Stiff, L. V., & Harvey, W. B. (1988). On the education of black children in mathematics. *Journal of Black Studies 19*(2), 190-203.

Stillman, G., & Balatti, J. (2001). Contribution of ethnomathematics to mainstream mathematics classroom practice. In B. Atweh, H. Forgasz, & B. Nebres (Eds.), *Sociocultural research on mathematics education.* Mahwah, NJ: Lawrence Erlbaum.

Tales of the magicians. (1990). In E. Wilson (Ed. and Trans.), *Egyptian literature* (pp. 159-169). London: Colonial Press, (Original work published 1901). Referenced in Anne Pellowski, *The World of Storytelling* (p. 4). New York: H. W. Wilson.

Teachings. (1986). Translated and referenced in M. Stead, *Egyptian life* (p. 21). Cambridge, MA: Harvard University Press and the British Museum.

Tolkien, J. R. R. (1981). *The lord of the rings.* New York: Ballantine.

Trentacosta, J., & Kenney. M. J. (Eds.). (1997). *Multicultural and gender equity in the mathematics classroom.* Reston, VA: National Council of Teachers of Mathematics.

Vasquez, J. A. (1991). Cognitive style and academic achievement. In J. Lynch, C. Modgil, & S. Modgil (Eds.), *Cultural diversity and the schools: consensus and controversy.* London: Falconer Press.

Vygotsky, L. S. (1978). *Mind in society: The development of higher psychological processes.* Cambridge, MA: Harvard University Press.

Waqainabete, R. (1996). *Fijian ethnomathematics.* Unpublished manuscript, James Cook University, Townsville, Queensland, Australia. Quoted by G. Stillman & J. Balatti in Contribution of ethnomathematics to mainstream mathematics classroom practice. In B. Atweh, H. Forgasz, & B. Nebres (Eds.), *Sociocultural research on mathematics education.* Mahwah, NJ: Lawrence Erlbaum, 2001.

Welchman-Tischler, R. (1992). *How to use children's literature to teach mathematics.* Reston, VA.: National Council of Teachers of Mathematics.

Wells, G. (1986). *The meaning makers.* Portsmouth, NH: Heinemann.

Whitin, D. J., & Wilde, S. (1992). *Read any good math lately?: Children's books for mathematical learning.* Portsmouth, NH: Heinemann.

Whitin, D. J., & Wilde, S. (1995). *It's the story that counts.* Portsmouth, NH: Heinemann.

Wilder, R. (1950). The cultural basis of mathematics. *Proceedings of the International Congress of Mathematicians, 1,* 258-271.

Wilder, R. (1968). *Evolution of mathematical concepts.* New York: John Wiley.

Wilder, R. (1981). *Mathematics as a cultural system.* Oxford, UK: Pergamon Press.

Wilson, E. (1986). *Ancient Egyptian designs.* New York: Dover.

Zaslavsky, C. (1996). *The multicultural mathematics classroom.* Portsmouth, NH: Heinemann.

Index

ABOUT THE AUTHOR

Michael Stephen Schiro teaches courses in mathematics education and curriculum theory at Boston College. In mathematics education he specializes in the use of children's literature, physical manipulatives, academic games, multicultural activities, and computers in elementary school mathematics. In curriculum theory he focuses on the role of ideology in teacher education and in the creation and use of instructional materials. He has published eleven books on such diverse topics as *Integrating Children's Literature and Mathematics in the Classroom; Mega-Fun Math Games;* and *Curriculum for Better Schools: The Great Ideological Debate.*

Dr. Schiro was born in the slums of Washington, D.C., and during his teenage years traveled extensively around the world. In the 1960s he worked for school desegregation in North Carolina and Philadelphia, Pennsylvania. In the 1970s he worked to improve urban education in Lowell, Massachusetts. He has taught at the elementary, middle, and high school levels. He received his baccalaureate from Tufts University and his doctorate from Harvard University. He was Chair of the Department of Teacher Education and School Administration at Boston College in the 1980s.

Dr. Schiro has two children, Stephanie and Arthur, for whom he has created, and to whom he has told, hundreds of fantasy stories.

CREDITS

Chapter 7

Figure 7.5. Fronts and Backs of Three Tomb Cards.

Anubis reprinted from *Ancient Egyptian Cut and Use Stencils* (1978) by Theodore Menten. Published by Dover Publications, Inc.

Heart Amulet reprinted from *From Fetish to God in Ancient Egypt* by Ernest Alfred Wallis Budge. Originally published by Oxford University Press, 1934. Reprinted by Dover Publications, Inc., 1988.

Ushabti Statue reprinted from *The Mummy* by Ernest Alfred Wallis Budge. Originally published by Cambridge University Press, 1925. Reprinted by Dover Publications, Inc., 1989.

Figure 7.18. Egyptian Paddle Dolls, dating to about 2000 B.C.

From *Ancient Egyptians Designs* by Eva Wilson. Copyright © 1986. Reprinted with permission from Dover Publications, Inc.

Figure 7.25. Samples of Ancient Egyptian Designs.

From *Ancient Egyptians Designs* by Eva Wilson. Copyright © 1986. Reprinted with permission from Dover Publications, Inc.

Chapter 11

Various quotes from *Ways with Words: Language, Life, and Work in Communities and Classrooms,* by S. B. Heath. Copyright © 1983. Reprinted with the permission of Cambridge University Press.

CD-ROM

"The Egypt Story": Days 3 and 4

Images appearing on p. 11are reprinted from *The Mummy* by Ernest Alfred Wallis Budge. Originally published by Cambridge University Press, 1894.

Image appearing on p. 13, Book of the Dead, is reprinted from *From Fetish to God in Ancient Egypt* by Ernest Alfred Wallis Budge. Originally published by Oxford University Press, 1934. Reprinted by Dover Publications, Inc., 1988.

Images appearing on p. 13, Ka Statue of a Scribe, Ushabti Statue, Coffins, Cartonnage Mask, and Names are reprinted from *The Mummy* by Ernest Alfred Wallis Budge. Originally published by Cambridge University Press, 1894.

Images appearing on p. 15, Ma'at, Troth, Shu, and Bes, are reprinted from *The Mummy* by Ernest Alfred Wallis Budge. Originally published by Cambridge University Press, 1894.

Images appearing on p. 15, Final Judgment and Amenait, are reprinted from *From Fetish to God in Ancient Egypt* by Ernest Alfred Wallis Budge. Originally published by Oxford University Press, 1934. Reprinted by Dover Publications, Inc., 1988.